Practical Education
Vol. II

by

Maria Edgeworth And Richard Lovell Edgeworth

Double 9 BOOKS

Practical Education
Vol. II
by Maria Edgeworth And Richard Lovell Edgeworth

ISBN: 978-93-67140-08-6

Published by

DOUBLE 9 BOOKS

2/13-B, Ansari Road
Daryaganj, New Delhi – 110002
info@double9books.com
www.double9books.com
Tel. 011-40042856

ABOUT THE AUTHOR

Maria Edgeworth and her father, Richard Lovell Edgeworth, were prominent Anglo-Irish writers known for their contributions to literature and education. Richard was deeply interested in education and developed progressive ideas about teaching, which influenced Maria's work. He authored several texts on education and wrote children's books, emphasizing moral instruction and practical knowledge.

Maria Edgeworth, novels, such as "Castle Rackrent" and "Belinda," explored themes of class, gender, and social reform, showcasing her keen observation of Irish society. Maria's writing often reflected her advocacy for women's education and empowerment, challenging societal norms of her time.

Their book - "Practical Education" explores innovative educational methods, emphasizing practical learning, moral development, and the importance of tailoring education to individual needs and societal context.

Together, they collaborated on several projects, reflecting their shared belief in the power of education to transform society. Their contributions laid the groundwork for future writers and educators, highlighting the interplay between literature and social reform.

CONTENTS

CHAPTER XIII
ON GRAMMAR, AND CLASSICAL LITERATURE

As long as gentlemen feel a deficiency in their own education, when they have not a competent knowledge of the learned languages, so long must a parent be anxious, that his son should not be exposed to the mortification of appearing inferiour to others of his own rank. It is in vain to urge, that language is only the key to science; that the names of things are not the things themselves; that many of the words in our own language convey scarcely any, or at best but imperfect, ideas; that the true genius, pronunciation, melody, and idiom of Greek, are unknown to the best scholars, and that it cannot reasonably be doubted, that if Homer or Xenophon were to hear their works read by a professor of Greek, they would mistake them for the sounds of an unknown language. All this is true; but it is not the ambition of a gentleman to read Greek like an ancient Grecian, but to understand it as well as the generality of his contemporaries; to know whence the terms of most sciences are derived, and to be able, in some degree, to trace the progress of mankind in knowledge and refinement, by examining the extent and combination of their different vocabularies.

In some professions, Greek is necessary; in all, a certain proficiency of Latin is indispensable; how, therefore, to acquire this proficiency in the one, and a sufficient knowledge of the other, with the least labour, the least waste of time, and the least danger to the understanding, is the material question. Some school-masters would add, that we must expedite the business as much as possible: of this we may be permitted to doubt. *Festina lente* is one of the most judicious maxims in education, and those who have sufficient strength of mind to adhere to it, will find themselves at the goal, when their competitors, after all their bustle, are panting for breath, or lashing their restive steeds. We see some untutored children start forward in learning with rapidity: they seem to acquire knowledge at the very time it is wanted, as if by intuition; whilst others, with whom infinite pains have been taken, continue in dull ignorance; or, having accumulated a mass of learning, are utterly at a loss how to display, or how to use their treasures. What is the reason of this phenomenon? and to which class of children would a parent wish his son to belong? In a certain number of years, after having spent eight hours a day in "durance vile," by the influence of bodily fear, or by the infliction of bodily punishment, a regiment of boys may be drilled by an indefatigable usher into what are called scholars; but, perhaps, in the whole regiment not one shall ever distinguish himself, or ever emerge from the ranks. Can it be necessary to spend so many years, so many of the best years of life, in toil and misery? We shall calculate the waste of time which arises from the study of ill written, absurd grammar, and exercise-books; from the habits of idleness contracted by school-boys, and from the custom of allowing holydays to young students; and we shall compare the result of this calculation with the time really necessary for the attainment of the same quantity of classical knowledge by rational methods. We do not enter into this comparison with any invidious intention, but simply to quiet the apprehensions of parents; to show them the possibility of their children's attaining a certain portion of learning within a given number of years, without the sacrifice of health, happiness, or the general powers of the understanding.

At all events, may we not begin by imploring the assistance of some able and friendly hand to reform the present generation of grammars and school-books? For instance, is it indispensably necessary that a boy of seven years old should learn by rote, that "relative sentences are independent, *i. e.* no word in a relative sentence is governed either of verb, or adjective, that stands in another sentence, or depends upon any appurtenances of the relative; and that the English word 'That' is always a relative when it may be turned into *which* in good sense, which must be tried by reading over the English sentence *warily*, and judging how the sentence will bear it, but when it cannot be altered, salvo sensu, it is a conjunction?" Cannot we, for pity's sake, to assist the learner's memory, and to improve his intellect, substitute some sentences a little more connected, and perhaps a little more useful, than the following?

"I have been a soldier—You have babbled—Has the crow ever looked white?—Ye have exercised—Flowers have withered—We were in a passion—Ye lay down—Peas were parched—The lions did roar a while ago."

In a book of Latin exercises, [1] the preface to which informs us, that "it is intended to contain such precepts of morality and religion, as ought most industriously to be inculcated into the heads of all learners, contrived so as that children may, as it were, insensibly suck in such principles as will be of use to them afterwards in the manly conduct and ordering of their lives," we might expect somewhat more of pure morality and sense, with rather more elegance of style, than appear in the following sentences:

"I struck my sister with a stick, and was forced to flee into the woods; but when I had tarried there awhile, I returned to my parents, and submitted myself to their mercy, and they forgave me my offence."

"When my dear mother, unknown to my father, shall send me money, I will pay my creditors their debts, and provide a supper for all my friends in my chamber, without my brother's consent, and will make presents to all my relations."

So the measure of maternal tenderness is the sum of money, which the dear mother, unknown to her husband, shall send to her son; the measure of the son's generosity is the supper he is to give to all his friends in his chamber, exclusive of his poor brother, of whose offence we are ignorant. His munificence is to be displayed in making presents to all his relations, but in the mean time he might possibly forget to pay his debts, for "justice is a slow-paced virtue, and cannot keep pace with generosity."

A reasonable notion of punishment, and a disinterested love of truth, is well introduced by the following picture. "My master's countenance was greatly changed when he found his beloved son guilty of a lie. Sometimes he was pale with anger; sometimes he was red with rage; and in the mean time, he, poor boy, was trembling, (for what?) for fear of punishment." Could the ideas of punishment and vengeance be more effectually joined, than in this portrait of the master red with rage? After truth has been thus happily recommended, comes honesty. "Many were fellow-soldiers with valiant Jason when he stole the golden fleece: many were companions with him, but he bore away the glory of the enterprise."

Valour, theft, and glory, are here happily combined. It will avail us nothing to observe, that the golden fleece has an allegorical meaning, unless we can explain satisfactorily the nature of an allegorical theft; though to our classical taste this valiant Jason may appear a glorious hero, yet to the simple judgment of children, he will appear a robber. It is fastidious, however, to object to Jason in the exercise-book, when we consider what children are to hear, and to hear with admiration, as they advance in their study of poetry and mythology.

Lessons of worldly wisdom, are not forgotten in our manual, which professes to teach "*the manly conduct and ordering of life*" to the rising generation. "Those men," we are told, "who have the most money, obtain the greatest honour amongst men." But then again, "a poor man is as happy without riches, *if* he can enjoy contentedness of mind, as the richest earl that coveteth greater honour." It may be useful to put young men upon their guard against hypocrites and knaves; but is it necessary to tell school-boys, that "it concerneth me, and all men, to look to ourselves, for the world is so full of knaves and hypocrites, that he is hard to be found who may be trusted?" That "they who behave themselves the most warily of all men, and live more watchfully than others, may happen to do something, which (if it be divulged) may very much damnify their reputation?" A knowledge of the world may be early requisite; but is it not going too far, to assure young people, that "the nations of the world are at this time come to that pass of wickedness, that the earth is like hell, and many men have degenerated into devils?"

A greater variety of ridiculous passages from this tenth edition of Garretson's Exercise-book, might be selected for the reader's entertainment; but the following specimens will be sufficient to satisfy him, that by this original writer, natural history is as well taught as morality:

Man. "Man is a creature of an upright body; he walketh upright when he is on a journey; and when night approaches, he lieth flat, and sleepeth."

Horses. "A journey an hundred and fifty miles long, tireth an horse that hath not had a moderate feed of corn."

Air, Earth, Fire, and Water. "The air is nearer the earth than the fire; but the water is placed nearest to the earth, because these two elements compose but one body."

It is an easy task, it will be observed, to ridicule absurdity. It is easy to pull down what has been ill built; but if we leave the ruins for others to stumble over, we do little good to society. Parents may reasonably say, if you take away from our children the books they have, give them better. They are not yet to be had, but if a demand for them be once excited, they will soon appear. Parents are now convinced, that the first books which children read, make a lasting impression upon them; but they do not seem to consider spelling-books, and grammars, and exercise-books, as books, but only as tools for different purposes: these tools are often very mischievous; if we could improve them, we should get our work much better done. The barbarous translations, which are put as models for imitation into the hands of school-boys, teach them bad habits of speaking and writing, which are sometimes incurable. For instance, in the fourteenth edition of Clarke's Cornelius Nepos, which the preface informs us was written by a man full of indignation for the common practices of grammar-schools, by a man who laments that youth should spend their time "in tossing over the leaves of a dictionary, and hammering out such a language as the Latin," we might expect some better translation than the following, to form the young student's style:

"No body ever heard any other entertainment for the ears at *his* (Atticus's) meals than a reader, which we truly think very pleasant. Nor was there ever a supper at his house without some reading, that their guests might be entertained in their minds as well as their stomachs; *for* he invited those whose manners were not different from his own."

"He (Atticus) likewise had a touch at poetry, that he might not be unacquainted with this pleasure, we suppose. *For* he has related in verses the lives of those who excelled the Roman people in honour, and the greatness of their exploits. *So* that he has described under each of their images, their actions and offices in no more than four or five verses, *which* is scarcely to be believed *that* such great things could be so briefly delivered."

Those who, in reading these quotations, have perhaps exclaimed, "Why must we go through this farrago of nonsense?" should reflect, that they have now wasted but a few minutes of their time upon what children are doomed to study for hours and years. If a few pages disgust, what must be the effect of volumes in the same style! and what sort of writing can we expect from pupils who are condemned to such reading? The analogy of ancient and modern languages, differs so materially, that a literal translation of any ancient author, can scarcely be tolerated. Yet, in general, young scholars are under a necessity of *rendering* their Latin lessons into English word for word, faithful to the taste of their dictionaries, or the notes in their translations. This is not likely to improve the freedom of their English style; or, what is of much more consequence, is it likely to preserve in the pupil's mind a taste for literature? It is not the time that is spent in pouring over lexicons, it is not the multiplicity of rules learnt by rote, nor yet is it the quantity of Latin words crammed into the memory, which can give the habit of attention or the power of voluntary exertion: without these, you will never have time enough to teach; with them, there will always be time enough to learn.—One half hour's vigorous application, is worth a whole day's constrained and yawning study. If we compare what from experience we know can be done by a child of ordinary capacity in a given time, with what he actually does in school-hours, we shall be convinced of the enormous waste of time incident to the common methods of instruction. Tutors are sensible of this; but they throw the blame upon their pupils— "You might have learned your lesson in half the time, if you had chosen it." The children also are sensible of this; but they are not able or willing to prevent the repetition of the reproach. But exertion does not always depend upon the will of the boy; it depends upon his previous habits, and upon the strength of the immediate motive which acts upon him. Some children of quick abilities, who have too much time allotted for their classical studies, are so fully sensible themselves of the pernicious effect this has upon their activity of mind, that they frequently defer *getting their lessons* to the last moment, that they may be forced by a sufficient motive to exert themselves. In *classes* at public schools, the quick and the slow, the active and indolent, the stumbling and sure-footed, are all yoked together, and are forced to keep pace with one another: stupidity may sometimes be dragged along by the vigour of genius; but genius is more frequently chained down by the weight of stupidity. We are well aware of the difficulties with which the public preceptor has to contend; he is often compelled by his situation to follow ancient usage, and to continue many customs which he wishes to see reformed. Any reformation in the manner of instruction in these public seminaries, must be gradual, and will necessarily follow the conviction that parents may feel of its utility. Perhaps nothing can be immediately done, more practicably useful, than to simplify grammar, and to lighten as much as possible the load that is laid upon the memory. Without a multiplicity of masters, it would be impossible to suit instruction to the different capacities, and previous acquirements, of a variety of pupils; but in a private education, undoubtedly the task may be rendered much easier to the scholar and to the teacher; much jargon may be omitted; and what appears from want of explanation to be jargon, may be rendered intelligible by proper skill and attention. During the first lessons in grammar, and in Latin, the pupil need not be disgusted with literature, and we may apply all the principles which we find on other occasions successful in the management of the attention. [2] Instead of keeping the attention feebly obedient for an idle length of time, we should fix if decidedly by some sufficient motive for as short a period as may be requisite to complete the work that we would have done. As we apprehend, that even where children are to be sent to school, it will be a great advantage to them to have some general notions of grammar, to lead them through the labyrinth of common school books, we think that we shall do the public preceptor an acceptable service, if we point out the means by which parents may, without much labour to themselves, render the first principles of grammar intelligible and familiar to their children.

We may observe, that children pay the strictest attention to the analogies of the language that they speak. Where verbs are defective or irregular, they supply the parts that are wanting with wonderful facility, according to the common form of other verbs. They make all verbs regular. I go*ed*, I read*ed*, I writ*ed*, &c. By a proper application of this faculty, much time may be saved in teaching children grammar, much perplexity, and much of that ineffectual labour which stupifies and dispirits the understanding. By gentle degrees, a child may be taught the relations of words to each other in common conversation, before he is presented with the first sample of grammatical eloquence in Lilly's Accidence. "There be eight parts of speech." A phrase which in some parts of this kingdom would perhaps be understood, but which to the generality of boys who go to school, conveys no meaning, and is got by heart without reflection, and without advantage. A child can, however, be made to understand these formidable parts of speech, if they are properly introduced to his acquaintance: he can comprehend, that some of the words which he hears express *that something is done;* he will readily perceive, that if something is done, somebody, or something must do it: he will distinguish with much facility the word in any common sentence which expresses an action, and that which denotes the agent. Let the reader try the experiment immediately upon any child of six or seven years old who has *not* learned grammar, and he may easily ascertain the fact.

A few months ago, Mr. — — gave his little daughter H— —, a child of five years old, her first lesson in English grammar; but no alarming book of grammar was produced upon the occasion, nor did the father put on an unpropitious gravity of countenance. He explained to the smiling child the nature of a verb, a pronoun, and a substantive.

Then he spoke a short familiar sentence, and asked H— —, to try if she could find out which word in it was a verb, which a pronoun, and which a substantive. The little girl found them all out most successfully, and formed no painful associations with her first grammatical lesson. But though our pupil may easily understand, he will easily forget our first explanations; but provided he understands them at the moment, we should pardon his forgetfulness, and we should patiently repeat the same exercise several days successively; a few minutes at each lesson will be sufficient, and the simplest sentences, such as children speak themselves, will be the best examples. Mr. — —, after having talked four or five times, for a few minutes at a time, with his son S— —, when S— — was between five and six years old, about grammar, asked him if he knew what a pronoun meant? The boy answered, "A word that is said instead of a substantive." As these words might have been merely remembered by rote, the father questioned his pupil further, and asked him to name any pronoun that he recollected. S— —immediately said, "*I* a pronoun." "Name another," said his father. The boy answered after some pause, as if he doubted whether it was or was not a pronoun, *A.* Now it would have been very imprudent to have made a sudden exclamation at the child's mistake. The father, without showing any surprise, gently answered, "No, my dear, *a* does not stand in the place of any substantive. We say *a man,* but the word *a* does not mean *a man,* when it is said by itself—Does it?"

S— —. No.

Father. Then try if you can find out a word that does.

S— —. He, and *Sir.*

Sir does stand, in conversation, in the place of a man, or gentleman; therefore the boy, even by this mistake, showed that he had formed, from the definition that had been given to him, a general idea of the nature of a pronoun, and at all events he exercised his understanding upon the affair, which is the principal point we ought to have in view.

An interjection is a part of speech familiar to children. Mr. Horne Tooke is bitter in his contempt for it, and will scarcely admit it into civilized company. "The brutish inarticulate interjection, which has nothing to do with speech, and is only the miserable refuge of the speechless, has been permitted to usurp a place amongst words, &c." — "The neighing of a horse, the lowing of a cow, the barking of a dog, the purring of a cat; sneezing, coughing, groaning, shrieking, and every other involuntary convulsion with oral sound, have almost as good a title to be called parts of speech, as interjections have."

Mr. Horne Tooke would have been pleased with the sagacity of a child of five years old (S——) who called *laughing* an interjection. Mr. —— gave S——a slight pinch, in order to produce "an involuntary convulsion with oral sound." And when the interjection Oh! was uttered by the boy, he was told by his father, that the word was an interjection; and, that "any word or noise, that expresses a sudden feeling of the mind, may be called an interjection." S——immediately said, "is laughing an interjection, then?" We hope that the candid reader will not imagine, that we produce these *sayings* of children of four or five years old, without some sense of the danger of ridicule; but we wish to give some idea of the sort of simple answers which children are likely to make in their first grammatical lessons. If too much is expected from them, the disappointment, which must be quickly felt, and will be quickly shown by the preceptor, will discourage the pupil. We must repeat, that the first steps should be frequently retraced: a child should be *for some weeks* accustomed to distinguish an active verb, and its agent, or nominative case, from every other word in a sentence, before we attempt to advance. The objects of actions are the next class of words that should be selected.

The fanciful, or at least what appears to the moderns fanciful, arrangement of the cases amongst grammarians, may be dispensed with for the present. The idea, that the nominative is a direct, upright *case*, and that the genitive declines with the smallest obliquity from it; the dative, accusative, and ablative, falling further and further from the perpendicularity of speech, is a species of metaphysics not very edifying to a child. Into what absurdity men of abilities may be led by the desire of explaining what they do not sufficiently understand, is fully exemplified in other sciences as well as grammar.

The discoveries made by the author of Epea Pteroenta, show the difference between a vain attempt to substitute analogy and rhetoric in the place of demonstration and common sense. When a child has been patiently taught in conversation to analyze what he says, he will take great pleasure in the exercise of his new talent; he will soon discover, that the cause of the action does not always come before the verb in a sentence, that sometimes it follows the verb. "John beats Thomas," and "Thomas is beaten by John," he will perceive mean the same thing; he may, with very little difficulty, be taught the difference between a verb active and a verb passive; that one brings first before the mind the person or thing which performs the action, and the other represents in the first place the person or thing upon whom the action is performed. A child of moderate capacity, after he has been familiarized to this general idea of a verb active and passive, and after he has been taught the names of the cases, will probably, without much difficulty, discover that the nominative case to a passive verb becomes the accusative case to a verb active. "School-masters are plagued by boys." A child sees plainly, that school-masters are the persons upon whom the action of plaguing is performed, and he will convert the sentence readily into "boys plague school-masters."

We need not, however, be in any hurry to teach our pupil the names of the cases; technical grammar may be easily learned, after a general idea of rational grammar has been obtained. For instance, *the verb* means only *the word*, or the principal word in a sentence; a child can easily learn this after he has learnt what is meant by a sentence; but it would be extremely difficult to make him comprehend it before he could distinguish a verb from a noun, and before he had any idea of the structure of a common sentence. From easy, we should proceed to more complicated, sentences. The grammatical construction of the following lines, for example, may not be immediately apparent to a child:

> "What modes of sight between each vast extreme,
> The mole's dim curtain, and the lynx's beam;
> Of smell the headlong lioness between,
> And hound sagacious on the tainted green."

"*Of Smell.*" A girl of ten years old (C— —) was asked if she could tell what substantive the word "*of*" relates to; she readily answered, "*modes.*" C— —had learned a general idea of grammar in conversation, in the manner which we have described. It is asserted from experience, that this method of instructing children in grammar by conversation, is not only practicable, but perfectly easy, and that the minds of children are adapted to this species of knowledge. During life, we learn with eagerness whatever is congenial with our present pursuits, and the acquisition of language is one of the most earnest occupations of childhood. After distinct and ready knowledge of the verb and nominative case has been acquired, the pupil should be taught to distinguish the object of an action, or, in other words, the objective or accusative case. He should be exercised in this, as in the former lessons, repeatedly, until it becomes perfectly familiar; and he should be encouraged to converse about these lessons, and to make his own observations concerning grammar, without fear of the preceptor's peremptory frown, or positive reference to "*his rules*." A child of five years old, was asked what the word "*Here!*" meant; he answered, "It means to give a thing."

"When I call a person, as, John! John! it seems to me," said a boy of nine years old (S——) "it seems to me, that the vocative case is both the verb and its accusative case." A boy who had ever been checked by his tutor for making his own observations upon the mysterious subject of grammar, would never have dared to have thought, or to have uttered a new thought, so freely.—Forcing children to learn any art or science by rote, without permitting the exercise of the understanding, must materially injure their powers both of reasoning and of invention. We acknowledge that Wilkins and Tooke have shown masters how to teach grammar a little better than it was formerly taught. Fortunately for the rising generation, all the words under the denomination of adverbs, prepositions, and conjunctions, which were absolute nonsense to us, may be easily explained to them, and the commencement of instruction need no longer lay the foundation of implicit acquiescence in nonsense. We refer to Mr. Horne Tooke's "Epea Pteroenta," forbearing to dilate upon the principles of his work, lest we should appear in the invidious light of authors who rob the works of others to adorn their own. We cannot help expressing a wish, that Mr. Horne Tooke would have the philanthropic patience to write an elementary work in a *simple style*, unfolding his grammatical discoveries to the rising generation.

When children have thus by gentle degrees, and by short and clear conversations, been initiated in general grammar, and familiarized to its technical terms, the first page of tremendous Lilly will lose much of its horror. It has been taken for granted, that at the age of which we have been speaking, a child can read English tolerably well, and that he has been used to employ a dictionary. He may now proceed to translate from some easy books a few short sentences: the first word will probably be an adverb or conjunction; either of them may readily be found in the Latin dictionary, and the young scholar will exult in having translated one word of Latin; but the next word, a substantive or verb, perhaps will elude his search. Now the grammar may be produced, and something of the various terminations of a noun may be explained. If *musam* be searched for in the dictionary, it cannot be found, but *musa* catches the eye, and, with the assistance of the grammar, it may be shown, that the meaning of words may be discovered by the united helps of the dictionary and grammar. After some days patient continuation of this exercise, the use of the grammar, and of its uncouth collection of words and syllables, will be apparent to the pupil: he will perceive that the grammar is a sort of appendix to the dictionary. The grammatical formulæ may then, by gentle degrees, be committed to memory, and when once got by heart, should be assiduously preserved in the recollection. After the preparation which we have recommended, the singular number of a declension will be learnt in a few minutes by a child of ordinary capacity, and after two or three days repetition, the plural number may be added. The whole of the first declension should be well fixed in the memory before a second is attempted. During this process, a few words at every lesson may be translated from Latin to English, and such nouns as are of the first declension, may be compared with *musa*, and may be declined according to the same form. Tedious as this method may appear, it will in the end be found expeditious. Omitting some of the theoretic or didactic part of the grammar, which should only be read, and which may be explained with care and patience, the whole of the declensions, pronouns, conjugations, the list of prepositions and conjunctions, interjections, some adverbs, the concords, and common rules of syntax, may be comprised with sufficient repetitions in about two or three hundred lessons of ten minutes each; that is to say, ten minutes application of the scholar in the presence of the teacher. A young boy should never be set to learn a lesson by heart when alone. Forty hours! Is this tedious? If you are afraid of losing time, begin a few months earlier; but begin when you will, forty hours is surely no great waste of time: the whole, or even half of this short time, is not spent in the labour of getting jargon by rote; each day some slight advance is made in the knowledge of words, and in the knowledge of their combinations. What we insist upon is, that *nothing should be done to disgust the pupil*: steady perseverance, with uniform gentleness, will induce habit, and nothing should ever interrupt the regular return of the daily lesson. If absence, business, illness, or any other cause, prevent the attendance of the teacher, a substitute must be appointed; the idea of relaxation on Sunday, or a holyday, should never be permitted. In most public seminaries above one third, in some nearly one half, of the year is permitted to idleness: it is the comparison between severe labour and dissipation, that renders learning hateful.

Johnson is made to say by one of his female biographers, [3] that no child loves the person who teaches him Latin; yet the author of this chapter would not take all the doctor's fame, and all the lady's wit and riches, in exchange for the hourly, unfeigned, unremitting friendship, which he enjoys with a son who had no other master than his father. So far from being laborious or troublesome, he has found it an agreeable employment to instruct his children in grammar and the learned languages. In the midst of a variety of other occupations, half an hour every morning for many years, during the time of dressing, has been allotted to the instruction of boys of different ages in languages, and no other time has been spent in this employment. Were it asserted that these boys made *a reasonable progress*, the expression would convey no distinct meaning to the reader; we shall, therefore, mention an experiment tried this morning, November 8th, 1796, to ascertain the progress of one of these pupils. Without previous study, he translated twenty lines of the story of Ceyx and Alcyone, from Ovid, consulting the dictionary only twice: he was then desired to translate the passage which he had read into English verse; and in two or three hours he produced the following version. Much of the time was spent in copying the lines fairly, as this opportunity was taken of exciting his attention to writing and spelling, to associate the habit of application with the pleasure of voluntary exertion. The *curious* may, if they think it worth their while, see the various *readings* and corrections of the translation (V. Chapter on Conversation, and Anecdotes of Children) which were carefully preserved, not as "*Curiosities of Literature*," but for the sake of truth, and with a desire to show, that the pupil had the patience to correct. A *genius* may hit off a few tolerable lines; but if a child is willing and able to criticise and correct what he writes, he shows that he selects his expressions from choice, and not from chance or imitation; and he gives to a judicious tutor the certain promise of future improvement.

"Far in a vale there lies a cave forlorn,
Which Phœbus never enters eve or morn,
The misty clouds inhale the pitchy ground,
And twilight lingers all the vale around.
No watchful cocks Aurora's beams invite;
No dogs nor geese, the guardians of the night:
No flocks nor herds disturb the silent plains;
Within the sacred walls mute quiet reigns,
And murmuring Lethe soothing sleep invites;
In dreams again the flying past delights:
From milky flowers that near the cavern grow,
Night scatters the collected sleep below."

S— —, the boy who made this translation, was just ten years old; he had made but three previous attempts in versification; his reading in poetry had been some of Gay's fables, parts of the Minstrel, three odes of Gray, the

Elegy in a Country Church-yard, the Tears of Old May-day, and parts of the second volume of Dr. Darwin's Botannic Garden; Dryden's translations of the fable of Ceyx and Alcyone he had never seen; the book had always been locked up. Phædrus and Ovid's Metamorphoses were the whole of his Latin erudition. These circumstances are mentioned thus minutely, to afford the inquisitive teacher materials for an accurate estimate of the progress made by our method of instruction. Perhaps most boys of S——'s age, in our great public seminaries, would, upon a similar trial, be found superior. Competition in the art of translation is not our object; our object is to show, that half an hour a day, steadily appropriated to grammar and Latin, would be sufficient to secure a boy of this age, from any danger of ignorance in classical learning; and that the ease and shortness of his labour will prevent that disgust, which is too often induced by forced and incessant application. We may add, that some attention to the *manner* in which the pupils repeat their Latin lessons, has been found advantageous: as they were never put in bodily fear, by the impatience of a pedagogue, they had leisure and inclination to read and recite, without awkward gestures and discordant tones. The whining tones and convulsive gestures often contracted by boys during the agony of repeating their long lessons, are not likely to be advantageous to the rising generation of orators. Practice, and the strong motive of emulation, may, in a public seminary, conquer these bad habits. After the pupil has learned to speak ill, he *may* be taught to speak well; but the chances are against him: and why should we have the trouble of breaking bad habits? It is much easier to prevent them. In private education, as the preceptor has less chance of curing his pupil of the habit of speaking ill, he should be peculiarly attentive to give the child constant habits of speaking and reading well. It is astonishing, that parents, who are extremely intent upon the education of their children, should overlook some of the essential means of success. A young man with his head full of Latin and law, will make but a poor figure at the bar, or in parliament, if he cannot enunciate distinctly, and if he cannot speak good English extempore, or produce his learning and arguments with grace and propriety. It is in vain to expect that a boy should speak well in public, who cannot, in common conversation, utter three connected sentences without a false concord or a provincial idiom; he may be taught with much care and cost to speak *tripod* sentences; [4] but bring the young orator to the test, bring him to actual business, rouse any of his passions, throw him off his guard, and then listen to his language; he will forget instantly his reading master, and all his rules of pronunciation and rhetoric, and he will speak the language to which he has been most accustomed. No master will then be near him to regulate the pitch and tones of his voice. We cannot believe that even Caius Gracchus could, when he was warmed by passion, have listened to Licinius's pitch-pipe. [5] Example, and constant attention to their manner of speaking in common conversation, we apprehend to be the most certain methods of preparing young men for public speakers. Much of the time that is spent in teaching boys to walk upon stilts, might be more advantageously employed in teaching them to walk well without them. It is all very well whilst the pupil is under the protection of his preceptor. The actor on the stage is admired whilst he is elevated by the cothurnus; but young men are not to exhibit their oratorical talents always with the advantages of stage effect and decorations. We should imagine, that much of the diffidence felt by young men of abilities, when they first rise to speak in public, may be attributed to their immediate perception of the difference between scholastic exhibitions and the real business of life; they feel that they have learned to speak two languages, which must not, on any account, be mixed together; the one, the vulgar language of common conversation; the other, the refined language of oratorical composition: the first they are most inclined to use when they are agitated; and they are agitated when they rise to speak before numbers: consequently there is an immediate struggle between custom and institution. Now, a young man, who in common conversation in his own family has never been accustomed to hear or to speak vulgar or ungrammatical language, cannot possibly apprehend that he shall suddenly utter ridiculous expressions; he knows, that, if he speaks at all, he shall at least speak good English; and he is not afraid, that, if he is pursued, he shall be obliged to throw away his cumbrous stilts. The practice of speaking in public, we are sensible, is a great advantage; but the habit of speaking accurately in private, is of still greater consequence: this habit depends upon the early and persevering care of the parent and the preceptor. There is no reason why children should not be made at the same time good scholars and good speakers; nor is there any reason why boys, whilst they learn to write Latin, should be suffered to forget how to write English.

It would be a great advantage to the young classical scholar, if his Latin and English literature were mixed; the taste for ancient authors and for modern literature, ought to be cultivated at the same time; and the beauties of composition, characteristic of different languages, should be familiarized to the student. Classical knowledge and taste afford such continual and innocent sources of amusement, that we should be extremely sorry that any of our pupils should not enjoy them in their fullest extent; but we do not include a talent for Latin composition amongst the *necessary* accomplishments of a gentleman. There are situations in life, where facility and elegance in writing Latin may be useful, but such situations are not common; when a young man is intended for them, he may be trained with more particular assiduity to this art; perhaps for this purpose the true Busbyean method is the best. The great Latin and Greek scholars of the age, have no reason to be displeased by the assertion, that classical proficiency equal to their own, is not a *necessary* accomplishment in a gentleman; if their learning become more rare, it may thence become more valuable. We see no reason why there should not be Latinists as well as special pleaders.

We have not laid down any course of classical study; those who consider the order in which certain authors are read, as of material consequence in the education of scholars, may consult Milton, Mrs. Macaulay, "Milne's Well-bred Scholar," &c. where they will find precise directions.

We have *lately* seen a collection of exercises for boys, [6] which in some measure supplies the defect of Mr. Garretson's curious performance. We wish most earnestly that dictionaries were improved. The author of "Stemmata Latinitatis," has conferred an essential service on the public; but still there is wanting a dictionary for schools, in which elegant and proper English might be substituted for the barbarous translations now in use. Such a dictionary could not be compiled, we should think, without an attention to the course of books that are most commonly used in schools. The first meanings given in the dictionary, should suit the first authors that a boy reads; this may probably be a remote or metaphoric meaning: then the radical word should be mentioned, and it would not cost a master any great trouble to trace the genealogy of words to the parent stock.

Cordery is a collection of such mean sentences, and uninstructive dialogue, as to be totally unfit for boys. Commenius's "Visible World displayed," is far superior, and might, with proper alterations and better prints, become a valuable *English* school-book. Both these books were intended for countries where the Latin language was commonly spoken, and consequently they are filled with the terms necessary for domestic life and conversation: for this very reason they are not good introductions to the classics. Selections from Bailey's Phædrus, will be proper for young beginners, upon account of the glossary. We prefer this mode of assisting them with glossaries to the use of translations, because they do not induce indolent habits, and yet they prevent the pupil from having unnecessary labour. Translations always give the pupil more trouble in the end, than they save in the beginning. The glossary to Bailey's Phædrus, which we have just mentioned, wants much to be modernized, and the language requires to be improved. Mr. Valpy's "Select Sentences," would be much more useful if they had a glossary annexed. As they are, they will, however, be useful after Phædrus. Ovid's Metamorphoses, with all its monstrous faults, appears to be the best introduction to the Latin classics, and to heathen mythology. Norris's Ovid may be safely put into the hands of children, as it is a selection of the least exceptionable fables. To accustom boys to read poetry and prose nearly at the same period, is advantageous. Cornelius Nepos, a *crabbed* book, but useful from its brevity, and from its being a proper introduction to Grecian and Roman history, may be read nearly at the same time with Ovid's Metamorphoses. After Ovid, the pupil may begin Virgil, postponing some of the Eclogues, and all the Georgics.

We recommend that some English books should be put into the hands of boys whilst they are going through Phædrus, Ovid, and Cornelius Nepos, which may suit with the ideas they acquire from these Latin authors. Plutarch's Lives, for instance, will be useful and interesting. When we mention Plutarch's Lives, we cannot help recollecting how many great people have acknowledged the effect of this book in their early education. Charles the Twelfth, Rousseau, Madame Roland, Gibbon, we immediately remember, and we are sure we have noticed many others. An abridgment of Plutarch, by Mrs. Helme, which we have looked into, appears (the preface excepted) to be well written; and we see another abridgment of Plutarch advertised, which we hope may prove serviceable: good prints to a Plutarch for children, would be very desirable.

As an English introduction to mythology, we recommend the first volume of Lord Chesterfield's Letters, as a most elegant view of heathen mythology. But if there be any danger that the first volume should introduce the remainder of Lord Chesterfield's work to the inexperienced reader, we should certainly forbear the experiment: it would be far better for a young man never to be acquainted with a single heathen deity, than to purchase Lord Chesterfield's classical knowledge at the hazard of contamination from his detestable system of morals. Without his Lordship's assistance, Mrs. Monsigny's Mythology can *properly* initiate the young pupil of either sex into the mysteries of ancient fables. The notes to Potter's Æschylus, are also well suited to our purpose. In Dr. Darwin's "Botanic Garden," there are some beautiful poetic allusions to ancient gems and ancient fables, which must fix themselves in the memory or in the imagination of the pupil. The sooner they are read, the better; we have felt the advantage of putting them into the hands of a boy of nine or ten years old. The ear should be formed to English as well as to Latin poetry.

Classical poetry, without the knowledge of mythology, is unintelligible: if children study the one, they must learn the other. Divested of the charms of poetry, and considered without classical prepossession, mythology presents a system of crimes and absurdities, which no allegorical, metaphysical, or literal interpreters of modern times, can perfectly reconcile to common sense, or common morality; but our poets have naturalized ancient fables, so that mythology is become essential even to modern literature. The associations of taste, though arbitrary, are not easily changed in a nation whose literature has attained to a certain pitch of refinement, and whose critical judgments must consequently have been for some generations traditional. There are subjects of popular allusion, which poets and orators regard as common property; to dispossess them of these, seems impracticable, after time has sanctioned the prescriptive right. But new knowledge, and the cultivation of new sciences, present objects of poetic allusion which, skilfully managed by men of inventive genius, will oppose to the habitual reverence for antiquity, the charms of novelty united to the voice of philosophy. [7]

In education we must, however, consider the actual state of manners in that world in which our pupils are to live, as well as our wishes or our hopes of its gradual improvement. [8] With a little care, preceptors may manage so as to teach mythology without in the least injuring their pupils. Children may be familiarized to the strange manners and strange personages of ancient fable, and may consider them as a set of beings who are not to be judged by any rules of morality, and who have nothing in common with ourselves. The caricatura of some of the passions, perhaps, will not shock children who are not used to their natural appearance; they will pass over the stories of love and jealousy, merely because they do not understand them. We should rather leave them completely unintelligible, than attempt, like Mr. Riley, in his mythological pocket dictionary for youth, to elucidate the whole at once, by assuring children that Saturn was Adam, that Atlas is Moses, and his brother Hesperus, Aaron; that Vertumnus and Pomona were Boaz and Ruth; that Mars *corresponds* with Joshua; that Apollo *accords* with David, since they both played upon the harp; that Mercury can be no other than our Archangel Michael, since they both have wings on their arms and feet; that, in short, to complete the concordance, Momus is a striking likeness of Satan. The ancients, Mr. Riley allows, have so much disfigured these personages, that it is hard to know many of the portraits again at first sight; however, he is persuaded that "the young student will find a peculiar gratification in tracing the likeness," and he has kindly furnished us with a catalogue to explain the exhibition, and to guide us through his new pantheon.

As books of reference, the convenient size, and compressed information, of *pocket* mythological dictionaries, will recommend them to general use; but we object to the miserable prints with which they are sometimes disgraced. The first impression made upon the imagination [9] of children, is of the utmost consequence to their future taste. The beautiful engravings [10] in Spence's Polymetis, will introduce the heathen deities in their most graceful and picturesque forms to the fancy. The language of Spence, though classical, is not entirely free from pedantic affectation, and his dialogues are, perhaps, too stiff and long winded for our young pupils. But a parent or preceptor can easily select the useful explanations; and in turning over the prints, they can easily associate some general notion of the history and attributes of the gods and goddesses with their forms: the little eager spectators will, as they crowd round the book, acquire imperceptibly all the necessary knowledge of mythology, imbibe the first pleasing ideas of taste, and store their imagination with classic imagery. The same precautions that are necessary to educate the eye, are also necessary to form the ear and understanding of taste. The first mythological descriptions which our pupils read, should be the best in their kind. Compare the following account of Europa in a pocket dictionary, with her figure in a poetical gem—"Europa, the daughter of Agenor, king of the Phœnicians, and sister of Cadmus. This princess was so beautiful, that, they say, one of the companions of Juno had robbed her of a pot of paint to bestow on this lady, which rendered her so handsome. She was beloved of Jupiter, who assumed the shape of a bull to run away with her, swam over the sea with her on his back, and carried her into that part of the world now called Europe, from her name." So far the dictionary; now for the poet.

> "Now lows a milk-white bull on Afric's strand,
> And crops with dancing head the daisy'd land;
> With rosy wreathes Europa's hand adorns
> His fringed forehead and his pearly horns;
> Light on his back the sportive damsel bounds,
> And, pleas'd, he moves along the flowery grounds;
> Bears with slow step his beauteous prize aloof,
> Dips in the lucid flood his ivory hoof;
> Then wets his velvet knees, and wading laves
> His silky sides, amid the dimpling waves.
> While her fond train with beckoning hands deplore,
> Strain their blue eyes, and shriek along the shore:
> Beneath her robe she draws her snowy feet,
> And, half reclining on her ermine seat,
> Round his rais'd neck her radiant arms she throws,
> And rests her fair cheek on his curled brows;
> Her yellow tresses wave on wanton gales,
> And high in air her azure mantle sails." [1]

[1] Garretson's Exercises, the tenth edition.

[2] V. Chapter on Attention.

[3] Mrs. Piozzi.

[4] V. Blair.

[5] V. Plutarch.

[6] Valpy's Exercises.

[7] V. Darwin's Poetry.

[8] Since the above was written, we have seen a letter from Dr. Aikin to his son on the *morality* and *poetic merit* of the fable of Circe, which convinces us that the observations that we have hazarded are not premature.

[9] Chapter on Imagination.

[10] We speak of these engravings as *beautiful*, for the times in which they were done; modern artists have arrived at higher perfection.

[11] Darwin. V. Botanic Garden.

CHAPTER XIV
ON GEOGRAPHY AND CHRONOLOGY

The usual manner of teaching Geography and Chronology, may, perhaps, be necessary in public seminaries, where a number of boys are to learn the same thing at the same time; but what is learned in this manner, is not permanent; something besides merely committing names and dates to the memory, is requisite to make a useful impression upon the memory. For the truth of this observation, an appeal is made to the reader. Let him recollect, whether the Geography and Chronology which he learned whilst a boy, are what he now remembers—Whether he has not obtained his present knowledge from other sources than the tasks of early years. When business, or conversation, calls upon us to furnish facts accurate as to place and time, we retrace our former heterogeneous acquirements, and select those circumstances which are connected with our present pursuit, and thus we form, as it were, a nucleus round which other facts insensibly arrange themselves. Perhaps no two men in the world, who are well versed in these studies, connect their knowledge in the same manner. Relation to some particular country, some favourite history, some distinguished person, forms the connection which guides our recollection, and which arranges our increasing nomenclature. By attending to what passes in our own minds, we may learn an effectual method of teaching without pain, and without any extraordinary burden to the memory, all that is useful of these sciences. The details of history should be marked by a few chronological æras, and by a few general ideas of geography. When these have been once completely associated in the mind, there is little danger of their being ever disunited: the sight of any country will recall its history, and even from representations in a map, or on the globe, when the mind is wakened by any recent event, a long train of concomitant ideas will recur.

The use of technical helps to the memory, has been condemned by many, and certainly, when they are employed as artifices to supply the place of real knowledge, they are contemptible; but when they are used as indexes to facts that have been really collected in the mind; when they serve to arrange the materials of knowledge in appropriate classes, and to give a sure and rapid clue to recollection, they are of real advantage to the understanding. Indeed, they are now so common, that pretenders cannot build the slightest reputation upon their foundation. Were an orator to attempt a display of long chronological accuracy, he might be wofully confounded by his opponent's applying at the first pause,

[12] Els*luk* he would have said!

Ample materials are furnished in Gray's Memoria Technica, from which a short and useful selection may be made, according to the purposes which are in view. For children, the little ballad of the Chapter of Kings, will not be found beneath the notice of mothers who attend to education. If the technical terminations of Gray are inserted, they will never be forgotten, or may be easily recalled. [13] We scarcely ever forget a ballad if the tune is popular.

For pupils at a more advanced age, it will be found advantageous to employ technical helps of a more scientific construction. Priestley's Chart of Biography may, from time to time, be hung in their view. Smaller charts, upon the same plan, might be provided with a few names as land-marks; these may be filled up by the pupil with such names as he selects from history; they may be bound in octavo, like maps, by the middle, so as to unfold both ways—Thirty-nine inches by nine will be a convenient size. Prints, maps, and medals, which are part of the constant furniture of a room, are seldom attended to by young people; but when circumstances excite an interest upon any particular subject, then is the moment to produce the symbols which record and communicate knowledge.

Mrs. Radcliffe, in her judicious and picturesque Tour through Germany, tells us, that in passing through the apartments of a palace which the archduchess Maria Christiana, the sister of the late unfortunate queen of France, had left a few hours before, she saw spread upon a table a map of all the countries then included in the seat of the war. The positions of the several corps of the allied armies were marked upon this chart with small pieces of various coloured wax. Can it be doubted, that the strong interest which this princess must have taken in the subject, would for ever impress upon her memory the geography of this part of the world?

How many people are there who have become geographers since the beginning of the present war. Even the common newspapers disseminate this species of knowledge, and those who scarcely knew the situation of Brest harbour a few years ago, have consulted the map with that eagerness which approaching danger excites; they consequently will tenaciously remember all the geographical knowledge they have thus acquired. The art of creating an interest in the study of geography, depends upon the dexterity with which passing circumstances are seized by a preceptor in conversation. What are maps or medals, statues or pictures, but technical helps to memory? If a mother possess good prints, or casts of ancient gems, let them be shown to any persons of taste and knowledge who visit her; their attention leads that of our pupils; imitation and sympathy are the parents of taste, and taste reads in the monuments of art whatever history has recorded.

In the Adele and Theodore of Madame de Silleri, a number of adventitious helps are described for teaching history and chronology. There can be no doubt that these are useful; and although such an apparatus cannot be procured by private families, fortunately the print-shops of every provincial town, and of the capital in particular, furnish even to the passenger a continual succession of instruction. Might not prints, assorted for the purposes which we have mentioned, be *lent* at circulating libraries?

To assist our pupils in geography, we prefer a globe to common maps. Might not a cheap, portable, and convenient globe, be made of oiled silk, to be inflated by a common pair of bellows? Mathematical exactness is not requisite for our purpose, and though we could not pretend to the precision of our best globes, yet a balloon of this sort would compensate by its size and convenience for its inaccuracy. It might be hung by a line from its north pole, to a hook screwed into the horizontal architrave of a door or window; and another string from its south pole might be fastened at a proper angle to the floor, to give the requisite elevation to the axis of the globe. An idea of the different projections of the sphere, may be easily acquired from this globe in its flaccid state, and any part of it might be consulted as a map, if it were laid upon a convex board of a convenient size. Impressions from the plates which are used for common globes, might be taken to try this idea without any great trouble or expense; but we wish to employ a much larger scale, and to have them five or six feet diameter. The inside of a globe of this sort might be easily illuminated, and this would add much to the novelty and beauty of its appearance.

In the country, with the assistance of a common carpenter and plasterer, a large globe of lath and plaster may be made for the instruction and entertainment of a numerous family of children. Upon this they should leisurely delineate from time to time, by their given latitudes and longitudes, such places as they become acquainted with in reading or conversation. The capital city, for instance, of the different countries of Europe, the rivers, and the neighbouring towns, until at last the outline might be added: for the sake of convenience, the lines, &c. may be first delineated upon a piece of paper, from which they may be accurately transferred to their proper places on the globe, by the intervention of black-leaded paper, or by pricking the lines through the paper, and pouncing powdered blue through the holes upon the surface of the globe.

We enter into this detail because we are convinced, that every addition to the active manual employment of children, is of consequence, not only to their improvement, but to their happiness.

Another invention has occurred to us for teaching geography and history together. Priestley's Chart of History, though constructed with great ingenuity, does not invite the attention of young people: there is an intricacy in the detail which is not obvious at first. To remedy what appears to us a difficulty, we propose that eight and twenty, or perhaps thirty, octavo maps of the globe should be engraved; upon these should be traced, in succession, the different situations of the different countries of the world, as to power and extent, during each respective century: different colours might denote the principal divisions of the world in each of these maps; the same colour always denoting the same country, with the addition of one strong colour; red, for instance, to distinguish that country which had at each period the principal dominion. On the upper and lower margin in these maps, the names of illustrious persons might be engraven in the manner of the biographical chart; and the reigning opinions of each century should also be inserted. Thus history, chronology, and geography, would appear at once to the eye in their proper order, and regular succession, divided into centuries and periods, which easily occur to recollection.

We forbear to expatiate upon this subject, as it has not been actually submitted to experiment; carefully avoiding in the whole of this work to recommend any mode of instruction which we have not actually put in practice. For this reason, we have not spoken of the abbé Gaultier's method of teaching geography, as we have only been able to obtain accounts of it from the public papers, and from reviews; we are, however, disposed to think favourably beforehand, of any mode which unites amusement with instruction. We cannot forbear recommending, in the strongest manner, a few pages of Rollin in his "Thoughts upon Education," which we think contain an excellent specimen of the manner in which a well informed preceptor might lead his pupils a geographical, historical, botanical, and physiological tour upon the artificial globe.

We conclude this chapter of hints, by repeating what we have before asserted, that though technical assistance may be of ready use to those who are really acquainted with that knowledge to which it refers, it never can supply the place of accurate information.

The causes of the rise and fall of empires, the progress of human knowledge, and the great discoveries of superior minds, are the real links which connect the chain of political knowledge.

[12] V. Gray's Memoria Technica, and the Critic.

[13] Instead of

William the conqueror long did reign,
And William his son by an arrow was slain.

Read,

William the Con*sau* long did reign,
And Ruf*koi* his son by an arrow was slain.

And so on from Gray's Memoria Technica to the end of the chapter.

CHAPTER XV
ON ARITHMETIC

The man who is ignorant that two and two make four, is stigmatized with the character of hopeless stupidity; except, as Swift has remarked, in the arithmetic of the customs, where two and two do not always make the same sum.

We must not judge of the understanding of a child by this test, for many children of quick abilities do not immediately assent to this proposition when it is first laid before them. "Two and two make four," says the tutor. "Well, child, why do you stare so?"

The child stares because the word *make* is in this sentence used in a sense which is quite new to him; he knows what it is to make a bow, and to make a noise, but how this active verb is applicable in the present case, where there is no agent to perform the action, he cannot clearly comprehend. "Two and two *are* four," is more intelligible; but even this assertion, the child, for want of a distinct notion of the sense in which the word *are* is used, does not understand. "Two and two *are called* four," is, perhaps, the most accurate phrase a tutor can use; but even these words will convey no meaning until they have been associated with the pupil's perceptions. When he has once perceived the combination of the numbers with real objects, it will then be easy to teach him that the words *are called, are,* and *make,* in the foregoing proposition, are synonymous terms.

We have chosen the first simple instance we could recollect, to show how difficult the words we generally use in teaching arithmetic, must be to our young pupils. It would be an unprofitable task to enumerate all the puzzling technical terms which, in their earliest lessons, children are obliged to hear, without being able to understand.

It is not from want of capacity that so many children are deficient in arithmetical skill; and it is absurd to say, "such a child has no genius for arithmetic. Such a child cannot be made to comprehend any thing about numbers." These assertions prove nothing, but that the persons who make them, are ignorant of the art of teaching. A child's seeming stupidity in learning arithmetic, may, perhaps, be a proof of intelligence and good sense.

It is easy to make a boy, who does not reason, repeat by rote any technical rules which a common writing-master, with magisterial solemnity, may lay down for him; but a child who reasons, will not be thus easily managed; he stops, frowns, hesitates, questions his master, is wretched and refractory, until he can discover why he is to proceed in such and such a manner; he is not content with seeing his preceptor make figures and lines upon a slate, and perform wondrous operations with the self-complacent dexterity of a conjurer. A sensible boy is not satisfied with merely seeing the total of a given sum, or the answer to a given question, *come out right*; he insists upon knowing why it is right. He is not content to be led to the treasures of science blindfold; he would tear the bandage from his eyes, that he might know the way to them again.

That many children, who have been thought to be slow in learning arithmetic, have, after their escape from the hands of pedagogues, become remarkable for their quickness, is a fact sufficiently proved by experience. We shall only mention one instance, which we happened to meet with whilst we were writing this chapter. John Ludwig, a Saxon peasant, was dismissed from school when he was a child, after four years ineffectual struggle to learn the common rules of arithmetic. He had been, during this time, beaten and scolded in vain. He spent several subsequent years in common country labour, but at length some accidental circumstances excited his ambition, and he became expert in all the common rules, and mastered the rule of three and fractions, by the help of an old school book, in the course of one year. He afterwards taught himself geometry, and raised himself, by the force of his abilities and perseverance, from obscurity to fame.

We should like to see the book which helped Mr. Ludwig to conquer his difficulties. Introductions to Arithmetic are, often, calculated rather for adepts in science, than for the ignorant. We do not pretend to have discovered any shorter method than what is common, of teaching these sciences; but, in conformity with the principles which are laid down in the former part of this work, we have endeavoured to teach their rudiments without disgusting our pupils, and without habituating them to be contented with merely technical operations.

In arithmetic, as in every other branch of education, the principal object should be, to preserve the understanding from implicit belief; to invigorate its powers; to associate pleasure with literature, and to induce the laudable ambition of progressive improvement.

As soon as a child can read, he should be accustomed to count, and to have the names of numbers early connected in his mind with the combinations which they represent. For this purpose, he should be taught to add first by things, and afterwards by signs or figures. He should be taught to form combinations of things by adding them together one after another. At the same time that he acquires the names that have been given to these combinations, he should be taught the figures or symbols that represent them. For example, when it is familiar to the child, that one almond, and one almond, are called two almonds; that one almond, and two almonds, are called three almonds, and so on, he should be taught to distinguish the figures that represent these assemblages; that 3 means one and two, &c. Each operation of arithmetic should proceed in this manner, from individuals to the abstract notation of signs.

One of the earliest operations of the reasoning faculty, is abstraction; that is to say, the power of classing a number of individuals under one name. Young children call strangers either men or women; even the most ignorant savages [15] have a propensity to generalize.

We may err either by accustoming our pupils too much to the consideration of tangible substances when we teach them arithmetic, or by turning their attention too much to signs. The art of forming a sound and active understanding, consists in the due mixture of facts and reflection. Dr. Reid has, in his "Essay on the Intellectual Powers of Man," page 297, pointed out, with great ingenuity, the admirable economy of nature in limiting the powers of reasoning during the first years of infancy. This is the season for cultivating the senses, and whoever, at this early age, endeavours to force the tender shoots of reason, will repent his rashness.

In the chapter "on Toys," we have recommended the use of plain, regular solids, cubes, globes, &c. made of wood, as playthings for children, instead of uncouth figures of men, women and animals. For teaching arithmetic, half inch cubes, which can be easily grasped by infant fingers, may be employed with great advantage; they can be easily arranged in various combinations; the eye can easily take in a sufficient number of them at once, and the mind is insensibly led to consider the assemblages in which they may be grouped, not only as they relate to number, but as they relate to quantity or shape; besides, the terms which are borrowed from some of these shapes, as squares, cubes, &c. will become familiar. As these children advance in arithmetic to square or cube, a number will be more intelligible to them than to a person who has been taught these words merely as the formula of certain rules. In arithmetic, the first lessons should be short and simple; two cubes placed *above* each other, will soon be called two; if placed in any other situations near each other, they will still be called two; but it is advantageous to accustom our little pupils to place the cubes with which they are taught in succession, either by placing them upon one another, or laying in columns upon a table, beginning to count from the cube next to them, as we cast up in addition. For this purpose, a board about six inches long, and five broad, divided into columns perpendicularly by slips of wood three eighths of an inch wide, and one eighth of an inch thick, will be found useful; and if a few cubes of colours *different from those already mentioned*, with numbers on their six sides, are procured, they may be of great service. Our cubes should be placed, from time to time, in a different order, or promiscuously; but when any arithmetical operations are to be performed with them, it is best to preserve the established arrangement.

One cube and one other, are called two.

Two what?

Two cubes.

One glass, and one glass, are called two glasses. One raisin, and one raisin, are called two raisins, &c. One cube, and one glass, are called what? *Two things* or two.

By a process of this sort, the meaning of the abstract term *two* may be taught. A child will perceive the word *two*, means the same as the words *one and one*; and when we say one and one are called two, unless he is prejudiced by something else that is said to him, he will understand nothing more than that there are two names for the same thing.

"One, and one, and one, are called three," is the same as saying "that three is the name for one, and one, and one." "Two and one are three," is also the same as saying "that three is the name of *two and one*." Three is also the name of one and two; the word three has, therefore, three meanings; it means one, and one, and one; *also*, two and one; also, one and two. He will see that any two of the cubes may be put together, as it were, in one parcel, and that this parcel may be called *two*; and he will also see that this parcel, when joined to another single cube, will *make* three, and that the sum will be the same, whether the single cube, or the two cubes, be named first.

In a similar manner, the combinations which form *four*, may be considered. One, and one, and one, and one, are four.

One and three are four.

Two and two are four.

Three and one are four.

All these assertions mean the same thing, and the term *four* is equally applicable to each of them; when, therefore, we say that two and two are four, the child may be easily led to perceive, and indeed to *see*, that it means the same thing as saying one *two*, and one *two*, which is the same thing as saying two *two's*, or saying the word *two* two times. Our pupil should be suffered to rest here, and we should not, at present, attempt to lead him further towards that compendious method of addition which we call multiplication; but the foundation is laid by giving him this view of the relation between two and two in forming four.

There is an enumeration in the note [16] of the different combinations which compose the rest of the Arabic notation, which consists only of nine characters.

Before we proceed to the number ten, or to the new series of numeration which succeeds to it, we should make our pupils perfectly masters of the combinations which we have mentioned, both in the direct order in which they are arranged, and in various modes of succession; by these means, not only the addition, but the subtraction, of numbers as far as nine, will be perfectly familiar to them.

It has been observed before, that counting by realities, and by signs, should be taught at the same time, so that the ear, the eye, and the mind, should keep pace with one another; and that technical habits should be acquired without injury to the understanding. If a child begins between four and five years of age, he may be allowed half a year for this essential, preliminary step in arithmetic; four or five minutes application every day, will be sufficient to teach him not only the relations of the first decade in numeration, but also how to write figures with accuracy and expedition.

The next step, is, by far the most difficult in the science of arithmetic; in treatises upon the subject, it is concisely passed over under the title of Numeration; but it requires no small degree of care to make it intelligible to children, and we therefore recommend, that, besides direct instruction upon the subject, the child should be led, by degrees, to understand the nature of classification in general. Botany and natural history, though they are not pursued as sciences, are, notwithstanding, the daily occupation and amusement of children, and they supply constant examples of classification. In conversation, these may be familiarly pointed out; a grove, a flock, &c. are constantly before the eyes of our pupil, and he comprehends as well as we do what is meant by two groves, two flocks, &c. The trees that form the grove are each of them individuals; but let their numbers be what they may when they are considered as a grove, the grove is but one, and may be thought of and spoken of distinctly, without any relation to the number of single trees which it contains. From these, and similar observations, a child may be led to consider *ten* as the name for a *whole*, an *integer*; a *one*, which may be represented by the figure (1): this same figure may also stand for a hundred, or a thousand, as he will readily perceive hereafter. Indeed, the term one hundred will become familiar to him in conversation long before he comprehends that the word *ten* is used as an aggregate term, like a dozen, or a thousand. We do not use the word ten as the French do *une dizaine*; ten does not, therefore, present the idea of an integer till we learn arithmetic. This is a defect in our language, which has arisen from the use of duodecimal numeration; the analogies existing between the names of other numbers in progression, is broken by the terms eleven and twelve. *Thirteen, fourteen*, &c. are so obviously compounded of three and ten, and four and ten, as to strike the ears of children immediately, and when they advance as far as twenty, they readily perceive that a new series of units begins, and proceeds to thirty, and that thirty, forty, &c. mean three tens, four tens, &c. In pointing out these analogies to children, they become interested and attentive, they show that species of pleasure which arises from the perception of *aptitude*, or of truth. It can scarcely be denied that such a pleasure exists independently of every view of utility and fame; and when we can once excite this feeling in the minds of our young pupils at any period of their education, we may be certain of success.

As soon as distinct notions have been acquired of the manner in which a collection of ten units becomes a new unit of a higher order, our pupil may be led to observe the utility of this invention by various examples, before he applies it to the rules of arithmetic. Let him count as far as ten with black pebbles, [17] for instance; let him lay aside a white pebble to represent the collection of ten; he may count another series of ten black pebbles, and lay aside another white one; and so on, till he has collected ten white pebbles: as *each* of the ten white pebbles represents ten black pebbles, he will have counted one hundred; and the ten white pebbles may now be represented by a single red one, which will stand for one hundred. This large number, which it takes up so much time to count, and which could not be comprehended at one view, is represented by a single sign. Here the difference of colour forms the distinction: difference in shape, or size, would answer the same purpose, as in the Roman notation X for ten, L for fifty, C for one hundred, &c. All this is fully within the comprehension of a child of six years old, and will lead him to the value of written figures by the *place* which they hold when compared with one another. Indeed he may be led to invent this arrangement, a circumstance which would encourage him in every part of his education. When once he clearly comprehends that the third place, counting from the right, contains only figures which represent hundreds, &c. he will have conquered one of the greatest difficulties of arithmetic. If a paper ruled with several perpendicular lines, a quarter of an inch asunder, be shown to him, he will see that the spaces or columns between these lines would distinguish the value of figures written in them, without the use of the sign (0) and he will see that (0) or zero, serves only to mark the place or situation of the neighbouring figures.

An idea of decimal arithmetic, but without detail, may now be given to him, as it will not appear extraordinary to *him* that a unit should represent ten by having its place, or column changed; and nothing more is necessary in decimal arithmetic, than to consider that figure which represented, at one time, an integer, or whole, as representing at another time the number of *tenth parts* into which that whole may have been broken.

Our pupil may next be taught what is called numeration, which he cannot fail to understand, and in which he should be frequently exercised. Common addition will be easily understood by a child who distinctly perceives that the perpendicular columns, or places in which figures are written, may distinguish their value under various different denominations, as gallons, furlongs, shillings, &c. We should not tease children with long sums in avoirdupois weight, or load their frail memories with tables of long-measure, and dry-measure, and ale-measure in the country, and ale-measure in London; only let them cast up a few sums in different denominations, with the tables before them, and let the practice of addition be preserved in their minds by short sums every day, and when they are between six and seven years old, they will be sufficiently masters of the first and most useful rule of arithmetic.

To children who have been trained in this manner, subtraction will be quite easy; care, however, should be taken to give them a clear notion of the mystery of *borrowing* and *paying*, which is inculcated in teaching subtraction.

From   94
Subtract   46

"Six from four I can't, but six from ten, and four remains; four and four *is* eight."

And then, "One that I borrowed and four are five, five from nine, and four remains."

This is the formula; but is it ever explained—or can it be? Certainly not without some alteration. A child sees that six cannot be subtracted (taken) from four: more especially a child who is familiarly acquainted with the component parts of the names six and four: he sees that the sum 46 is less than the sum 94, and he knows that the lesser sum may be subtracted from the greater; but he does not perceive the means of separating them figure by figure. Tell him, that though six cannot be deducted from four, yet it can from fourteen, and that if one of the tens which are contained in the (9) ninety in the uppermost row of the second column, be supposed to be taken away, or borrowed, from the ninety, and added to the four, the nine will be reduced to 8 (eighty), and the four will become fourteen. *Our* pupil will comprehend this most readily; he will see that 6, which could not be subtracted from 4, may be subtracted from fourteen, and he will remember that the 9 in the next column is to be considered as only (8). To avoid confusion, he may draw a stroke across the (9) and write 8 over [18] it [8 over (9)] and proceed to the remainder of the operation. This method for beginners is certainly very distinct, and may for some time, be employed with advantage; and after its rationale has become familiar, we may explain the common method which depends upon this consideration.

"If one number is to be deducted from another, the remainder will be the same, whether we add any given number to the smaller number, or take away the same given number from the larger." For instance:

Let the larger number be	9
And the smaller	4
If you deduct 3 from the larger it will be	6
From this subtract the smaller	4
The remainder will be	2
Or if you add 3 to the smaller number, it will be	7
Subtract this from the larger number	9
	7
The remainder will be	2

Now in the common method of subtraction, the *one* which is borrowed is taken from the uppermost figure in the adjoining column, and instead of altering that figure to *one* less, we add one to the lowest figure, which, as we have just shown, will have the same effect. The terms, however, that are commonly used in performing this operation, are improper. To say "one that I borrowed, and four" (meaning the lowest figure in the adjoining column) implies the idea that what was borrowed is now to be repaid to that lowest figure, which is not the fact. As to multiplication, we have little to say. Our pupil should be furnished, in the first instance, with a table containing the addition of the different units, which form the different products of the multiplication table: these he should, from time to time, add up as an exercise in addition; and it should be frequently pointed out to him, that adding these figures so many times over, is the same as multiplying them by the number of times that they are added; as three times 3 means 3 added three times. Here one of the figures represents a quantity, the other does not represent a quantity, it denotes nothing but the times, or frequency of repetition. Young people, as they advance, are apt to confound these signs, and to imagine, for instance, in the rule of three, &c. that the sums which they multiply together, mean quantities; that 40 yards of linen may be multiplied by three and six-pence, &c.—an idea from which the misstatements in sums that are intricate, frequently arise.

We have heard that the multiplication table has been set, like the Chapter of Kings, to a cheerful tune. This is a species of technical memory which we have long practised, and which can do no harm to the understanding; it prevents the mind from no beneficial exertion, and may save much irksome labour. It is certainly to be wished, that our pupil should be expert in the multiplication table; if the cubes which we have formerly mentioned, be employed for this purpose, the notion of *squaring* figures will be introduced at the same time that the multiplication table is committed to memory.

In division, what is called the Italian method of arranging the divisor and quotient, appears to be preferable to the common one, as it places them in such a manner as to be easily multiplied by each other, and as it agrees with algebraic notation.

The usual method is this:

Italian method:

$$\text{Divisor} \atop 71)83467(1175$$

$$\begin{array}{c} \text{Dividend} \\ 83467 \end{array} \,\Big|\, \begin{array}{c} 71 \\ \hline 1175 \end{array}$$

The rule of three is commonly taught in a manner merely technical: that it may be learned in this manner, so as to answer the common purposes of life, there can be no doubt; and nothing is further from our design, than to depreciate any mode of instruction which has been sanctioned by experience: but our purpose is to point out methods of conveying instruction that shall improve the reasoning faculty, and habituate our pupil to think upon every subject. We wish, therefore, to point out the course which the mind would follow to solve problems relative to proportion without the rule, and to turn our pupil's attention to the circumstances in which the rule assists us.

The calculation of the price of any commodity, or the measure of any quantity, where the first term is one, may be always stated as a sum in the rule of three; but as this statement retards, instead of expediting the operation, it is never practised.

If one yard costs a shilling, how much will three yards cost?

The mind immediately perceives, that the price added three times together, or multiplied by three, gives the answer. If a certain number of apples are to be equally distributed amongst a certain number of boys, if the share of one is one apple, the share of ten or twenty is plainly equal to ten or twenty. But if we state that the share of three boys is twelve apples, and ask what number will be sufficient for nine boys, the answer is not obvious; it requires consideration. Ask our pupil what made it so easy to answer the last question, he will readily say, "Because I knew what was the share of one."

Then you could answer this new question if you knew the share of one boy?

Yes.

Cannot you find out what the share of one boy is when the share of three boys is twelve?

Four.

What number of apples then will be enough, at the same rate, for nine boys?

Nine times four, that is thirty-six.

In this process he does nothing more than divide the second number by the first, and multiply the quotient by the third; 12 divided by 3 is 4, which multiplied by 9 is 36. And this is, in truth, the foundation of the rule; for though the golden rule facilitates calculation, and contributes admirably to our convenience, it is not absolutely necessary to the solution of questions relating to proportion.

Again, "If the share of three boys is five apples, how many will be sufficient for nine?"

Our pupil will attempt to proceed as in the former question, and will begin by endeavouring to find out the share of one of the three boys; but this is not quite so easy; he will see that each is to have one apple, and part of another; but it will cost him some pains to determine exactly how much. When at length he finds that one and two-thirds is the share of one boy, before he can answer the question, he must multiply one and two-thirds by nine, which is an operation *in fractions*, a rule of which he at present knows nothing. But if he begins by multiplying the second, instead of dividing it previously by the first number, he will avoid the embarrassment occasioned by fractional parts, and will easily solve the question.

$$3 : 5 : 9 : 15$$

Multiply	5
by	9

it makes 45

which product 45, divided by 3, gives 15.

Here our pupil perceives, that if a given number, 12, for instance, is to be divided by one number, and multiplied by another, *it will come to the same thing*, whether he begins by dividing the given number, or by multiplying it.

12 divided by 4 is 3, which
multiplied by 6 is 18;
And
12 multiplied by 6 is 72, which
divided by 4 is 18.

We recommend it to preceptors not to fatigue the memories of their young pupils with sums which are difficult only from the number of figures which they require, but rather to give examples *in practice*, where aliquot parts are to be considered, and where their ingenuity may be employed without exhausting their patience. A variety of arithmetical questions occur in common conversation, and from common incidents; these should be made a subject of inquiry, and our pupils, amongst others, should try their skill: in short, whatever can be taught in conversation, is clear gain in instruction.

We should observe, that every explanation upon these subjects should be recurred to from time to time, perhaps every two or three months; as there are no circumstances in the business of every day, which recall abstract speculations to the minds of children; and the pupil who understands them to-day, may, without any deficiency of memory, forget them entirely in a few weeks. Indeed, the perception of the chain of reasoning, which connects demonstration, is what makes it truly advantageous in education. Whoever has occasion, in the business of life, to make use of the rule of three, may learn it effectually in a month as well as in ten years; but the habit of reasoning cannot be acquired late in life without *unusual* labour, and uncommon fortitude.

[15] V. A strange instance quoted by Mr. Stewart, "On the Human Mind," page 152.

```
1
1   1
1   1   1   2
1   2   3   2
—   —   —   —
4   4   4   4


1
1   1
1   1   1
1   1   1       1
1   1   1   1   2   3
1   2   3   4   2   2
—   —   —   —   —   —
5   5   5   5   5   5


1
1   1
1   1   1               1
1   1   1   1           1   2   1           1
1   1   1   1   1       2   2   3   4       2   3
1   2   3   4   5       2   2   2   2       3   3
—   —   —   —   —   —   —   —   —   —   —
6   6   6   6   6   6   6   6   6   6   6


1
1   1
1   1   1                   1
1   1   1   1               1   1   1
1   1   1   1   1           1   2   1   1       2   1
1   1   1   1   1   1       2   2   3   4   5   2   3   4
1   2   3   4   5   6       2   2   2   2   2   3   3   3
—   —   —   —   —   —   —   —   —   —   —   —   —   —
7   7   7   7   7   7   7   7   7   7   7   7   7   7
```

```
1
1  1
1  1  1
1  1  1  1                    1
1  1  1  1                    1  1        1
1  1  1  1  1                 1  1  2  1  1  1
1  1  1  1  1  1              1  2  2  1  2  1  2  1
1  1  1  1  1  1  1           2  2  2  2  2  3  3  4
1  2  3  4  5  6  7           2  2  2  3  3  3  3  3
_____          _____
8  8  8  8  8  8  8           8  8  8  8  8  8  8  8
```

```
   1
   1  2  1     1
5  2  2  3  4  2  2
3  4  4  4  4  5  6
_____
8  8  8  8  8  8  8
```

```
1
1  1
1  1  1
1  1  1  1                    1
1  1  1  1  1                 1  1        1
1  1  1  1  1  1              1  1  2  1  1  2  1
1  1  1  1  1  1  1           1  2  2  1  2  2  1
1  1  1  1  1  1  1  1        2  2  2  2  2  2  3
1  2  3  4  5  6  7  8        2  2  2  3  3  3  3
_____ _____
9  9  9  9  9  9  9  9        9  9  9  9  9  9  9
```

```
                              1
1     1                 1  1           1
2  3  1  2  1           1  2  1     1  2  1
3  3  4  4  5  6  2  2  4  5  2  2  2  2
3  3  3  3  3  3  4  4  4  4  5  5  6  7
_____
9  9  9  9  9  9  9  9  9  9  9  9  9  9
```

[17] The word calculate is derived from the Latin calculus, a pebble.

[18] This method is recommended in the Cours de Math, par Camus, p. 38.

CHAPTER XVI
GEOMETRY

There is certainly no royal road to geometry, but the way may be rendered easy and pleasant by timely preparations for the journey.

Without any previous knowledge of the country, or of its peculiar language, how can we expect that our young traveller should advance with facility or pleasure? We are anxious that our pupil should acquire a taste for accurate reasoning, and we resort to Geometry, as the most perfect, and the purest series of ratiocination which has been invented. Let us, then, sedulously avoid whatever may disgust him; let his first steps be easy, and successful; let them be frequently repeated until he can trace them without a guide.

We have recommended in the chapter upon Toys, that children should, from their earliest years, be accustomed to the shape of what are commonly called regular solids; they should also be accustomed to the figures in mathematical diagrams. To these should be added their respective names, and the whole language of the science should be rendered as familiar as possible.

Mr. Donne, an ingenious mathematician of Bristol, has published a prospectus of an Essay on Mechanical Geometry: he has executed, and employed with success, models in wood and metal for demonstrating propositions in geometry in a *palpable* manner. We have endeavoured, in vain, to procure a set of these models for our own pupils, but we have no doubt of their entire utility.

What has been acquired in childhood, should not be suffered to escape the memory. Dionysius [19] had mathematical diagrams described upon the floors of his apartments, and thus recalled their demonstrations to his memory. The slightest addition that can be conceived, if it be continued daily, will imperceptibly, not only preserve what has been already acquired, but will, in a few years, amount to as large a stock of mathematical knowledge as we could wish. It is not our object to make mathematicians, but to make it easy to our pupil to become a mathematician, if his interest, or his ambition, make it desirable; and, above all, to habituate him to clear reasoning, and close attention. And we may here remark, that an early acquaintance with the accuracy of mathematical demonstration, does not, within our experience, contract the powers of the imagination. On the contrary, we think that a young lady of twelve years old, who is now no more, and who had an uncommon propensity to mathematical reasoning, had an imagination remarkably vivid and inventive. [20]

We have accustomed our pupils to form in their minds the conception of figures generated from points and lines, and surfaces supposed to move in different directions, and with different velocities. It may be thought, that this would be a difficult occupation for young minds; but, upon trial, it will be found not only easy to them, but entertaining. In their subsequent studies, it will be of material advantage; it will facilitate their progress not only in pure mathematics, but in mechanics and astronomy, and in every operation of the mind which requires exact reflection.

To demand steady thought from a person who has not been trained to it, is one of the most unprofitable and dangerous requisitions that can be made in education.

> "Full in the midst of Euclid dip at once,
> And petrify a genius to a dunce."

In the usual commencement of mathematical studies, the learner is required to admit that a point, of which he sees the prototype, a dot before him, has neither length, breadth, nor thickness. This, surely, is a degree of faith not absolutely necessary for the neophyte in science. It is an absurdity which has, with much success, been attacked in "Observations on the Nature of Demonstrative Evidence," by Doctor Beddoes.

We agree with the doctor as to the impropriety of calling a visible dot, a point without dimensions. But, notwithstanding the high respect which the author commands by a steady pursuit of truth on all subjects of human knowledge, we cannot avoid protesting against part of the doctrine which he has endeavoured to inculcate. That the names point, radius, &c. are derived from sensible objects, need not be disputed; but surely the word centre can be understood by the human mind without the presence of any visible or tangible substance.

Where two lines meet, their junction cannot have dimensions; where two radii of a circle meet, they constitute the centre, and the name centre may be used for ever without any relation to a tangible or visible point. The word boundary, in like manner, means the extreme limit we call a line; but to assert that it has thickness, would, from the very terms which are used to describe it, be a direct contradiction. Bishop Berkely, Mr. Walton, Philathetes

Cantabrigiensis, and Mr. Benjamin Robins, published several pamphlets upon this subject about half a century ago. No man had a more penetrating mind than Berkely; but we apprehend that Mr. Robins closed the dispute against him. This is not meant as an appeal to authority, but to apprize such of our readers as wish to consider the argument, where they may meet an accurate investigation of the subject. It is sufficient for our purpose, to warn preceptors not to insist upon their pupils' acquiescence in the dogma, that a point, represented by a dot, is without dimensions; and at the same time to profess, that we understand distinctly what is meant by mathematicians when they speak of length without breadth, and of a superfices without depth; expressions which, to our minds, convey a meaning as distinct as the name of any visible or tangible substance in nature, whose varieties from shade, distance, colour, smoothness, heat, &c. are infinite, and not to be comprehended in any definition.

In fact, this is a dispute merely about words, and as the extension of the art of printing puts it in the power of every man to propose and to defend his opinions at length, and at leisure, the best friends may support different sides of a question with mutual regard, and the most violent enemies with civility and decorum. Can we believe that Tycho Brahe lost half his nose in a dispute with a Danish nobleman about a mathematical demonstration?

[19] Plutarch.—Life of Dion.

[20] V. Rivuletta, a little story written *entirely* by her in 1786.

CHAPTER XVII
ON MECHANICS

Parents are anxious that children should be conversant with Mechanics, and with what are called the Mechanic Powers. Certainly no species of knowledge is better suited to the taste and capacity of youth, and yet it seldom forms a part of early instruction. Every body talks of the lever, the wedge, and the pulley, but most people perceive, that the notions which they have of their respective uses, are unsatisfactory, and indistinct; and many endeavour, at a late period of life, to acquire a scientific and exact knowledge of the effects that are produced by implements which are in every body's hands, or that are absolutely necessary in the daily occupations of mankind.

An itinerant lecturer seldom fails of having a numerous and attentive auditory; and if he does not communicate much of that knowledge which he endeavours to explain, it is not to be attributed either to his want of skill, or to the insufficiency of his apparatus, but to the novelty of the terms which he is obliged to use. Ignorance of the language in which any science is taught, is an insuperable bar to its being suddenly acquired; besides a precise knowledge of the meaning of terms, we must have an instantaneous idea excited in our minds whenever they are repeated; and, as this can be acquired only by practice, it is impossible that philosophical lectures can be of much service to those who are not familiarly acquainted with the technical language in which they are delivered; and yet there is scarcely any subject of human inquiry more obvious to the understanding, than the laws of mechanics. Only a small portion of geometry is necessary to the learner, if he even wishes to become master of the more difficult problems which are usually contained in a course of lectures, and most of what is practically useful, may be acquired by any person who is expert in common arithmetic.

But we cannot proceed a single step without deviating from common language; if the theory of the balance, or the lever, is to be explained, we immediately speak of *space* and *time*. To persons not versed in literature, it is probable that these terms appear more simple and unintelligible than they do to a man who has read Locke, and other metaphysical writers. The term *space* to the bulk of mankind, conveys the idea of an interval; they consider the word *time* as representing a definite number of years, days, or minutes; but the metaphysician, when he hears the words *space* and *time*, immediately takes the alarm, and recurs to the abstract notions which are associated with these terms; he perceives difficulties unknown to the unlearned, and feels a confusion of ideas which distracts his attention. The lecturer proceeds with confidence, never supposing that his audience can be puzzled by such common terms. He means by *space*, the distance from the place whence a body begins to fall, to the place where its motion ceases; and by time, he means the number of seconds, or of any determinate divisions of *civil* time which elapse from the commencement of any motion to its end; or, in other words, the duration of any given motion. After this has been frequently repeated, any intelligent person perceives the sense in which they are used by the tenour of the discourse; but in the interim, the greatest part of what he has heard, cannot have been understood, and the premises upon which every subsequent demonstration is founded, are unknown to him. If this be true, when it is affirmed of two terms only, what must be the situation of those to whom eight or ten unknown technical terms occur at the commencement of a lecture? A complete knowledge, such a knowledge as is not only full, but familiar, of all the common terms made use of in theoretic and practical mechanics, is, therefore, absolutely necessary before any person can attend public lectures in natural philosophy with advantage.

What has been said of public lectures, may, with equal propriety, be applied to private instruction; and it is probable, that inattention to this circumstance is the reason why so few people have distinct notions of natural philosophy. Learning by rote, or even reading repeatedly, definitions of the technical terms of any science, must undoubtedly facilitate its acquirement; but conversation, with the habit of explaining the meaning of words, and the structure of common domestic implements, to children, is the sure and effectual method of preparing the mind for the acquirement of science.

The ancients, in learning this species of knowledge, had an advantage of which we are deprived: many of their terms of science were the common names of familiar objects. How few do we meet who have a distinct notion of the words radius, angle, or valve. A Roman peasant knew what a radius or a valve meant, in their original signification, as well as a modern professor; he knew that a valve was a door, and a radius a spoke of a wheel; but an English child finds it as difficult to remember the meaning of the word angle, as the word parabola. An angle is usually confounded, by those who are ignorant of geometry and mechanics, with the word triangle, and the long reasoning of many a laborious instructer has been confounded by this popular mistake. When a glass pump is shown to an admiring spectator, he is desired to watch the motion of the valves: he looks "above, about, and underneath;" but, ignorant of the word *valve*, he looks in vain. Had he been desired to look at the motion of the little doors that opened and shut, as the handle of the pump was moved up and down, he would have followed the lecturer with ease, and would have understood all his subsequent reasoning. If a child attempts to push any thing heavier than himself, his feet slide away from it, and the object can be moved only at intervals, and by sudden starts; but if he be desired to prop his feet against the wall, he finds it easy to push what before eluded his little strength. Here the use of a fulcrum, or fixed point, by means of which bodies may be moved, is distinctly understood. If two boys lay a board across a narrow block of wood, or stone, and balance each other at the opposite ends of it, they acquire another idea of a centre of motion. If a poker is rested against a bar of a grate, and employed to lift up the coals, the same notion of a centre is recalled to their minds. If a boy, sitting upon a plank, a sofa, or form, be lifted up by another boy's applying his strength at one end of the seat, whilst the other end of the seat rests on the ground, it will be readily perceived by them, that the point of rest, or centre of motion, or fulcrum, is the ground, and that the fulcrum is not, as in the first instance, between the force that lifts, and the thing that is lifted; the fulcrum is at one end, the force which is exerted acts at the other end, and the weight is in the middle. In trying, these simple experiments, the terms *fulcrum, centre of motion,* &c. should be constantly employed, and in a very short time they would be as familiar to a boy of eight years old as to any philosopher. If for some years the same words frequently recur to him in the same sense, is it to be supposed that a lecture upon the balance and the lever would be as unintelligible to him as to persons of good abilities, who at a more advanced age hear these terms from the mouth of a lecturer? A boy in such circumstances would appear as if he had a genius for mechanics, when, perhaps, he might have less taste for the science, and less capacity, than the generality of the audience. Trifling as it may at first appear, it will not be found a trifling advantage, in the progress of education, to attend to this circumstance. A distinct knowledge of a few terms, assists a learner in his first attempts; finding these successful, he advances with confidence, and acquires new ideas without difficulty or disgust. Rousseau, with his usual eloquence, has inculcated the necessity of annexing ideas to words; he declaims against the splendid ignorance of men who speak by rote, and who are rich in words amidst the most deplorable poverty of ideas. To store the memory of his pupil with images of things, he is willing to neglect, and leave to hazard, his acquirement of language. It requires no elaborate argument to prove that a boy, whose mind was stored with accurate images of external objects, of experimental knowledge, and who had acquired habitual dexterity, but who was unacquainted with the usual signs by which ideas are expressed, would be incapable of accurate reasoning, or would, at best, reason only upon particulars. Without general terms, he could not abstract; he could not, until his vocabulary was enlarged, and familiar to him, reason upon general topics, or draw conclusions from general principles: in short, he would be in the situation of those who, in the solution of difficult and complicated questions relative to quantity, are obliged to employ tedious and perplexed calculations, instead of the clear and comprehensive methods that unfold themselves by the use of signs in algebra.

It is not necessary, in teaching children the technical language of any art or science, that we should pursue the same order that is requisite in teaching the science itself. Order is required in reasoning, because all reasoning is employed in deducing propositions from one another in a regular series; but where terms are employed merely as names, this order may be dispensed with. It is, however, of great consequence to seize the proper time for introducing a new term; a moment when attention is awake, and when accident has produced some particular interest in the object. In every family, opportunities of this sort occur without any preparation, and such opportunities are far preferable to a formal lecture and a splendid apparatus for the first lessons in natural philosophy and chemistry. If the pump belonging to the house is out of order, and the pump-maker is set to work, an excellent opportunity presents itself for variety of instruction. The centre pin of the handle is taken out, and a long rod is drawn up by degrees, at the end of which a round piece of wood is seen partly covered with leather. Your pupil immediately asks the name of it, and the pump-maker prevents your answer, by informing little master that it is called a sucker. You show it to the child, he handles it, feels whether the leather is hard or soft, and at length discovers that there is a hole through it which is covered with a little flap or door. This, he learns from the workmen, is called a clack. The child should now be permitted to plunge *the piston* (by which name it should *now* be called) into a tub of water; in drawing it backwards and forwards, he will perceive that the clack, which should now be called the valve, opens and shuts as the piston is drawn backwards and forwards. It will be better not to inform the child how this mechanism is employed in the pump. If the names sucker and piston, clack and valve, are fixed in his memory, it will be sufficient for his first lesson. At another opportunity, he should be present when the fixed or lower valve of the pump is drawn up; he will examine it, and find that it is similar to the valve of the piston; if he sees it put down into the pump, and sees the piston put into its place, and set to work, the names that he has learned will be fixed more deeply in his mind, and he will have some general notion of the whole apparatus. From time to time these names should be recalled to his memory on suitable occasions, but he should not be asked to repeat them by rote. What has been said, is not intended as a lesson for a child in mechanics, but as a sketch of a method of teaching which has been employed with success.

Whatever repairs are carried on in a house, children should be permitted to see: whilst every body about them seems interested, they become attentive from sympathy; and whenever action accompanies instruction, it is sure to make an impression. If a lock is out of order, when it is taken off, show it to your pupil; point out some of its principal parts, and name them; then put it into the hands of a child, and let him manage it as he pleases. Locks are full of oil, and black with dust and iron; but if children have been taught habits of neatness, they may be clock-makers and white-smiths, without spoiling their clothes, or the furniture of a house. Upon every occasion of this sort, technical terms should be made familiar; they are of great use in the every-day business of life, and are peculiarly serviceable in giving orders to workmen, who, when they are spoken to in a language that they are used to, comprehend what is said to them, and work with alacrity.

An early use of a rule and pencil, and easy access to prints of machines, of architecture, and of the implements of trades, are of obvious use in this part of education. The machines published by the Society of Arts in London; the prints in Desaguliers, Emerson, le Spectacle de la Nature, Machines approuvées par l'Académie, Chambers's Dictionary, Berthoud sur l'Horlogerie, Dictionaire des Arts et des Métiers, may, in succession, be put into the hands of children. The most simple should be first selected, and the pupils should be accustomed to attend minutely to one print before another is given to them. A proper person should carefully point out and explain to them the first prints that they examine; they may afterwards be left to themselves.

To understand prints of machines, a previous knowledge of what is meant by an elevation, a profile, a section, a perspective view, and a (vue d'oiseau) bird's eye view, is necessary. To obtain distinct ideas of sections, a few models of common furniture, as chests of drawers, bellows, grates, &c. may be provided, and may be cut asunder in different directions. Children easily comprehend this part of drawing, and its uses, which may be pointed out in books of architecture; its application to the common business of life, is so various and immediate, as to fix it for ever in the memory; besides, the habit of abstraction, which is acquired by drawing the sections of complicated architecture or machinery, is highly advantageous to the mind. The parts which we wish to express, are concealed, and are suggested partly by the elevation or profile of the figure, and partly by the connection between the end proposed in the construction of the building, machine, &c. and the means which are adapted to effect it.

A knowledge of perspective, is to be acquired by an operation of the mind directly opposite to what is necessary in delineating the sections of bodies; the mind must here be intent only upon the objects that are delineated upon the retina, exactly what we see; it must forget or suspend the knowledge which it has acquired from experience, and must see with the eye of childhood, no further than the surface. Every person, who is accustomed to drawing in perspective, sees external nature, when he pleases, merely as a picture: this habit contributes much to form a taste for the fine arts; it may, however, be carried to excess. There are improvers who prefer the most dreary ruin to an elegant and convenient mansion, and who prefer a blasted stump to the glorious foliage of the oak.

Perspective is not, however, recommended merely as a means of improving the taste, but as it is useful in facilitating the knowledge of mechanics. When once children are familiarly acquainted with perspective, and with the representations of machines by elevations, sections, &c. prints will supply them with an extensive variety of information; and when they see real machines, their structure and uses will be easily comprehended. The noise, the seeming confusion, and the size of several machines, make it difficult to comprehend and combine their various parts, without much time, and repeated examination; the reduced size of prints lays the whole at once before the eye, and tends to facilitate not only comprehension, but contrivance. Whoever can delineate progressively as he invents, saves much labour, much time, and the hazard of confusion. Various contrivances have been employed to facilitate drawing in perspective, as may be seen in "Cabinet de Servier, Memoires of the French Academy, Philosophical Transactions, and lately in the Repertory of Arts." The following is simple, cheap, and *portable*.

PLATE 1. FIG. 1.

A B C, three mahogany boards, two, four, and six inches long, and of the same breadth respectively, so as to double in the manner represented.

PLATE 1. FIG. 2.

The part A is screwed, or *clamped* to a table of a convenient height, and a sheet of paper, one edge of which is put under the piece A, will be held fast to the table.

The index P is to be set (at pleasure) with it sharp point to any part of an object which the eye sees through E, the eye-piece.

The machine is now to be doubled as in Fig. 2, taking care that the index be not disturbed; the point, which was before perpendicular, will then approach the paper horizontally, and the place to which it points on the paper, must be marked with a pencil. The machine must be again unfolded, and another point of the object is to be ascertained in the same manner as before; the space between these points may be then connected with a line; fresh points should then be taken, marked with a pencil, and connected with a line; and so on successively, until the whole object is delineated.

Besides the common terms of art, the technical terms of science should, by degrees, be rendered familiar to our pupils. Amongst these the words Space and Time occur, as we have observed, the soonest, and are of the greatest importance. Without exact definitions, or abstract reasonings, a general notion of the use of these terms may be inculcated by employing them frequently in conversation, and by applying them to things and circumstances which occur without preparation, and about which children are interested, or occupied. "There is a great space left between the words in that printing." The child understands, that *space* in this sentence means white paper between black letters. "You should leave a greater space between the flowers which you are planting"—he knows that you mean more *ground*. "There is a great space between that boat and the ship"—space of water. "I hope the hawk will not be able to catch that pigeon, there is a great space between them"—space of air. "The men who are pulling that sack of corn into the granary, have raised it through half the space between the door and the ground." A child cannot be at any loss for the meaning of the word space in these or any other practical examples which may occur; but he should also be used to the word space as a technical expression, and then he will not be confused or stopped by a new term when employed in mechanics.

The word *time* may be used in the same manner upon numberless occasions to express the duration of any movement which is performed by the force of men, or horses, wind, water, or any mechanical power.

"Did the horses in the mill we saw yesterday, go as fast as the horses which are drawing the chaise?" "No, not as fast as the horses go at present on level ground; but they went as fast as the chaise-horses do when they go up hill, or as fast as horses draw a waggon."

"How many times do the sails of that wind-mill go round in a minute? Let us count; I will look at my watch; do you count how often the sails go round; wait until that broken arm is uppermost, and when you say *now*, I will begin to count the *time*; when a minute has past, I will tell you."

After a few trials, this experiment will become easy to a child of eight or nine years old; he may sometimes attend to the watch, and at other times count the turns of the sails; he may easily be made to apply this to a horse-mill, or to a water-mill, a corn-fan, or any machine that has a rotatory motion; he will be entertained with his new employment; he will compare the *velocities* of different machines; the meaning of this word will be easily added to his vocabulary.

"Does that part of the arms of the wind-mill which is near the *axle-tree*, or *centre*, I mean that part which has no cloth or sail upon it, go as fast as the ends of the arms that are the farthest from the centre?"

"No, not near so fast."

"But that part goes as often round in a minute as the rest of the sail."

"Yes, but it does not go as fast."

"How so?"

"It does not go so *far* round."

"No, it does not. The *extremities* of the *sails go through more space in the same time* than the part near the centre."

By conversations like these, the technical meaning of the word *velocity* may be made quite familiar to a child much younger than what has been mentioned; he may not only comprehend that velocity means time and space considered together, but if he is sufficiently advanced in arithmetic, he may be readily taught how to express and compare in numbers *velocities* composed of certain portions of time and space. He will not inquire about the abstract meaning of the word *space*; he has seen space measured on paper, on timber, on the water, in the air, and he perceives distinctly that it is a term equally applicable to all distances that can exist between objects of any sort, or that he can see, feel, or imagine.

Momentum, a less common word, the meaning of which is not quite so easy to convey to a child, may, by degrees, be explained to him: at every instant he feels the effect of momentum in his own motions, and in the motions of every thing that strikes against him; his feelings and experience require only proper terms to become the subject of his conversation. When he begins to inquire, it is the proper time to instruct him. For instance, a boy of ten years old, who had acquired the meaning of some other terms in science, this morning asked the meaning of the word momentum; he was desired to explain what he thought it meant.

He answered, "Force."

"What do you mean by force?"

"Effort."

"Of what?"

"Of gravity."

"Do you mean that force by which a body is drawn down to the earth?"

"No."

"Would a feather, if it were moving with the greatest conceivable swiftness or velocity, throw down a castle?"

"No." [21]

"Would a mountain torn up by the roots, as fabled in Milton, if it moved with the least conceivable velocity, throw down a castle?"

"Yes, I think it would."

The difference between an uniform, and an uniformly accelerated motion, the measure of the velocity of falling bodies, the composition of motions communicated to the same body in different directions at the same time, and the cause of the curvilinear track of projectiles, seem, at first, intricate subjects, and above the capacity of boys of ten or twelve years old; but by short and well-timed lessons, they may be explained without confounding or fatiguing their attention. We tried another experiment whilst this chapter was writing, to determine whether we had asserted too much upon this subject. After a conversation between two boys upon the descent of bodies towards the earth, and upon the measure of the increasing velocity with which they fall, they were desired, with a view to ascertain whether they understood what was said, to invent a machine which should show the difference between an uniform and an accelerated velocity, and in particular to show, by occular demonstration, "that if one body moves in a given time through a given space, with an uniform motion, and if another body moves through the same space in the same time with an uniformly accelerated motion, the uniform motion of the one will be equal to half the accelerated motion of the other." The eldest boy, H——, thirteen years old, invented and executed the following machine for this purpose:

Plate I, Fig. 3. *b* is a bracket 9 inches by 5, consisting of a back and two sides of hard wood: two inches from the back two slits are made in the sides of the bracket half an inch deep, and an eighth of an inch wide, to receive the two wire pivots of a roller; which roller is composed of a cylinder, three inches long and half an inch diameter; and a cone three inches long and one inch diameter in its largest part or base. The cylinder and cone are not separate, but are turned out of one piece; a string is fastened to the cone at its base *a*, with a bullet or any other small weight at the other end of it; and another string and weight are fastened to the cylinder at *c*; the pivot *p* of wire is bent into the form of a handle; if the handle is turned either way, the strings will be respectively wound up upon the cone and cylinder; their lengths should now be adjusted, so that when the string on the cone is wound up as far as the cone will permit, the two weights may be at an equal distance from the bottom of the bracket, which bottom we suppose to be parallel with the pivots; the bracket should now be fastened against a wall, at such a height as to let the weights lightly touch the floor when the strings are unwound: silk or *bobbin* is a proper kind of string for this purpose, as it is woven or plaited, and therefore is not liable to twist. When the strings are wound up to their greatest heights, if the handle be suddenly let go, both the weights will begin to fall at the same moment; but the weight 1, will descend at first but slowly, and will pass through but small space compared with the weight 2. As they descend further, No. 2 still continues to get before No. 1; but after some time, No. 1 begins to overtake No. 2, and at last they come to the ground together. If this machine is required to show exactly the space that a falling body would describe in given times, the cone and cylinder must have grooves cut spirally upon their circumference, to direct the string with precision. To describe these spiral lines, became a new subject of inquiry. The young mechanics were again eager to exert their powers of invention; the eldest invented a machine upon the same principle as that which is used by the best workmen for cutting clock fusees; and it is described in Berthoud. The youngest invented the engine delineated, Plate 1, Fig. 4.

The roller or cone (or both together) which it is required to cut spirally, must be furnished with a handle, and a toothed wheel *w*, which turns a smaller wheel or pinion *w*. This pinion carries with it a screw *s*, which draws forward the puppet *p*, in which the graver of chisel *g* slides *without shake*. This graver has a point or edge shaped properly to form the spiral groove, with a shoulder to regulate the depth of the groove. The iron rod *r*, which is firmly fastened in the puppet, slides through mortices at *mm*, and guides the puppet in a straight line.

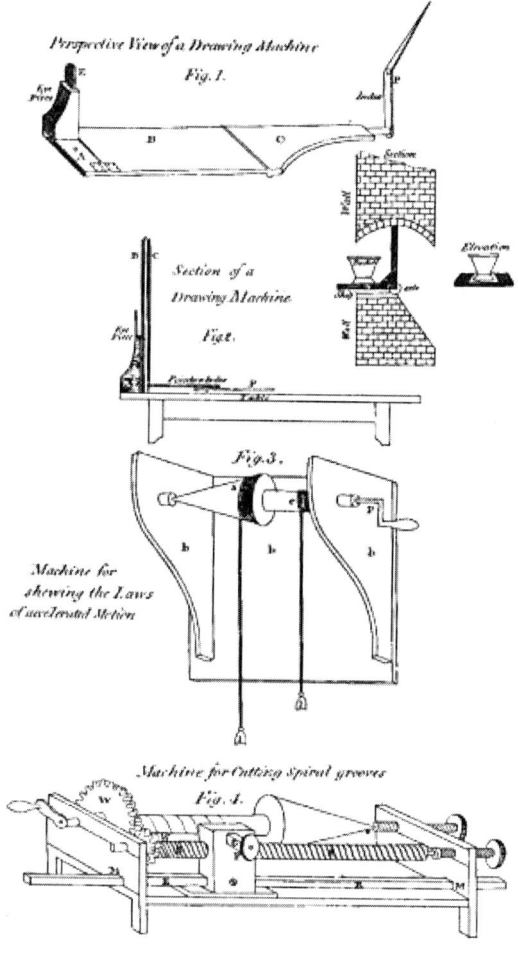

Plate 1.

The rest of the machine is intelligible from the drawing.

A simple method of showing the nature of compound forces was thought of at the same time. An ivory ball was placed at the corner of a board sixteen inches broad, and two feet long; two other similar balls were let fall down inclined troughs against the first ball in different directions, but at the same time. One fell in a direction parallel to the length of the board; the other ball fell back in a direction parallel to its breadth. By raising the troughs, such a force was communicated to each of the falling balls, as was sufficient to drive the ball that was at rest to that side or end of the board which was opposite, or at right angles, to the line of its motion.

When both balls were let fall together, they drove the ball that was at rest diagonally, so as to reach the opposite corner. If the same board were placed as an inclined plane, at an angle of five or six degrees, a ball placed at one of its uppermost corners, would fall with an accelerated motion in a direct line; but if another ball were made (by descending through an inclined trough) to strike the first ball at right angles to the line of its former descent, at the moment when it began to descend, it would not, as in the former experiment, move diagonally, but would describe a curve.

The reason why it describes a curve, and why that curve is not circular, was easily understood. Children who are thus induced to invent machines or apparatus for explaining and demonstrating the laws of mechanism, not only fix indelibly those laws in their own minds, but enlarge their powers of invention, and preserve a certain originality of thought, which leads to new discoveries.

We therefore strongly recommend it to teachers, to use as few precepts as possible in the rudiments of science, and to encourage their pupils to use their own understandings as they advance. In mechanism, a general view of the powers and uses of engines is all that need be taught; where more is necessary, such a foundation, with the assistance of good books, and the examination of good machinery, will perfect the knowledge of theory and facilitate practice.

At first we should not encumber our pupils with accurate demonstration. The application of mathematics to mechanics is undoubtedly of the highest use, and has opened a source of ingenious and important inquiry. Archimedes, the greatest name amongst mechanic philosophers, scorned the mere practical application of his sublime discoveries, and at the moment when the most stupendous effects were producing by his engines, he was so deeply absorbed in abstract speculation as to be insensible to the fear of death. We do not mean, therefore, to undervalue either the application of strict demonstration to problems in mechanics, or the exhibition of the most accurate machinery in philosophical lectures; but we wish to point out a method of giving a general notion of the mechanical organs to our pupils, which shall be immediately obvious to their comprehension, and which may serve as a sure foundation for future improvement. We are told by a vulgar proverb, that though we believe what we see, we have yet a higher belief in what we *feel*. This adage is particularly applicable to mechanics. When a person perceives the effect of his own bodily exertions with different engines, and when he can compare in a rough manner their relative advantages, he is not disposed to reject their assistance, or expect more than is reasonable from their application. The young theorist in mechanics thinks he can produce a perpetual motion! When he has been accustomed to refer to the plain dictates of common sense and experience, on this, as well as on every other subject, he will not easily be led astray by visionary theories.

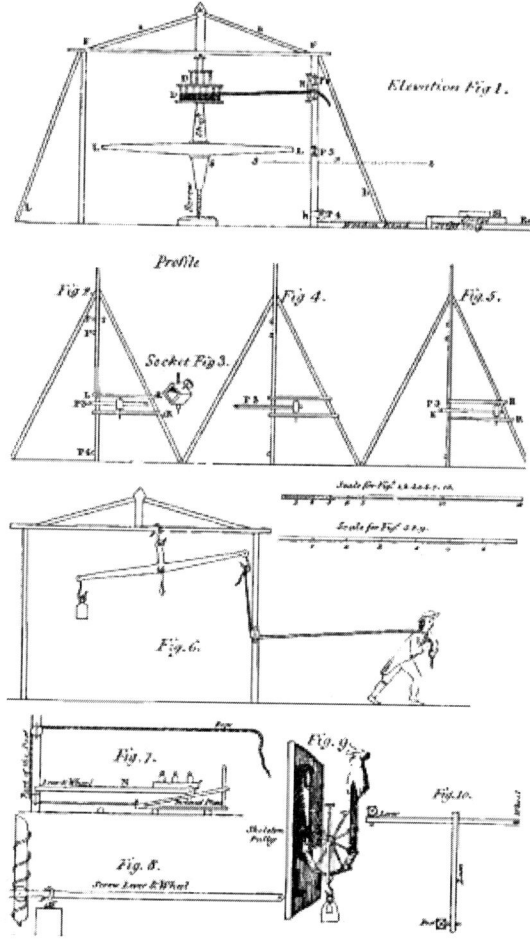

Plate 2.

To bring the sense of feeling to our assistance in teaching the uses of the mechanic powers, the following apparatus was constructed, to which we have given the name Panorganon.

It is composed of two principal parts: a frame to contain the moving machinery; and a *capstan* or *windlass*, which is erected on a *sill* or plank, that is sunk a few inches into the ground: the frame is by this means, and by six braces or props, rendered steady. The cross rail, or *transom*, is strengthened by braces and a king-post to make it lighter and cheaper. The *capstan* consists of an upright shaft, upon which are fixed two *drums*; about which a rope may be wound up, and two levers or arms by which it may be turned round. There is also a screw of iron coiled round the lower part of the shaft, to show the properties of the screw as a mechanic power. The rope which goes round the *drum* passes over one of the pulleys near to the top of the frame, and under another pulley near the bottom of the frame. As two *drums* of different sizes are employed, it is necessary to have an upright roller to conduct the rope in a proper direction to the pulleys, when either of the *drums* is used. Near the frame, and in the direction in which the rope runs, is laid a platform or road of deal boards, one board in breadth, and twenty or thirty feet long, upon which a small sledge loaded with different weights may be drawn. Plate 2. Fig. 1.

F. F. The frame.

b. b. Braces to keep the frame steady.

a. a. a. Angular braces to strengthen the transom; and also a *king-post*.

S. A round, taper shaft, strengthened above and below the mortises with iron hoops.

L L. Two arms, or levers, by which the shaft, &c. are to be moved round.

D D. The drum, which has two rims of different circumferences.

R. The roller to conduct the rope.

P. The pulley, round which the rope passes to the larger drum.

P 2. Another pulley to answer to the smaller drum.

P 3. A pulley through which the rope passes when experiments are tried with levers, &c.

P 4. Another pulley through which the rope passes when the sledge is used.

Ro. The road of deal boards for the sledge to move on.

Sl. The sledge, with pieces of hard wood attached to it, to guide it on the road.

Uses of the Panorganon

As this machine is to be moved by the force of men or children, and as their force varies not only with the strength and weight of each individual, but also according to the different manner in which that strength or weight is applied; it is, in the first place, requisite to establish one determinate mode of applying human force to the machine; and also a method of determining the relative force of each individual whose strength is applied to it.

To estimate the force with which a person can draw horizontally by a rope over his shoulder

EXPERIMENT I

Hang a common long scale-beam (without scales or chains) from the top or *transom* of the frame, so as that one end of it may come within an inch of one side or post of the machine. Tie a rope to the hook of the scale-beam, where the chains of the scale are usually hung, and pass it through the pulley P 3, which is about four feet from the ground; let the person pull this rope from 1 towards 2, turning his back to the machine, and pulling the rope over his shoulder—Pl. 2. Fig. 6. As the pulley may be either too high or too low to permit the rope to be horizontal, the person who pulls it should be placed ten or fifteen feet from the machine, which will lessen the angular direction of the cord, and the inaccuracy of the experiment. Hang weights to the other end of the scale-beam, until the person who pulls can but just walk forward, pulling fairly without propping his feet against any thing. This weight will estimate the force with which he can draw horizontally by a rope over his shoulder. [22] Let a child who tries this, walk on the board with dry shoes; let him afterwards chalk his shoes, and afterwards try it with his shoes soaped: he will find that he can pull with different degrees of force in these different circumstances; but when he tries the following experiments, let his shoes be always dry, that his force may be always the same.

To show the power of the three different sorts of levers

EXPERIMENT II

Instead of putting the cord that comes from the scale-beam, as in the last experiment, over the shoulder of the boy, hook it to the end 1 of the lever L, Fig. 2. Plate 2. This lever is passed through a socket—Plate 2. Fig. 3.—in which it can be shifted from one of its ends towards the other, and can be fastened at any place by the screw of the socket. This socket has two gudgeons, upon which it, and the lever which it contains, can turn. This socket and its gudgeons can be lifted out of the holes in which it plays, between the rail R R, Plate 2. Fig. 2. and may be put into other holes at R R, Fig. 5. Loop another rope to the other end of this lever, and let the boy pull as before. Perhaps it should be pointed out, that the boy must walk in a direction contrary to that in which he walked before, viz. from 1 towards 3. The height to which the weight ascends, and the distance to which the boy advances, should be carefully marked and measured; and it will be found, that he can raise the weight to the same height, advancing through the same space as in the former experiment. In this case, as both ends of the lever moved through equal spaces, the lever only changed the direction of the motion, and added no mechanical power to the direct strength of the boy.

EXPERIMENT III

Shift the lever to its extremity in the *socket*; the middle of the lever will be now opposite to the pulley, Pl. 2. Fig. 4.—hook to it the rope that goes through the pulley P 3, and fasten to the other end of the lever the rope by which the boy is to pull. This will be *a lever of the second kind*, as it is called in books of mechanics; in using which, *the resistance is placed between the centre of motion or fulcrum, and the moving power*. He will now raise double the weight that he did in Experiment II, and he will advance through double the space.

EXPERIMENT IV

Shift the lever, and the socket which forms the axis (without shifting the lever from the place in which it was in the socket in the last experiment) to the holes that are prepared for it at R R, Plate 2. Fig. 5. The free end of the lever E will now be opposite to the rope, and to the pulley (over which the rope comes from the scale-beam.) Hook this rope to it, and hook the rope by which the boy pulls, to the middle of the lever. The effect will now be different from what it was in the two last experiments; the boy will advance only half as far, and will raise only half as much weight as before. This is called *a lever of the third sort*. The first and second kinds of levers are used in quarrying; and the operations of many tools may be referred to them. The third kind of lever is employed but seldom, but its properties may be observed with advantage whilst a long ladder is raised, as the man who raises it, is obliged to exert an increasing force until the ladder is nearly perpendicular. When this lever is used, it is obvious, from what has been said, that the power must always pass through less space than the thing which is to be moved; it can never, therefore, be of service in gaining power. But the object of some machines, is to increase velocity, instead of obtaining power, as in a sledge-hammer moved by mill-work. (V. the plates in Emerson's Mechanics, No. 236.)

The experiments upon levers may be varied at pleasure, increasing or diminishing the mechanical advantage, so as to balance the power and the resistance, to accustom the learners to calculate the relation between the power and the effect in different circumstances; always pointing out, that whatever excess there is in the power, [23] or in the resistance, is always compensated by the difference of space through which the inferiour passes.

The experiments which we have mentioned, are sufficiently satisfactory to a pupil, as to the immediate relation between the power and the resistance; but the different spaces through which the power and the resistance move when one exceeds the other, cannot be obvious, without they pass through much larger spaces than levers will permit.

EXPERIMENT V

Place the sledge on the farthest end of the wooden road—Plate 2. Fig. 1.—fasten a rope to the sledge, and conduct it through the lowest pulley P 4, and through the pulley P 3, so as that the boy may be enabled to draw it by the rope passed over his shoulder. The sledge must now be loaded, until the boy can but just advance with short steps steadily upon the wooden road; this must be done with care, as there will be but just room for him beside the rope. He will meet the sledge exactly on the middle of the road, from which he must step aside to pass the sledge. Let the time of this experiment be noted. It is obvious that the boy and the sledge move with equal velocity; there is, therefore, no mechanical advantage obtained by the pulleys. The weight that he can draw will be about half a hundred, if he weigh about nine stone; but the exact force with which the boy draws, is to be known by Experiment I.

The wheel and axle

This organ is usually called in mechanics, *The axis in peritrochio*. A *hard* name, which might well be spared, as the word windlass or capstan would convey a more distinct idea to our pupils.

EXPERIMENT VI

To the largest drum, Plate 2. Fig. 1. fasten a cord, and pass it through the pulley P downwards, and through the pulley P 4 to the sledge placed at the end of the wooden road, which is farthest from the machine. Let the boy, by a rope fastened to the extremity of one of the arms of the capstan, and passed over his shoulder, draw the capstan round; he will wind the rope round the drum, and draw the sledge upon its road. To make the sledge advance twenty-four feet upon its road, the boy must have walked circularly 144 feet, which is six times as far, and he will be able to draw about three hundred weight, which is six times as much as in the last experiment.

It may now be pointed out, that the difference of space, passed through by the power in this experiment, is exactly equal to the difference of weight, which the boy could draw without the capstan.

EXPERIMENT VII

Let the rope be now attached to the smaller drum; the boy will draw nearly twice as much weight upon the sledge as before, and will go through double the space.

EXPERIMENT VIII

Where there are a number of boys, let five or six of them, whose power of drawing (estimated as in Experiment I) amounts to six times as much as the force of the boy at the capstan, pull at the end of the rope which *was* fastened to the sledge; they will balance the force of the boy at the capstan: either they, or he, by a sudden pull, may advance, but if they pull fairly, there will be no advantage on either part. In this experiment, the rope should pass through the pulley P 3, and should be coiled round the larger drum. And it must be also observed, that in all experiments upon the motion of bodies, in which there is much friction, as where a sledge is employed, the results are never so uniform as in other circumstances.

The Pulley

Upon the pulley we shall say little, as it is in every body's hands, and experiments may be tried upon it without any particular apparatus. It should, however, be distinctly inculcated, that the power is not increased by a fixed pulley. For this purpose, a wheel without a rim, or, to speak with more propriety, a number of spokes fixed in a nave, should be employed. (Plate 2. Fig. 9.) Pieces like the heads of crutches should be fixed at the ends of these spokes, to receive a piece of girth-web, which is used instead of a cord, because a cord would be unsteady; and a strap of iron with a hook to it should play upon the centre, by which it may at times be suspended, and from which at other times a weight may be hung.

EXPERIMENT IX

Let the skeleton of a pulley be hung by the iron strap from the transom of the frame; fasten a piece of web to one of the radii, and another to the end of the opposite radius. If two boys of equal weight pull these pieces of girth-web, they will balance each other; or two equal weights hung to these webs, will be in equilibrio. If a piece of girth-web be put round the uppermost radius, two equal weights hung at the ends of it will remain immoveable; but if either of them be pulled, or if a small additional weight be added to either of them, it will descend, and the web will apply itself successively to the ascending radii, and will detach itself from those that are descending. If this movement be carefully considered, it will be perceived, that the web, in unfolding itself, acts in the same manner upon the radii as two ropes would if they were hung to the extremities of the opposite radii in succession. The two radii which are opposite, may be considered as a lever of the first sort, where the centre is in the middle of the lever; as each end moves through an equal space, there is no mechanical advantage. But if this skeleton-pulley be employed as a common *block* or *tackle*, its motions and properties will be entirely different.

EXPERIMENT X. PLATE 2. FIG. 9

Nail a piece of girth-web to a post, at the distance of three or four feet from the ground; fasten the other end of it to one of the radii. Fasten another piece of web to the opposite radius, and let a boy hold the skeleton-pulley suspended by the web; hook weights to the strap that hangs from the centre. The end of the radius to which the fixed girth-web is fastened, will remain immoveable; but, if the boy pulls the web which he holds in his hand upwards, he will be able to lift nearly double the weight, which he can raise from the ground by a simple rope, without the machine, and he will perceive that his hand moves through twice as great a space as the weight ascends: he has, therefore, the mechanical advantage which he would have by a lever of the second sort, as in Experiment iii. Let a piece of web be put round the under radii, let one end of it be nailed to the post, and the other be held by the boy, and it will represent the application of a rope to a moveable pulley; if its motion be carefully considered, it will appear that the radii, as they successively apply themselves to the web, represent a series of levers of the second kind. A pulley is nothing more than an infinite number of such levers; the cord at one end of the diameter serving as a fulcrum for the *organ* during its progress. If this *skeleton-pulley* be used horizontally, instead of perpendicularly, the circumstances which have been mentioned, will appear more obvious.

Upon the wooden road lay down a piece of girth-web; nail one end of it to the road; place the pulley upon the web at the other end of the board, and, bringing the web over the radii, let the boy, taking hold of it, draw the loaded sledge fastened to the hook at the centre of the pulley: he will draw nearly twice as much in this manner as he could without the pulley. [24]

Here the web lying on the road, shows more distinctly, that it is quiescent where the lowest radius touches it; and if the radii, as they tread upon it, are observed, their points will appear at rest, whilst the centre of the pulley will go as fast as the sledge, and the top of each radius successively (and the boy's hand which unfolds the web) will move twice as fast as the centre of the pulley and the sledge.

If a person, holding a stick in his hand, observes the relative motions of the top, and the middle, and the bottom of the stick, whilst he inclines it, he will see that the bottom of the stick has no motion on the ground, and that the middle has only half the motion of the top. This property of the pulley has been dwelt upon, because it elucidates the motion of a wheel rolling upon the ground; and it explains a common paradox, which appears at first inexplicable. "The bottom of a rolling wheel never moves *upon* the road." This is asserted only of a wheel moving over hard ground, which, in fact, may be considered rather as laying down its circumference upon the road, than as moving upon it.

The inclined Plane and the Wedge

The *inclined plane* is to be next considered. When a heavy body is to be raised, it is often convenient to lay a sloping artificial road of planks, up which it may be pushed or drawn. This mechanical power, however, is but of little service without the assistance of wheels or rollers; we shall, therefore, speak of it as it is applied in another manner, under the name of *the wedge*, which is, in fact, a moving inclined plane; but if it is required to explain the properties of the inclined plane by the panorganon, the wooden road may be raised and set to any inclination that is required, and the sledge may be drawn upon it as in the former experiments.

Let one end of a lever, N. Plate 2. Fig. 7. with a wheel at one end of it, be hinged to the post of the frame, by means of a gudgeon driven or screwed into the post. To prevent this lever from deviating sideways, let a slip of wood be connected with it by a nail, which shall be fast in the lever, but which moves freely in a hole in the rail. The other end of this slip must be fastened to a stake driven into the ground at three or four feet from the lever, at one side of it, and towards the end in which the wheel is fixed (Plate 2. Fig 10. which is a *vue d'oiseau*) in the same manner as the treadle of a common lathe is managed, and as the treadle of a loom is sometimes guided. [25]

EXPERIMENT XI

Under the wheel of this lever place an inclined plane or half-wedge (Plate 2. Fig. 7.) on the wooden road, with rollers under it, to prevent friction; [26] fasten a rope to the foremost end of the wedge, and pass it through the pulleys (P 4. and P 3.) as in the fifth experiment. Let a boy draw the sledge by this rope over his shoulder, and he will find, that as it advances it will raise the weight upwards; the wedge is five feet long, and elevated one foot. Now, if the perpendicular ascent of the weight, and the space through which he advances, be compared, he will find, that the space through which he has passed will be five times as great as that through which the weight has ascended; and that *this* wedge has enabled him to raise five times as much as he could raise without it, if his strength were applied, as in Experiment i, without any mechanical advantage. By making this wedge in two parts hinged together, with a graduated piece to keep them asunder, the wedge may be adjusted to any given obliquity; and it will be always found, that the mechanical advantage of the wedge may be ascertained by comparing its perpendicular elevation with its base. If the base of the wedge is 2, 3, 4, 5, or any other number of times greater than its height, it will enable the boy to raise respectively 2, 3, 4, 5 times more weight than he could do in Experiment i, by which his power is estimated.

The Screw

The screw is an inclined plane wound round a cylinder; the height of all its revolutions round the cylinder taken together, compared with the space through which the power that turns it passes, is the measure of its *mechanical advantage*. [27] Let the lever, used in the last experiment, be turned in such a manner as to reach from its gudgeon to the shaft of the Panorganon, guided by an attendant lever as before. (Plate 2. Fig. 8.) Let the wheel rest upon the lowest *helix* or thread of the screw: as the arms of the shaft are turned round, the wheel will ascend, and carry up the weight which is fastened to the lever. [28] As the situation of the screw prevents the weight from being suspended exactly from the centre of the screw, proper allowance must be made for this in estimating the force of the screw, or determining the mechanical advantage gained by the lever: this can be done by measuring the perpendicular ascent of the weight, which in all cases is better, and more expeditious, than measuring the parts of a machine, and estimating its force by calculation; because the different diameters of ropes, and other small circumstances, are frequently mistaken in estimates.

The space passed through by the moving power, and by that which it moves, are infallible data for estimating the powers of engines. Two material subjects of experiments, yet remain for the Panorganon; friction, and wheels of carriages: but we have already extended this article far beyond its just proportion to similar chapters in this work. We repeat, that it is not intended in this, or in any other part of our design, to write treatises upon science; but merely to point out methods for initiating young people in the rudiments of knowledge, and of giving them a clear and distinct view of those principles upon which they are founded. No preceptor, who has had experience, will cavil at the superficial knowledge of a boy of twelve or thirteen upon these subjects; he will perceive, that the general view, which we wish to give our pupils of the useful arts and sciences, must certainly tend to form a taste for literature and investigation. The *sciolist* has learned only to *talk*—we wish to teach our pupils to *think*, upon the various objects of human speculation.

The Panorganon may be employed in trying the resistance of air and water; the force of different muscles; and in a great variety of amusing and useful experiments. In academies, and private families, it may be erected in the place allotted for amusement, where it will furnish entertainment for many a vacant hour. When it has lost its novelty, the shaft may from time to time be taken down, and a swing may be suspended in its place. It may be constructed at the expense of five or six pounds: that which stands before our window, was made for less than three guineas, as we had many of the materials beside us for other purposes.

[21] When this question was sometime afterwards repeated to S——, he observed, that the feather would throw down the castle, if its swiftness were so great as to make up for its want of weight.

[22] Were it thought necessary to make these experiments perfectly accurate, a segment of a pulley, the radius of which is half the length of the scale-beam, should be attached to the end of the beam; upon which the cord may apply itself, and the pulley (P 3) should be raised or lowered, to bring the rope horizontally from the man's shoulder when in the attitude of drawing.

[23] The word *power* is here used in a popular sense, to denote the strength or efficacy that is employed to produce an effect by means of any engine.

[24] In all these experiments with the skeleton-pulley, somebody must keep it in its proper direction; as from

its structure, which is contrived for illustration, not for practical use, it cannot retain its proper situation without assistance.

[25] In a loom this secondary lever is called *a lamb*, by mistake, for *lam*; from *lamina*, a slip of wood.

[26] There should be three rollers used; one of them must be placed before the sledge, under which it will easily find its place, if the bottom of the sledge near the foremost end is a little sloped upwards. To retain this foremost roller in its place until the sledge meets it, it should be stuck lightly on the road with two small bits of wax or pitch.

[27] *Mechanical advantage* is not a proper term, but our language is deficient in proper technical terms. The word *power* is used so indiscriminately, that it is scarcely possible to convey our meaning, without employing it more strictly.

[28] In this experiment, the boy should pull as near as possible to the shaft, within a foot of it, for instance, else he will have such mechanical advantage as cannot be counterbalanced by any weight which the machine would be strong enough to bear.

CHAPTER XVIII
CHEMISTRY

In the first attempts to teach chemistry to children, objects should be selected, the principal properties of which may be easily discriminated by the senses of touch, taste or smell; and such terms should be employed as do not require accurate definition.

When a child has been caught in a shower of snow, he goes to the fire to warm and dry himself. After he has been before the fire for some time, instead of becoming dry, he finds that he is wetter than he was before: water drops from his hat and clothes, and the snow with which he was covered disappears. If you ask him what has become of the snow, and why he has become wetter, he cannot tell you. Give him a tea-cup of snow, desire him to place it before the fire, he perceives that the snow melts, that it becomes water. If he puts his finger into the water, he finds that it is warmer than snow; he then perceives that the fire which warmed him, warmed likewise the snow, which then became water; or, in other words, he discovers, that the heat which came from the fire goes into the snow and melts it: he thus acquires the idea of the dissolution of snow by heat.

If the cup containing the water, or melted snow, be taken from the fire, and put out of the window on a frosty day, he perceives, that in time the water grows colder; that a thin, brittle skin spreads over it; which grows thicker by degrees, till at length all the water becomes ice; and if the cup be again put before the fire, the ice returns to water. Thus he discovers, that by diminishing the heat of water, it becomes ice; by adding heat to ice, it becomes water.

A child watches the drops of melted sealing-wax as they fall upon paper. When he sees you stir the wax about, and perceives, that what was formerly hard, now becomes soft and very hot, he will apply his former knowledge of the effects of heat upon ice and snow, and he will tell you that the heat of the candle melts the wax. By these means, the principle of the solution of bodies by heat, will be imprinted upon his memory; and you may now enlarge his ideas of solution.

When a lump of sugar is put into a dish of hot tea, a child sees that it becomes less and less, till at last it disappears. What has become of the sugar? Your pupil will say that it is melted by the heat of the tea: but if it be put into cold tea, or cold water, he will find that it dissolves, though more slowly. You should then show him some fine sand, some clay, and chalk, thrown into water; and he will perceive the difference between mechanical mixture and diffusion, or chemical mixture. Chemical mixture, as that of sugar in water, depends upon the attraction that subsists between the parts of the solid and fluid which are combined. Mechanical mixture is only the suspension of the parts of a solid in a fluid. When fine sand, chalk, or clay, are put into water, the water continues for some time turbid or muddy; but by degrees the sand, &c. falls to the bottom, and the water becomes clear. In the chemical mixture of sugar and water, there is no muddiness, the fluid is clear and transparent, even whilst it is stirred, and when it is at rest, there is no sediment, the sugar is joined with the water; a new, fluid substance, is formed out of the two simple bodies sugar and water, and though the parts which compose the mixture are not discernible to the eye, yet they are perceptible by the taste.

After he has observed the mixture, the child should be asked, whether he knows any method by which he can separate the sugar from the water. In the boiling of a kettle of water, he has seen the steam which issues from the mouth of the vessel; he knows that the steam is formed by the heat from the fire, which joining with the water drives its parts further asunder, and makes it take another form, that of vapour or steam. He may apply this knowledge to the separation of the sugar and water; he may turn the water into steam, and the sugar will be left in the vessel in a solid form. If, instead of evaporating the water, the boy had added a greater quantity of sugar to the mixture, he would have seen, that after a certain time, the water would have dissolved no more of the sugar; the superfluous sugar would fall to the bottom of the vessel as the sand had done: the pupil should then be told that the liquid is *saturated* with the solid.

By these simple experiments, a child may acquire a general knowledge of solution, evaporation, and saturation, without the formality of a lecture, or the apparatus of a chemist. In all your attempts to instruct him in chemistry, the greatest care should be taken that he should completely understand one experiment, before you proceed to another. The common metaphorical expression, that the mind should have time to digest the food which it receives, is founded upon fact and observation.

Our pupil should see the solution of a variety of substances in fluids, as salt in water; marble, chalk, or alkalies, in acids; and camphire in spirits of wine: this last experiment he may try by himself, as it is not dangerous.

Certainly many experiments are dangerous, and therefore unfit for children; but others may be selected, which they may safely try without any assistance; and the dangerous experiments may, when they are necessary, be shown to them by some careful person. Their first experiments should be such as they can readily execute, and of which the result may probably be successful: this success will please and interest the pupils, and will encourage them to perseverance.

A child may have some spirit of wine and some camphire given to him; the camphire will dissolve in the spirit of wine, till the spirit is saturated; but then he will be at a loss how to separate them again. To separate them, he must pour into the mixture a considerable quantity of water; he will immediately see the liquor, which was transparent, become muddy and white: this is owing to the separation of the camphire from the spirit; the camphire falls to the bottom of the vessel in the form of a curd. If the child had weighed the camphire, both before and after its solution, he would have found the result nearly the same. He should be informed, that this *chemical operation* (for technical terms should now be used) is called *precipitation*: the substance that is separated from the mixture by the introduction of another body, is cast down, or precipitated from the mixture. In this instance, the spirit of wine attracted the camphire, and therefore dissolved it. When the water was poured in, the spirit of wine attracted the water more strongly than it did the camphire; the camphire being let loose, fell to the bottom of the vessel.

The pupil has now been shown two methods, by which a solid may be separated from a fluid in which it has been dissolved.

A still should now be produced, and the pupil should be instructed in the nature of distillation. By experiments he will learn the difference between the *volatility* of different bodies; or, in other words, he will learn that some are made fluid, or are turned into vapour, by a greater or less degree of heat than others. The degrees of heat should be shown to him by the thermometer, and the use of the thermometer, and its nature, should be explained. As the pupil already knows that most bodies expand by heat, he will readily understand, that an increase of heat extends the mercury in the bulb of the thermometer, which, having no other space for its expansion, rises in the small glass tube; and that the degree of heat to which it is exposed, is marked by the figures on the scale of the instrument.

The business of distillation, is to separate the more volatile from the less volatile of two bodies. The whole mixture is put into a vessel, under which there is fire: the most volatile liquor begins first to turn into vapour, and rises into a higher vessel, which, being kept cold by water or snow, condenses the evaporated fluid; after it has been condensed, it drops into another vessel. In the experiment that the child has just tried, after having separated the camphire from the spirit of wine by precipitation, he may separate the spirit from the water by distillation. When the substance that rises, or that is separated from other bodies by heat, is a solid, or when what is collected after the operation, is solid, the process is not called distillation, but sublimation.

Our pupil may next be made acquainted with the general qualities of acids and alkalies. For instructing him in this part of chemistry, definition should as much as possible be avoided; example, and occular demonstration, should be pursued. Who would begin to explain by words the difference between an acid and an alkali, when these can be shown by experiments upon the substances themselves? The first great difference which is perceptible between an acid and an alkali, is their taste. Let a child have a distinct perception of the difference of their tastes; let him be able to distinguish them when his eyes are shut; let him taste the strongest of each so as not to hurt him, and when he has once acquired distinct notions of the pungent taste of an alkali, and of the sour taste of an acid, he will never forget the difference. He must afterwards see the effects of an acid and alkali on the blue colour of vegetables at *separate times*, and not on the same day; by these means he will more easily remember the experiments, and he will not confound their different results. The blue colour of vegetables is turned red by acids, and green by alkalies. Let your pupil take a radish, and scrape off the blue part into water; it should be left for some time, until the water becomes of a blue colour: let him pour some of this liquor into two glasses; add vinegar or lemon juice to one of them, and the liquor will become red; dissolve some alkali in water, and pour this into the other glass, and the dissolved radish will become green. If into the red mixture alkali be poured, the colour will change into green; and if into the liquor which was made green, acid be poured, the colour will change to red: thus alternately you may pour acid or alkali, and produce a red or green colour successively. Paper stained with the blue colour of vegetables, is called *test* paper; this is changed by the least powerful of the acids or alkalies, and will, therefore, be peculiarly useful in the first experiments of our young pupils. A child should for safety use the weakest acids in his first trials, but he should be shown that the effects are similar, whatever acids we employ; only the colour will be darker when we make use of the strong, than when we use the weak acids. By degrees the pupil should be accustomed to employ the strong acids; such as the vitriolic, the nitric, and the muriatic, which three are called fossil acids, to distinguish them from the vegetable, or weaker acids. We may be permitted to advise the young chemist to acquire the habit of wiping the neck of the vessel out of which he pours any strong acid, as the drops of the liquor will not then burn his hand when he takes hold of the bottle; nor will they injure the table upon which he is at work. This custom, trivial as it may seem, is of advantage, as it gives an appearance of order, and of ease, and steadiness, which are all necessary in trying chemical experiments. The little pupil may be told, that the custom which we have just mentioned, is the constant practice of the great chemist, Dr. Black.

We should take care how we first use the term *salt* in speaking to children, lest they should acquire indistinct ideas: he should be told, that the kind of salt which he eats is not the only salt in the world; he may be put in mind of the kind of salts which he has, perhaps, smelt in smelling-bottles; and he should be further told, that there are a number of earthy, alkaline, and metallic salts, with which he will in time become acquainted.

When an acid is put upon an alkali, or upon limestone, chalk, or marle, a bubbling may be observed, and a noise is heard; a child should be told, that this is called *effervescence*. After some time the effervescence ceases, and the limestone, &c. is dissolved in the acid. This effervescence, the child should be informed, arises from the escape of a considerable quantity of a particular sort of air, called fixed air, or carbonic acid gas. In the solution of the lime in the acid, the lime and acid have an attraction for one another; but as the present mixture has no attraction for the gas, it escapes, and in rising, forms the bubbling or effervescence. This may be proved to a child, by showing him, that if an acid is poured upon caustic lime (lime which has had this gas taken from it by fire) there will be no effervescence.

There are various other chemical experiments with which children may amuse themselves; they may be employed in analyzing marle, or clays; they may be provided with materials for making ink or soap. It should be pointed out to them, that the common domestic and culinary operations of making butter and cheese, baking, brewing, &c. are all chemical processes. We hope the reader will not imagine, that we have in this slight sketch pretended to point out the *best* experiments which can be devised for children; we have only offered a few of the simplest which occurred to us, that parents may not, at the conclusion of this chapter, exclaim, "What is to be done? How are we to *begin*? What experiments are suited to children? If we knew, our children should try them."

It is of little consequence what particular experiment is selected for the first; we only wish to show, that the minds of children may be turned to this subject; and that, by accustoming them to observation, we give them not only the power of learning what has been already discovered, but of adding, as they grow older, something to the general stock of human knowledge.

CHAPTER XIX
ON PUBLIC AND PRIVATE EDUCATION

The anxious parent, after what has been said concerning tasks and classical literature, will inquire whether the whole plan of education recommended in the following pages, is intended to relate to public or to private education. It is intended to relate to both. It is not usual to send children to school before they are eight or nine years old: our first object is to show how education may be conducted to that age in such a manner, that children may be well prepared for the acquisition of all the knowledge usually taught at schools, and may be perfectly free from many of the faults that pupils sometimes have acquired before they are sent to any public seminary. It is obvious, that public preceptors would be saved much useless labour and anxiety, were parents to take some pains in the previous instruction of their children; and more especially, if they were to prevent them from learning a taste for total idleness, or habits of obstinacy and of falsehood, which can scarcely be conquered by the utmost care and vigilance. We can assure parents, from experience, that if they pursue steadily a proper plan with regard to the understanding and the moral habits, they will not have much trouble with the education of their children after the age we have mentioned, as long as they continue to instruct them at home; and if they send them to public schools, their superiority in intellect and in conduct will quickly appear. Though we have been principally attentive to all the circumstances which can be essential to the management of young people during the first nine or ten years of their lives, we have by no means confined our observations to this period alone; but we have endeavoured to lay before parents a general view of the human mind (as far as it relates to our subject) of proper methods of teaching, and of the objects of rational instruction—so that they may extend the principles which we have laid down, through all the succeeding periods of education, and may apply them as it may best suit their peculiar situations, or their peculiar wishes. We are fully conscious, that we have executed but very imperfectly even our own design; that experimental education is yet but in its infancy, and that boundless space for improvement remains; but we flatter ourselves, that attentive parents and preceptors will consider with candour the practical assistance which is offered to them, especially as we have endeavoured to express our opinions without dogmatical presumption, and without the illiberal exclusion of any existing institutions or prevailing systems. People who, even with the best intentions, attack with violence any of these, and who do not consider what is practicable, as well as what ought to be done, are not likely to persuade, or to convince mankind to increase the general sum of happiness, or their own portion of felicity. Those who really desire to be of service to society, should point out decidedly, but with temperate indulgence for the feelings and opinions of others, whatever appears to them absurd or reprehensible in any prevailing customs: having done this, they will rest in the persuasion that what is most reasonable, will ultimately prevail.

Mankind, at least the prudent and rational part of mankind, have an aversion to pull down, till they have a moral certainty that they can build up a better edifice than that which has been destroyed. Would you, says an eminent writer, convince me, that the house I live in is a bad one, and would you persuade me to quit it; build a better in my neighbourhood; I shall be very ready to go into it, and shall return you my very sincere thanks. Till another house be ready, a wise man will stay in his old one, however inconvenient its arrangement, however seducing the plans of the enthusiastic projector. We do not set up for projectors, or reformers: we wish to keep steadily in view the actual state of things, as well as our own hopes of progressive improvement; and to seize and combine all that can be immediately serviceable: all that can assist, without precipitating improvements. Every well informed parent, and every liberal school-master, must be sensible, that there are many circumstances in the management of public education which might be condemned with reason; that too much time is sacrificed to the study of the learned languages; that too little attention is paid to the general improvement of the understanding and formation of the moral character; that a school-master cannot pay attention to the temper or habits of each of his numerous scholars; and that parents, during that portion of the year which their children spend with them, are not sufficiently solicitous to co-operate with the views of the school-master; so that the public is counteracted by the private education. These, and many other things, we have heard objected to schools; but what are we to put in the place of schools? How are vast numbers who are occupied themselves in public or professional pursuits, how are men in business or in trade, artists or manufacturers, to educate their families, when they have not time to attend to them; when they may not think themselves perfectly prepared to undertake the classical instruction and entire education of several boys; and when, perhaps, they may not be in circumstances to engage the assistance of such a preceptor as they could approve? It is obvious, that if in such situations parents were to attempt to educate their children at home, they would harass themselves, and probably spoil their pupils irrecoverably. It would, therefore, be in every respect impolitic and cruel to disgust those with public schools, who have no other resource for the education of their families. There is another reason which has perhaps operated upon many in the middle ranks of life unperceived, and which determines them in favour of public education. Persons of narrow fortune, or persons who have acquired wealth in business, are often desirous of breeding up their sons to the liberal professions: and they are conscious that the company, the language, and the style of life, which their children would be accustomed to at home, are beneath what would be suited to their future professions. Public schools efface this rusticity, and correct the faults of provincial dialect: in this point of view they are highly advantageous. We strongly recommend it to such parents to send their children to large public schools, to Rugby, Eton, or Westminster; not to any small school; much less to one in their own neighbourhood. Small schools are apt to be filled with persons of nearly the same stations, and out of the same neighbourhood: from this circumstance, they contribute to perpetuate uncouth antiquated idioms, and many of those obscure prejudices which cloud the intellect in the future business of life.

Whilst we admit the necessity which compels the largest portion of society to prefer public seminaries of education, it is incumbent upon us to caution parents from expecting that the moral character, the understandings, or the tempers of their children, should be improved at large schools; there the learned languages, we acknowledge, are successfully taught. Many satisfy themselves with the assertion, that public education is the least troublesome, that a boy once sent to school is settled for several years of life, and will require only short returns of parental care twice a year at the holydays. It is hardly to be supposed, that those who think in this manner, should have paid any anxious, or at least any judicious attention to the education of their children, previously to sending them to school. It is not likely that they should be very solicitous about the commencement of an education which they never meant to finish: they would think, that what could be done during the first few years of life, is of little consequence; that children from four to seven years old are too young to be taught; and that a school would speedily supply all deficiencies, and correct all those faults which begin at that age to be troublesome at home. Thus to a public school, as to a general infirmary for mental disease, all desperate subjects are sent, as the last resource. They take with them the contagion of their vices, which quickly runs through the whole tribe of their companions, especially amongst those who happen to be nearly of their own age, whose sympathy peculiarly exposes them to the danger of infection. We are often told, that as young people have the strongest sympathy with each other, they will learn most effectually from each other's example. They do learn quickly from example, and this is one of the dangers of a public school: a danger which is not necessary, but incidental; a danger against which no school-master can possibly guard, but which parents can, by the previous education of the pupils, prevent. Boys are led, driven, or carried to school; and in a school-room they first meet with those who are to be their fellow prisoners. They do not come with fresh unprejudiced minds to commence their course of social education; they bring with them all the ideas and habits which they have already learned at their respective homes. It is highly unreasonable to expect, that all these habits should be reformed by a public preceptor. If he had patience, how could he have time for such an undertaking? Those who have never attempted to break a pupil of any one bad habit, have no idea of the degree of patience requisite to success. We once heard an officer of dragoons assert, that he would rather break twenty horses of their bad habits, than one man of his. The proportionate difficulty of teaching boys, may be easily calculated.

It is sometimes asserted, that the novelty of a school life, the change of situation, alters the habits, and forms in boys a new character. Habits of eight or nine years standing, cannot be instantaneously, perhaps can never be radically, destroyed; they will mix themselves imperceptibly with the new ideas which are planted in their minds, and though these may strike the eye by the rapidity of their growth, the others, which have taken a strong root, will not easily be dispossessed of the soil. In this new character, as it is called, there will, to a discerning eye, appear a strong mixture of the old disposition. The boy, who at home lived with his father's servants, and was never taught to have any species of literature, will not acquire a taste for it at school, merely by being compelled to learn his lessons; the boy, who at home was suffered to be the little tyrant of a family, will, it is true, be forced to submit to superior strength or superior numbers at school; [29] but does it improve the temper to practise alternately the habits of a tyrant and a slave? The lesson which experience usually teaches to the temper of a school-boy, is, that strength, and power, and cunning, will inevitably govern in society: as to reason, it is out of the question, it would be hissed or laughed out of the company. With respect to social virtues, they are commonly amongst school-boys so much mixed with party spirit, that they mislead even the best dispositions. A boy at home, whose pleasures are all immediately connected with the idea of self, will not feel a sudden enlargement of mind from entering a public school. He will, probably, preserve his selfish character in his new society; or, even suppose he catches that of his companions, the progress is not great in moral education from selfishness to spirit of party: the one is a despicable, the other a dangerous, principle of action. It has been observed, that what we are when we are twenty, depends on what we were when we were ten years old. What a young man is at college, depends upon what he was at school; and what he is at school, depends upon what he was before he went to school. In his father's house, the first important lessons, those which decide his future abilities and character, must be learned. We have repeated this idea, and placed it in different points of view, in hopes that it will catch and fix the attention. Suppose that parents educated their children well for the first eight or nine years of their lives, and then sent them all to public seminaries, what a difference this must immediately make in public education: the boys would be disposed to improve themselves with all the ardour which the most sanguine preceptor would desire; their tutors would find that there was nothing to be *unlearned*; no habits of idleness to conquer; no perverse stupidity would provoke them; no capricious contempt of application would appear in pupils of the quickest abilities. The moral education could then be made a part of the preceptor's care, with some hopes of success; the pupils would all have learned the first necessary moral principles and habits; they would, consequently, be all fit companions for each other; in each other's society they would continue to be governed by the same ideas of right and wrong by which they had been governed all their lives; they would not have any new character to learn; they would improve, by mixing with numbers, in the social virtues, without learning party spirit; and though they would love their companions, they would not, therefore, combine together to treat their instructers as pedagogues and tyrants. This may be thought an Utopian idea of a school; indeed it is very improbable, that out of the numbers of parents who send their children to large schools, many should suddenly be much moved, by any thing that we can say, to persuade them to take serious trouble in their previous instruction. But much may be effected by gradual attempts. Ten well educated boys, sent to a public seminary at nine or ten years old, would, probably, far surpass their competitors in every respect; they would inspire others with so much emulation, would do their parents and preceptors so much credit, that numbers would eagerly inquire into the causes of their superiority; and these boys would, perhaps, do more good by their example, than by their actual acquirements. We do not mean to promise, that a boy judiciously educated, shall appear at ten years old a prodigy of learning; far from it: we should not even estimate his capacity, or the chain of his future progress, by the quantity of knowledge stored in his memory, by the number of Latin lines he had got by rote, by his expertness in repeating the rules of his grammar, by his pointing out a number of places readily in a map, or even by his knowing the latitude and longitude of all the capital cities in Europe; these are all useful articles of knowledge: but they are not the test of a good education. We should rather, if we were to examine a boy of ten years old, for the credit of his parents, produce proofs of his being able to reason accurately, of his quickness in invention, of his habits of industry and application, of his having learned to generalize his ideas, and to apply his observations and his principles: if we found that he had learned all, or any of these things, we should be in little pain about grammar, or geography, or even Latin; we should be tolerably certain that he would not long remain deficient in any of these; we should know that he would overtake and surpass a competitor who had only been technically taught, as certainly as that the giant would overtake the panting dwarf, who might have many miles the start of him in the race. We do not mean to say, that a boy should not be taught the principles of grammar, and some knowledge of geography, at the same time that his understanding is cultivated in the most enlarged manner: these objects are not incompatible, and we particularly recommend it to *parents who intend to send their children to school*, early to give them confidence in themselves, by securing the rudiments of literary education; otherwise their pupils, with a real superiority of understanding, may feel depressed, and may, perhaps, be despised, when they mix at a public school with numbers who will estimate their abilities merely by their proficiency in particular studies.

Mr. Frend, [30] in recommending the study of arithmetic for young people, has very sensibly remarked, that boys bred up in public schools, are apt to compare themselves with each other merely as classical scholars; and, when they afterwards go into the world excellent Greek and Latin scholars, are much astonished to perceive, that many of the companions whom they had under-valued at school, get before them when they come to actual business, and to active life. Many, in the pursuit of their classical studies, have neglected all other knowledge, especially that of arithmetic, that useful, essential branch of knowledge, without which neither the abstract sciences nor practical arts can be taught. The precision which the habit of applying the common rules of arithmetic, gives to the understanding, is highly advantageous, particularly to young people of vivacity, or, as others would say, of genius. The influence which the habit of estimating has upon that part of the moral character called prudence, is of material consequence. We shall further explain upon this subject when we speak of the means of teaching arithmetic and reasoning to children; we only mention the general ideas here, to induce intelligent parents to attend early to these particulars. If they mean to send their children to public classical schools, it must be peculiarly advantageous to teach them early the rudiments of arithmetic, and to give them the habit of applying their knowledge in the common business of life. We forbear to enumerate other useful things, which might easily be taught to young people before they leave home, because we do not wish to terrify with the apprehension, that a perplexing variety of things are to be taught. One thing well taught, is better than a hundred taught imperfectly.

The effect of the pains which are taken in the first nine or ten years of a child's life, may not be apparent immediately to the view, but it will gradually become visible. To careless observers, two boys of nine years old, who have been very differently educated, may appear nearly alike in abilities, in temper, and in the promise of future character. Send them both to a large public school, let them be placed in the same new situation, and exposed to the same trials, the difference will then appear: the difference in a few years will be such as to strike every eye, and people will wonder what can have produced in so short a time such an amazing change. In the Hindoo art of dyeing, the same liquors communicate different colours to particular spots, according to the several bases previously applied: to the ignorant eye, no difference is discernible in the ground, nor can the design be distinctly traced till the air, and light, and open exposure, bring out the bright and permanent colours to the wondering eye of the spectator.

Besides bestowing some attention upon early education, parents, who send their children to school, may much assist the public preceptor by judicious conduct towards children during that portion of the year which is usually spent at home. [31] Mistaken parental fondness, delights to make the period of time which children spend at home, as striking a contrast as possible with that which they pass at school. The holydays are made a jubilee, or rather resemble the Saturnalia. Even if parents do not wish to represent a school-master as a tyrant, they are by no means displeased to observe, that he is not the friend or favourite of their children. They put themselves in mean competition with him for their affection, instead of co-operating with him in all his views for their advantage. How is it possible, that any master can long retain the wish or the hope of succeeding in any plan of education, if he perceives that his pupils are but partially under his government; if his influence over their minds be counteracted from time to time by the superior influence of their parents? An influence which he must not wish to destroy. To him is left the power to punish, it is true; but parents reserve to themselves the privilege to reward. The ancients did not suppose, that even Jupiter could govern the world without the command of pain and pleasure. Upon the vases near his throne, depended his influence over mankind.

And what are these holyday delights? And in what consists parental rewards? In dissipation and idleness. With these are consequently associated the idea of happiness and the name of pleasure; the name is often sufficient, without the reality. During the vacation, children have a glimpse of what is called *the world*; and then are sent back to their prison with heads full of visions of liberty, and with a second-sight of the blessed lives which they are to lead when they have left school for ever. What man of sense, who has studied the human mind, who knows that the success of any plan of education must depend upon the concurrence of every person, and every circumstance, for years together, to the same point, would undertake any thing more than the partial instruction of pupils, whose leading associations and habits must be perpetually broken? When the work of school is undone during the holydays, what hand could have the patience perpetually to repair the web?

During the vacations spent at home, children may be made extremely happy in the society and in the affections of their friends, but they need not be taught, that idleness is pleasure: on the contrary, occupation should, by all possible methods, be rendered agreeable to them; their school acquisitions, their knowledge and taste, should be drawn out in conversation, and they should be made to feel the value of what they have been taught; by these means, there would be some connection, some unity of design, preserved in their education. Their school-masters and tutors should never become the theme of insipid ridicule; nor should parents ever put their influence in competition with that of a preceptor: on the contrary, his pupils should uniformly perceive, that from his authority there is no appeal, except to the superior power of reason, which should be the avowed arbiter to which all should be submitted.

Some of the dangerous effects of that mixed society at schools, of which we have complained, may be counteracted by the judicious conduct of parents during the time which children spend at home. A better view of society, more enlarged ideas of friendship and of justice, may be given to young people, and the vile principle of party spirit may be treated with just contempt and ridicule. Some standard, some rules may be taught to them, by which they may judge of character independently of prejudice, or childish prepossession.

> "I do not like you, Doctor Fell;
> The reason why, I cannot tell:
> But this I know full well,
> I do not like you, Doctor Fell" —

is an exact specimen of the usual mode of reasoning, of the usual method in which an ill educated school-boy expresses his opinion and feelings about all persons, and all things. "The reason why," should always be inquired whenever children express preference or aversion.

To connect the idea of childhood with that of inferiority and contempt, is unjust and impolitic; it should not be made a reproach to young people to be young, nor should it be pointed out to them, that when they are some years older, they will be more respected; the degree of respect which they really command, whether in youth or age, will depend upon their own conduct, their knowledge, and their powers of being useful and agreeable to others. If they are convinced of this, children will not at eight years old long to be fifteen, or at fifteen to be one and twenty; proper subordination would be preserved, and the scale of happiness would not have a forced and false connection with that of age. If parents did not first excite foolish wishes in the minds of their children, and then imprudently promise that these wishes shall be gratified at certain periods of their existence, children would not be impatient to pass over the years of childhood; those years which idle boys wish to pass over as quickly as possible, men without occupation regret as the happiest of their existence. To a child, who has been promised that he shall put on manly apparel on his next birthday, the pace of time is slow and heavy until that happy era arrive. Fix the day when a boy shall leave school, and he wishes instantly to mount the chariot, and lash the horses of the sun. Nor when he enters the world, will his restless spirit be satisfied; the first step gained, he looks anxiously forward to the height of manly elevation,

"And the brisk minor pants for twenty-one"

These juvenile anticipations diminish the real happiness of life; those who are in continual expectation, never enjoy the present; the habit of expectation is dangerous to the mind, it suspends all industry, all voluntary exertion. Young men, who early acquire this habit, find existence insipid to them without the immediate stimuli of hope and fear: no matter what the object is, they must have something to sigh for; a curricle, a cockade, or an opera-dancer.

Much may be done by education to prevent this boyish restlessness. Parents should refrain from those imprudent promises, and slight inuendoes, which the youthful imagination always misunderstands and exaggerates.— Never let the moment in which a young man quits a seminary of education, be represented as a moment in which all instruction, labour, and restraints, cease. The idea, that he must restrain and instruct himself, that he must complete his own education, should be excited in a young man's mind; nor should he be suffered to imagine that his education is finished, because he has attained to some given age.

When a common school-boy bids adieu to that school which he has been taught to consider as a prison, he exults in his escape from books and masters, and from all the moral and intellectual discipline, to which he imagines that it is the peculiar disgrace and misery of childhood to be condemned. He is impatient to be thought a man, but his ideas of the manly character are erroneous, consequently his ambition will only mislead him. From his companions whilst at school, from his father's acquaintance, and his father's servants, with whom he has been suffered to consort during the vacations, he has collected imperfect notions of life, fashion, and society. These do not mix well in his mind with the examples and precepts of Greek and Roman virtue: a temporary enthusiasm may have been kindled in his soul by the eloquence of antiquity; but, for want of sympathy, this enthusiasm necessarily dies away. His heroes are not the heroes of the present times; the maxims of his sages are not easily introduced into the conversation of the day. At the tea-table he now seldom hears even the name of Plato; and he often blushes for not knowing a line from a popular English poet, whilst he could repeat a cento from Horace, Virgil, and Homer; or an antistrophe from Æschylus or Euripides. He feels ashamed to produce the knowledge he has acquired, because he has not learned sufficient address to produce it without pedantry. On his entrance into the world, there remains in his mind no grateful, no affectionate, no respectful remembrance of those under whose care he has passed so many years of his life. He has escaped from the restraints imposed by his school-master, and the connection is dissolved for ever.

But when a son separates from his father, if he has been well educated, he wishes to continue his own education: the course of his ideas is not suddenly broken; what he has been, joins immediately with what he is to be; his knowledge applies to real life, it is such as he can use in all companies; there is no sudden metamorphosis in any of the objects of his ambition; the boy and man are the same individual. Pleasure will not influence him merely by her name, or by the contrast of her appearance with the rigid discipline of scholastic learning; he will feel the difference between pleasure and happiness, and his early taste for domestic life will remain or return upon his mind. His old precepts and new motives are not at war with each other; his experience will confirm his education, and external circumstances will call forth his latent virtues. When he looks back, he can trace the gradual growth of his knowledge; when he looks forward, it is with the delightful hope of progressive improvement. A desire in some degree to repay the care, to deserve the esteem, to fulfil the animating prophecies, or to justify the fond hopes of the parent who has watched over his education, is one of the strongest motives to an ingenuous young man; it is an incentive to exertion in every honourable pursuit. A son who has been judiciously and kindly educated, will feel the value of his father's friendship. The perception, that no man can be more entirely interested in every thing that concerns him, the idea, that no one more than his father can share in his glory or in his disgrace, will press upon his heart, will rest upon his understanding. Upon these ideas, upon this common family interest, the real strength of the connection between a father and his son depends. No public preceptor can have the same advantages; his connection with his pupil is not necessarily formed to last.

After having spoken with freedom, but we hope with moderation, of public schools, we may, perhaps, be asked our opinion of universities. Are universities the most splendid repositories of learning? We are not afraid to declare an opinion in the negative. Smith, in his Wealth of Nations, has stated some objections to them, we think, with unanswerable force of reasoning. We do not, however, wish to destroy what we do not entirely approve. Far be that insanity from our minds which would, like Orlando, tear up the academic groves; the madness of innovation is as destructive as the bigotry of ancient establishments. The learning and the views of the rising century must have different objects from those of the wisdom and benevolence of Alfred, Balsham, or Wolsey; and, without depreciating or destroying the magnificence or establishments of universities, may not their institutions be improved? May not their splendid halls echo with other sounds than the exploded metaphysics of the schools? And may not other learning be as much rewarded and esteemed as pure *latinity*?

We must here distinctly point out, that young men designed for the army or the navy, should not be educated in private families. The domestic habits, the learned leisure of private education, are unsuited to them; it would be absurd to waste many years in teaching them the elegancies of classic literature, which can probably be of no essential use to them; it would be cruel to give them a nice and refined choice of right and wrong, when it will be their professional duty to act under the command of others; when implicit, prompt, unquestioning obedience must be their first military virtue. Military academies, where the sciences practically essential to the professions are taught, must be the best situations for all young sailors and soldiers; strict institution is the best education for them. We do not here inquire how far these professions are necessary in society; it is obvious, that in the present state of European cultivation, soldiers and sailors are indispensable to every nation. We hope, however, that a taste for peace may, at some future period in the history of the world, succeed to the passion for military glory; and in the mean time, we may safely recommend it to parents, never to trust a young man designed for a soldier, to the care of a philosopher, even if it were possible to find one who would undertake the charge.

We hope that we have shown ourselves the friends of the public preceptor, that we have pointed out the practicable means of improving public institutions by parental care and parental co-operation. But, until such a meliorating plan shall actually have been carried into effect, we cannot hesitate to assert, that even when the abilities of the parent are inferiour to those of the public preceptor, the means of ensuring success preponderate in favour of private education. A father, who has time, talents, and temper, to educate his family, is certainly the best possible preceptor; and his reward will be the highest degree of domestic felicity. If, from his situation, he is obliged to forego this reward, he may select some man of literature, sense, and integrity, to whom he can confide his children. Opulent families should not think any reward too munificent for such a private preceptor. Even in an economic point of view, it is prudent to calculate how many thousands lavished on the turf, or lost at the gaming table, might have been saved to the heirs of noble and wealthy families by a judicious education.

[29] V. Barne's Essay on public and private education.
Manchester Society.

[30] V. Mr. Frend's Principles of Algebra.

[31] V. Williams's Lectures on Education.

CHAPTER XX
ON FEMALE ACCOMPLISHMENTS, MASTERS, AND GOVERNESSES

Some years ago, an opera dancer at Lyon's, whose charms were upon the wane, applied to an English gentleman for a recommendation to some of his friends in England, as a governess for young ladies. "Do you doubt," said the lady (observing that the gentleman was somewhat confounded by the easy assurance of her request) "do you doubt my capability? Do I not speak good Parisian French? Have I any provincial accent? I will undertake to teach the language grammatically. And for music and dancing, without vanity, may I not pretend to teach them to any young person?" The lady's excellence in all these particulars was unquestionable. She was beyond dispute a highly accomplished woman. Pressed by her forcible interrogatories, the gentleman was compelled to hint, that an English mother of a family might be inconveniently inquisitive about the private history of a person who was to educate her daughters. "Oh," said the lady, "I can change my name; and, at my age, nobody will make further inquiries."

Before we can determine how far this lady's pretensions were ill founded, and before we can exactly decide what qualifications are most desirable in a governess, we must form some estimate of the positive and relative value of what are called accomplishments.

We are not going to attack any of them with cynical asperity, or with the ambition to establish any new dogmatical tenets in the place of old received opinions. It can, however, do no harm to discuss this important subject with proper reverence and humility. Without alarming those mothers, who declare themselves above all things anxious for the rapid progress of their daughters in every fashionable accomplishment, it may be innocently asked, what price such mothers are willing to pay for these *advantages*. Any price within the limits of our fortune! they will probably exclaim.

There are other standards by which we can measure the value of objects, as well as by money. "Fond mother, would you, if it were in your power, accept of an opera dancer for your daughter's governess, upon condition that you should live to see that daughter dance the best minuet at a birth-night ball?"

"Not for the world," replies the mother. "Do you think I would hazard my daughter's innocence and reputation, for the sake of seeing her dance a good minuet? Shocking! Absurd! What can you mean by such an outrageous question?"

"To fix your attention. Where the mind has not precisely ascertained its wishes, it is sometimes useful to consider extremes; by determining what price you will *not* pay, we shall at length ascertain the value which you set upon the object. Reputation and innocence, you say, you will not, upon any account, hazard. But would you consent that your daughter should, by universal acclamation, be proclaimed the most accomplished woman in Europe, upon the simple condition, that she should pass her days in a nunnery?"

"I should have no right to make such a condition; domestic happiness I ought certainly to prefer to public admiration for my daughter. Her accomplishments would be of little use to her, if she were to be shut up from the world: who is to be the judge of them in a nunnery?"

"I will say no more about the nunnery. But would not you, as a good mother, consent to have your daughter turned into an automaton for eight hours in every day for fifteen years, for the promise of hearing her, at the end of that time, pronounced the first private performer at the most fashionable and most crowded concert in London?"

"Eight hours a day for fifteen years, are too much. No one need practise so much to become the first performer in England."

"That is another question. You have not told me whether you would sacrifice so much of your daughter's existence for such an object, supposing that you could obtain it at no other price."

"For *one* concert?" says the hesitating mother; "I think it would be too high a price. Yet I would give any thing to have my daughter play better than any one in England. What a distinction! She would be immediately taken notice of in all companies! She might get into the first circles in London! She would want neither beauty nor fortune to recommend her! She would be a match for any man, who has any taste for music! And music is universally admired, even by those who have the misfortune to have no taste for it. Besides, it is such an elegant accomplishment in itself! Such a constant source of innocent amusement! Putting every thing else out of the question, I should wish my daughter to have every possible accomplishment, because accomplishments are such charming *resources* for young women; they keep them out of harm's way; they make a vast deal of their idle time pass so pleasantly to themselves and others! This is my *chief* reason for liking them."

Here are so many reasons brought together at once, along with the chief reason, that they are altogether unanswerable; we must separate, class, and consider them one at a time. Accomplishments, it seems, are valuable, as being the objects of universal admiration. Some accomplishments have another species of value, as they are tickets of admission to fashionable company. Accomplishments have another, and a higher species of value, as they are supposed to increase a young lady's chance of a prize in the matrimonial lottery. Accomplishments have also a value as resources against ennui, as they afford continual amusement and innocent occupation. This is ostensibly their chief praise; it deserves to be considered with respect. False and odious must be that philosophy which would destroy any one of the innocent pleasures of our existence. No reward was thought too high for the invention of a new pleasure; no punishment would be thought too severe for those who would destroy an old one. Women are peculiarly restrained in their situation, and in their employments, by the customs of society: to diminish the number of these employments, therefore, would be cruel; they should rather be encouraged, by all means, to cultivate those tastes which can attach them to their home, and which can preserve them from the miseries of dissipation. Every sedentary occupation must be valuable to those who are to lead sedentary lives; and every art, however trifling in itself, which tends to enliven and embellish domestic life, must be advantageous, not only to the female sex, but to society in general. As far as accomplishments can contribute to all or any of these excellent purposes, they must be just objects of attention in early education.

A number of experiments have already been tried; let us examine the result. Out of the prodigious number of young women who learn music and drawing, for instance, how many are there, who, after they become mistresses of their own time, and after they have the choice of their own amusements, continue to practise these accomplishments for the pure pleasure of occupation? As soon as a young lady is married, does she not frequently discover, that "she really has not *leisure* to cultivate talents which take up so much time?" Does she not complain of the labour of practising four or five hours a day to keep up her musical character? What motive has she for perseverance? She is, perhaps, already tired of playing to all her acquaintance. She may really take pleasure in hearing good music; but her own performance will not then please her ear so much as that of many others. She will prefer the more indolent pleasure of hearing the best music that can be heard for money at public concerts. She will then of course leave off playing, but continue very fond of music. How often is the labour of years thus lost for ever!

Those who have excelled in drawing, do not appear to abandon the occupation so suddenly; it does not demand such an inordinate quantity of time to keep up the talent; the exertion of the imitative powers with apparent success, is agreeable; the employment is progressive, and, therefore, the mind is carried on to complete what has been begun. Independently of all applause, which may be expected for the performance, there is a pleasure in going on with the work. But setting aside enthusiasm and habit, the probability that any sensible person will continue to pursue a given employment, must depend, in a great measure, upon their own conviction of its utility, or of its being agreeable to those whom they wish to please. The pleasure which a lady's friends receive from her drawings, arises chiefly from the perception of their comparative excellence. Comparative excellence is all to which gentlewomen artists usually pretend, all to which they expect to attain; positive excellence is scarcely attained by one in a hundred. Compared with the performances of other young ladies of their acquaintance, the drawings of Miss X or Y may be justly considered as charming! admirable! and astonishing! But there are few drawings by young ladies which can be compared with those of a professed artist. The wishes of obliging friends are satisfied with a few drawings in handsome frames, to be hung up for the young lady's credit; and when it is allowed amongst their acquaintance, that she draws in a *superior* style, the purpose of this part of her education is satisfactorily answered. We do not here speak of those few individuals who really *excel* in drawing, who have learnt something more than the common routine which is usually learnt from a drawing master, who have acquired an agreeable, talent, not for the mere purpose of exhibiting themselves, but for the sake of the occupation it affords, and the pleasure it may give to their *friends*. We have the pleasure of knowing some who exactly answer to this description, and who must feel themselves distinct and honourable exceptions to these general observations.

From whatever cause it arises, we may observe, that after young women are settled in life, their taste for drawing and music gradually declines. For this fact, we can appeal only to the recollection of individuals. We may hence form some estimate of the real value which ought to be put upon what are called accomplishments, *considered as occupations*. Hence we may also conclude, that parents do not form their judgments from the facts which they see every day in real life; or else may we not infer, that they deceive themselves as to their own motives; and that, amongst the reasons which make them so anxious about the accomplishments of their daughters, there are some secret motives more powerful than those which are usually openly acknowledged?

It is admitted in the cabinet council of mothers, that some share of the value of accomplishments depends upon the demand for them in the fashionable world. "A young lady," they say, "is nobody, and nothing, without accomplishments; they are as necessary to her as a fortune: they are indeed considered as part of her fortune, and sometimes are even found to supply the place of it. Next to beauty, they are the best tickets of admission into society which she can produce; and every body knows, that on the company she keeps, depends the chance of a young woman's settling advantageously in the world."

To judge of what will please and attach men of superior sense and characters—we are not quite certain that these are the men who are to be considered first, when we speak of a young lady's settling *advantageously* in the world; but we will take this for granted—to judge of what will please and attach men of superior sense and characters, we must observe their actual conduct in life, and listen to their speculative opinions. Superficial accomplishments do not appear to be the objects of their preference. In enumerating the perfections of his wife, or in retracing the progress of his love, does a man of sense dwell upon his mistress's skill in drawing, or dancing, or music? No. These, he tells you, are extremely agreeable talents, but they could have never attached him; they are subordinate parts in her character; he is angry that you can rank them amongst her perfections; he knows that a thousand women possess these accomplishments, who have never touched his heart. He does not, perhaps, deny, that in Chloe, altogether, they have power to please, but he does not think them essential to her power.

The opinion of women, who have seen a good deal of the world, is worth attending to upon this subject; especially if we can obtain it when their passions are wholly uninterested in their decision. Whatever may be the judgment of individuals concerning the character and politics of the celebrated Madame Roland, her opinion as a woman of abilities, and a woman who had seen a variety of life, will be thought deserving of attention. Her book was written at a time when she was in daily expectation of death, when she could have no motive to conceal her real sentiments upon any subject. She gives an account of her employments in prison, and, amongst others, mentions music and drawing.

"I then employed myself in drawing till dinner time. I had so long been out of the habit of using a pencil, that I could not expect to be very dexterous; but we commonly retain the power of repeating with pleasure, or at least of attempting with ease, whatever we have successfully practised in our youth. Therefore the study of the fine arts, considered as a part of female education, should be attended to, much less with a view to the acquisition of superior talents, than with a desire to give women a taste for industry, the habit of application, and a greater variety of employments; for these assist us to escape from *ennui*, the most cruel disease of civilized society; by these we are preserved from the dangers of vice, and even from those seductions which are far more likely to lead us astray.

"I would not make my daughter a *performer*. [32] I remember, that my mother was afraid that I should become a great musician, or that I should have devoted myself entirely to painting: she wished that I should, above all other things, love the duties of my sex: that I should be a good economist, a good mistress, as well as a good mother of a family. I wish my Eudora to be able to accompany her voice agreeably on the harp. I wish that she may play agreeably on the piano-forte; that she may know enough of drawing, to feel pleasure from the sight and from the examination of the finest pictures of the great painters; that she may be able to draw a flower that happens to please her; and that she may unite in her dress elegance and simplicity. I should wish that her talents might be such, that they should neither excite the admiration of others, nor inspire her with vanity; I should wish that she should please by the general effect of her whole character, without ever striking any body with astonishment at first sight; and that she should attach by her good qualities, rather than shine by her accomplishments."

Women cannot foresee what may be the tastes of the individuals with whom they are to pass their lives. Their own tastes should not, therefore, be early decided; they should, if possible, be so educated that they may attain any talent in perfection which they may desire, or which their circumstances may render necessary. If, for instance, a woman were to marry a man who was fond of music, or who admired painting, she should be able to cultivate these talents for his amusement and her own. If he be a man of sense and feeling, he will be more pleased with the motive than with the thing that is actually done. But if it be urged, that all women cannot expect to marry men of sense and feeling; and if we are told, that nevertheless they must look to "an advantageous establishment," we must conclude, that men of rank and fortune are meant by that comprehensive phrase. Another set of arguments must be used to those who speculate on their daughters accomplishments in this line. They have, perhaps, seen some instances of what they call success; they have seen some young women of their acquaintance, whose accomplishments have attracted men of fortune superior to their own; consequently, maternal tenderness is awakened, and many mothers are sanguine in their expectations of the effect of their daughters education.

But they forget that every body now makes the same reflections, that parents are, and have been for some years, speculating in the same line; consequently, the market is likely to be overstocked, and, of course, the value of the commodities must fall. Every young lady (and every young woman is now a young lady) has some pretensions to accomplishments. She draws a little; or she plays a little, or she speaks French a little. Even the blue-board boarding schools, ridiculed by Miss Allscript in the Heiress, profess to perfect young ladies in some or all of these necessary parts of education. Stop at any good inn on the London roads, and you will probably find that the landlady's daughter can show you some of her own framed drawings, can play a tune upon her spinnet, or support a dialogue in French of a reasonable length, in the customary questions and answers. Now it is the practice in high life to undervalue, and avoid as much as possible, every thing which descends to the inferiour classes of society. The dress of to-day is unfashionable to-morrow, because every body wears it. The dress is not preferred because it is pretty or useful, but because it is the distinction of well bred people. In the same manner accomplishments have lost much of that value which they acquired from opinion, since they have become common. They are now so common, that they cannot be considered as the distinguishing characteristics of even a gentlewoman's education. The higher classes in life, and those individuals who aim at distinction, now establish another species of monopoly, and secure to themselves a certain set of expensive masters in music, drawing, dancing, &c. and they endeavour to believe, and to make others believe, that no one can be well educated without having served an apprenticeship of so many lessons under some of these privileged masters. But it is in vain that they intrench themselves, they are pursued by the intrusive vulgar. In a wealthy, mercantile nation, there is nothing which can be bought for money, which will long continue to be an envied distinction. The hope of attaining to that degree of eminence in the fine arts which really deserves celebrity, becomes every day more difficult to private practitioners, because the number of competitors daily increases; and it is the interest of masters to forward their pupils by every possible means. Both genius and perseverance must now be united to obtain the prize of distinction; and how seldom are they found, or kept together, in the common course of education!

Considering all these circumstances, is not there some reason to apprehend, that in a few years the taste for several fashionable appendages of female education, may change, and that those will consequently be treated with neglect, who have no other claim to public regard, than their proficiency in what may, perhaps, then be thought vulgar or obsolete accomplishments? Our great grandmothers distinguished themselves by truly substantial tentwork chairs and carpets, by needle-work pictures of Solomon and the queen of Sheba. These were admirable in their day, but their day is over; and these useful, ingenious, and laborious specimens of female talents, are consigned to the garret, or they are produced but as curiosities, to excite wonder at the strange patience and miserable destiny of former generations: the taste for tapestry and embroidery is thus past; the long labours of the loom have ceased. Cloth-work, crape-work, chenille-work, ribbon-work, wafer-work, with a long train of etceteras, have all passed away in our own memory; yet these conferred much evanescent fame, and a proportional quantity of vain emulation. A taste for drawing, or music, cannot be classed with any of these trifling performances; but there are many faded drawings of the present generations, which cannot stand in competition with the glowing and faithful colours of the silk and worsted of former times; and many of the hours spent at a *stammering* harpsichord, might, surely, with full as much domestic advantage, have been devoted to the embellishment of chairs and carpets. We hope that no one will so perversely misunderstand us, as to infer from these remarks, that we desire to see the revival of old tapestry work; or that we condemn the elegant accomplishments of music and drawing. We condemn only the abuse of these accomplishments; we only wish that they should be considered as domestic occupations, not as matters of competition, or of exhibition, nor yet as the means of attracting temporary admiration. We are not afraid that any, who are really conscious of having acquired accomplishments with these prudent and honourable views, should misapprehend what has been said. Mediocrity may, perhaps, attempt to misrepresent our remarks, and may endeavour to make it appear that we have attacked, and that we would discourage, every effort of female taste and ingenuity in the fine arts; we cannot, therefore, be too explicit in disclaiming such illiberal views.

We have not yet spoken of dancing, though it is one of the most admired of female accomplishments. This evidently is an amusement, not an occupation; it is an agreeable exercise, useful to the health, and advantageous, as it confers a certain degree of habitual ease and grace. Mr. Locke seems to think, that it gives young people confidence in themselves when they come into company, and that it is, therefore, expedient to teach children early to dance: but there are so many other methods of inspiring young people with this confidence in themselves, that it appears unnecessary to lay much stress upon this argument. If children live in good company, and see constantly people with agreeable manners, they will acquire manners which the dancing master does not always teach; and they will easily vary their forms of politeness with the fashion of the day. Nobody comes into a room regularly as their dancing master taught them to make their entrance;

we should think a strict adherence to his lessons ridiculous and awkward in well bred company; therefore much must be left to the discretion and taste of the pupil, after the dancing master has made his last bow. Ease of manners is not always attained by those who have been strictly disciplined by a Vestris, because the lessons are not always practised in precisely the same circumstances in which they were learnt: this confuses and confounds the pupils, and they rather lose than gain confidence in themselves, from perceiving that they cannot immediately apply what they have been taught. But we need not expatiate upon this subject, because there are few parents of good sense, in any rank of life, who will not perceive that their daughter's manners cannot be formed or polished by a dancing-master. We are not to consider dancing in a grave and moral light; it is an amusement much more agreeable to young people, and much better suited to them in every respect, than cards, or silent assemblies of formal visiters. It promotes cheerfulness, and prevents, in some measure, the habits of gossiping conversation, and the love of scandal. So far we most willingly agree with its most vivacious advocates, in its common eulogium. But this is not, we fear, saying enough. We see, or fancy that we see, the sober matron lay down her carefully assorted cards upon the card-table, and with dictatorial solemnity she pronounces, "That dancing is something more than an amusement; that girls must learn to dance, because they must appear well in public; because the young ladies who dance the best, are usually most *taken notice* of in public; most admired by the other sex; most likely, in short, not only to-have their choice of the best partner in a ball room, but sometimes of the best partner for life."

With submission to maternal authority, these arguments do not seem to be justified of late years. Girls, who dance remarkably well, are, it is true, admired in a ball room, and followed, perhaps, by those idle, thoughtless young men, who frequent public places merely for want of something else to do. This race of beings are not particularly calculated to make good husbands in any sense of the word; nor are they usually disposed to think of marriage in any other light than as the last desperate expedient to repair their injured fortunes. They set their wits against the sex in general, and consider themselves as in danger of being jockeyed into the matrimonial state. Some few, perhaps, who have not brought their imagination sufficiently under the command of the calculating faculty, are *caught* by beauty and accomplishments, and marry against the common rules of interest. These men are considered with pity, or with ridicule, by their companions, as dupes who have suffered themselves to be taken in: others are warned by their fate; and the future probability of similar *errours*, of course, must be diminished. The fashionable apathy, whether real or affected, with which young men lounge in public places, with scarcely the appearance of attention to the fair exhibitors before them, sufficiently marks the temper of the times; and if the female sex have lost any thing of the respect and esteem which ought to be paid to them in society, they can scarcely expect to regain their proper influence by concessions to the false and vitiated taste of those who combine to treat them with neglect bordering upon insolence. If the system of female education, if the system of female manners, conspire to show in the fair sex a degrading anxiety to attract worthless admiration, wealthy or titled homage, is it surprising that every young man, who has any pretensions to birth, fortune, or fashion, should consider himself as the arbiter of their fate, and the despotic judge of their merit? Women, who understand their real interests, perceive the causes of the contempt with which the sex is treated by fashionable coxcombs, and they feel some indignation at the meanness with which this contempt, tacitly or openly expressed, is endured. Women, who feel none of this indignation, and who, either from their education, or their circumstances, are only solicitous to obtain present amusement, or what they think the permanent advantages of a fortunate alliance, will yet find themselves mistaken by persisting in their thoughtless career; they will not gain even the objects to which they aspire. How many accomplished belles run the usual round of dissipation in all public places of exhibition, tire the public eye, and, after a season or two, fade and are forgotten! How many accomplished belles are there, who, having gained the object of their own, or of their mother's ambition, find themselves doomed to misery for life! Those unequal marriages, which are sometimes called *excellent matches*, seldom produce much happiness. And where happiness is not, what *is* all the rest?

If all, or any of these reflections, should strike the heart, and convince the understanding, of an anxious, but reasonable mother, she will, probably, immediately determine upon her own conduct in the education of her daughters: she will resolve to avoid the common errours of the frivolous or the interested; she will not be influenced by the importunity of every idle acquaintance, who may talk to her of the necessity of her daughter's being taken notice of in public, of the chances of an *advantageous* establishment, of the good fortune of Miss Y— —, or lady Angelina X— —, in meeting with a coxcomb or a spendthrift for a husband; nor will she be moved with maternal emulation when she is further told, that these young ladies owed their *success* entirely to the superiority of their accomplishments: she will consider, for one moment, what is meant by the word success; she will, perhaps, not be of opinion that "'tis best repenting in a coach and six;" she will, perhaps, reflect, that even the "soft sounds" of titled grandeur lose their power to please, and "salute the ear" almost unobserved. The happiness, the permanent happiness of her child, will be the first, the last object of the good and the enlightened mother: to this all her views and all her efforts will tend; and to this she will make every fashionable, every elegant accomplishment subservient.

As to the means of acquiring these accomplishments, it would be absurd, and presumptuous, to present here any vague precepts, or tedious details, upon the mode of learning drawing, dancing, and music. These can be best learned from the masters who profess to teach them, as far as the technical part is necessary. But success will not ultimately depend upon any technical instructions that a master can give: he may direct the efforts of industry so as to save much useless labour; he may prevent his pupils from acquiring bad practical habits; he may assist, but he cannot inspire, the spirit of perseverance. A master, who is not expected, or indeed allowed, to interfere in the general education of his pupils, can only diligently attend to them whilst he is giving his lessons; he has not any power, except that pernicious motive, competition, to excite them to excel; his instructions cannot be peculiarly adapted to their tempers or their understandings, because with these he is unacquainted. Now a sensible mother has it in her power to supply all these deficiencies; even if she does not herself excel in any of the accomplishments which her daughters are learning, her knowledge of their minds, her taste, her judgment, her affection, her superintending intelligence, will be of inestimable value to her children. If she has any skill in any accomplishment, she will, for the first years of her daughters' lives, be undoubtedly the best person to instruct them. By skill, we do not mean superior talents, or proficiency in music or drawing; without these, she may be able to teach all that is necessary in the early part of education. One of the best motives which a woman can have to cultivate her talents after she marries, is the hope and belief, that she may be essentially serviceable in the instruction of her family. And that she may be essentially serviceable, let no false humility lead her to doubt. She need not be anxious for the rapid progress of her little pupils; she need not be terrified if she see their equals in age surpass them under what she thinks more able tuition; she may securely satisfy herself, that if she but inspires her children with a desire to excel, with the habits of attention and industry, they will certainly succeed, sooner or later, in whatever it is desirable that they should learn. The exact age at which the music, dancing, or drawing master, should begin their instructions, need not be fixed. If a mother should not be so situated as to be able to procure the best masters for her daughters whilst they are yet children, she need not be in despair; a rapid progress is made in a short time by well educated young people; those who have not acquired any bad habits, are easily taught: it should, therefore, seem prudent, if the best masters cannot be procured at any given period of education, to wait patiently, than to hazard their first impressions, and the first habits which might be given by any inferiour technical instruction. It is said, that the celebrated musician Timotheus, whose excellence in his art Alexander the conqueror of the world was forced to acknowledge, when pupils flocked to him from all parts of the world, had the prudence to demand double *entrance money* from every scholar who had had any other music master.

Besides the advantage of being entirely free from other bad habits, children who are not taught by inferiour masters, will not contract habits of listless application. Under the eye of an indolent person, children seldom give their entire attention to what they are about. They become mere machines, and, without using their own understanding in the least, have recourse to the convenient master upon every occasion. The utmost that children in such circumstances can learn, is all the technical part of the art which the master can teach. When the master is at last dismissed, and her education completed, the pupil is left both fatigued and helpless. "Few have been taught to any purpose, who have not been their own teachers," says Sir Joshua Reynolds. This reflection upon the art of teaching, may, perhaps, be too general; but those persons who look back upon their education, will, in many respects, allow it to be just. They will perceive that they have been too much taught, that they have learned every thing which they know as an art, and nothing as a science. Few people have sufficient courage to re-commence their own education, and for this reason few people get beyond a certain point of mediocrity. It is easy to them to practise the lessons which they have learned, if they practise them in intellectual darkness; but if you let in upon them one ray of philosophic light, you dazzle and confound them, so that they cannot even perform their customary feats. A young man, [33] who had been blind from his birth, had learned to draw a cross, a circle, and a square, with great accuracy; when he was twenty, his eyes were couched, and when he could see perfectly well, he was desired to draw his circle and square. His new sense of seeing, so far from assisting him in this operation, was extremely troublesome to him; though he took more pains than usual, he performed very ill: confounded by the new difficulty, he concluded that sight was useless in all operations to be performed by the hand, and he thought his eyes would be of no use to him in future. How many people find their reason as useless and troublesome to them as this young man found his eye-sight!

Whilst we are learning any mechanical operation, or whilst we are acquiring any technical art, the mind is commonly passive. In the first attempts, perhaps, we reason or invent ways of abridging our own labour, and the awkwardness of the unpractised hand is assisted by ingenuity and reflection; but as we improve in manual dexterity, attention and ingenuity are no longer exerted; we go on habitually without thought.—Thought would probably interrupt the operation, and break the chain of associated actions. [34] An artificer stops his hand the moment you ask him to explain what he is about: he can work and talk of indifferent objects; but if he reflects upon the manner in which he performs certain slight of hand parts of his business, it is ten to one but he cannot go on with them. A man, who writes a free running hand, goes on without thinking of the manner in which he writes; fix his attention upon the manner in which he holds his pen, or forms his letters, and he probably will not write quite so fast, or so well, as usual. When a girl first attempts to dress herself at a glass, the glass perplexes, instead of assisting her, because she thinks and reasons about every motion; but when by habit she has learned how to move her hands in obedience to the *flugel*-image, [35] which performs its exercise in the mirror, no further thought is employed. Make the child observe that she moves her left hand forward when the image in the glass moves in a contrary manner, turn the child's attention to any of her own motions, and she will make mistakes as she did before her habits were formed.

Many occupations, which are generally supposed to depend upon the understanding, and which do probably depend in the first instance upon the *understanding*, become by practice purely mechanical. This is the case in many of the imitative arts. A person unused to drawing, exerts a great deal of attention in copying any new object; but custom soon supplies the place of thought. By custom, [36] as a great artist assures us, he will become able to draw the human figure tolerably correctly, with as little effort of the mind, as to trace with a pen the letters of the alphabet.

We must further observe, that the habit of pursuing any occupation, which requires no mental exertion, induces an indolence or incapacity of intellect. Mere artists are commonly as stupid as mere artificers, and these are little more than machines.

The length of time which is required to obtain practical skill and dexterity in certain accomplishments, is one reason why there are so few people who obtain any thing more than mechanical excellence. They become the slaves of custom, and they become proud of their slavery. At first they might have considered custom as a tyrant; but when they have obeyed her for a certain time, they do her voluntary homage ever after, as to a sovereign by divine right. To prevent this species of intellectual degradation, we must in education be careful to rank mere mechanical talents below the exercise of the mental powers. Thus the ambition of young people will be directed to high objects, and all inferiour qualifications may be attained without contracting the understanding. Praise children for patience, for perseverance, for industry; encourage them to reason and to invent upon all subjects, and you may direct their attention afterwards as you think proper. But if you applaud children merely for drawing a flower neatly, or copying a landscape, without exciting their ambition to any thing higher, you will never create superior talents, or a superior character. The proficiency that is made in any particular accomplishment, at any given age, should not be considered so much, even by those who highly value accomplishments, as the power, the energy, that is excited in the pupil's mind, from which future progress is ensured. The writing and drawing automaton performs its advertised wonders to the satisfaction of the spectators; but the machine is not *"instinct with spirit;"* you cannot expect from its pencil the sketch of a Raphael, or from its pen the thoughts of a Shakespeare. It is easy to guide the hand, but who can transfuse a soul into the image?

It is not an uncommon thing to hear young people, who have been long under the tuition of masters, complain of their own want of genius. They are sensible that they have not made any great progress in any of the accomplishments which they have endeavoured to learn; they see others, who have not, perhaps, had what they call such *opportunities* and *advantages* in their education, suddenly surpass them; this they attribute to natural genius, and they say to themselves in despair, "Certainly I have no taste for drawing; I have no genius for music; I have learned so many years, I have had so many lessons from the best masters, and yet here is such and such a one, who has had no master, who has taught herself, and, perhaps, did not begin till late in life, has got before me, because she has a natural genius for these things. She must have a natural taste for them, because she can sit whole hours at these things for her own pleasure. Now I never would take a pencil in my hand from my own choice; and I am glad, at all events, that the time for lessons and masters is over. My education is finished, for I am of age."

The disgust and despair, which are thus induced by an injudicious education, absolutely defeat its own trivial purposes. So that, whatever may be the views of parents, whether they consider ornamental accomplishments as essential to their daughter's *success* in the world, or whether they value them rather as secondary objects, subordinate to her happiness; whether they wish their daughter actually to excel in any particular accomplishment, or to have the power of excelling in any to which circumstances may direct her, it is in all cases advisable to cultivate the general power of the pupil's understanding, instead of confining her to technical practices and precepts, under the eye of any master who does not possess that which is the *soul* of every art.

We do not mean any illiberal attack upon masters; but in writing upon education, it is necessary to examine the utility of different modes of instruction, without fear of offending *any class* of men. We acknowledge, that it is seldom found, that those who can communicate their knowledge the best, *possess the most*, especially if this knowledge be that of an artist or a linguist. Before any person is properly qualified *to teach*, he must have the power of recollecting exactly how *he learned*; he must go back step by step to the point at which he began, and he must be able to conduct his pupil through the same path without impatience or precipitation. He must not only have acquired a knowledge of the process by which his own ideas and habits were formed, but he must have extensive experience of the varieties of the human mind. He must not suppose, that the operations of intellect are carried on precisely in the same manner in all minds; he must not imagine, that there is but one method of teaching, which will suit all persons alike. The analogies which strike his own mind, the arrangement of ideas, which to him appears the most perspicuous, to his pupil may appear remote and confused. He must not attribute this to his pupil's inattention, stupidity, or obstinacy; but he must attribute it to the true causes; the different association of ideas in different minds, the different habits of thinking, which arise from their various tempers and previous education. He must be acquainted with the habits of all tempers: the slow, the quick, the inventive, the investigating; and he must adapt his instructions accordingly. There is something more requisite: a master must not only know what he professes to teach of his own peculiar art or science, but he ought to know all its bearings and dependencies. He must be acquainted not only with the local topography of his own district, but he must have the whole map of human knowledge before him; and whilst he dwells most upon his own province, he must yet be free from local prejudices, and must consider himself as a citizen of the world. Children who study geography in small separate maps, understand, perhaps, the view of each country tolerably well; but we see them quite puzzled when they are to connect these maps in their idea of the world. They do not know the relative size or situation of England or France; they cannot find London or Paris when they look for the first time upon the globe, and every country seems to be turned upside down in their imagination. Young people who learn particular arts and sciences from masters who have confined their view to the boundaries of each, without having given an enlarged idea of the whole, are much in the same situation with these unfortunate geographers.

The persisting to teach things separately, which ought to be taught as a whole, must prevent the progress of mental cultivation. [37] The division and subdivision of different parts of education, which are monopolised as trades by the masters who profess to teach them, must tend to increase and perpetuate errour. These intellectual *casts* are pernicious.

It is said, that the Persians had masters to teach their children each separate virtue: one master to teach justice, another fortitude, another temperance, and so on. How these masters could preserve the boundaries of their several moral territories, it is not easy to imagine, especially if they all insisted upon independent sovereignty. There must have been some danger, surely, of their disputing with one another concerning the importance of their respective professions, like the poor bourgeois gentilhomme's dancing-master, music-master, master of morality, and master of philosophy, who all fell to blows to settle their pretensions, forgetful of the presence of their pupil. Masters, who are only expected to teach one thing, may be sincerely anxious for the improvement of their pupils in that particular, without being in the least interested for their general character or happiness. Thus the drawing-master has done his part, and is satisfied if he teaches his pupil to draw well: it is no concern of his what her temper may be, any more than what sort of hand she writes, or how she dances. The dancing-master, in his turn, is wholly indifferent about the young lady's progress in drawing; all he undertakes, is to teach her to dance.

We mention these circumstances to show parents, that masters, even when they do the utmost that they engage to do, cannot educate their children; they can only partially instruct them in particular arts. Parents must themselves preside over the education of their children, or must entirely give them into the care of some person of an enlarged and philosophic mind, who can supply all the deficiencies of common masters, and who can take advantage of all the positive good that can be obtained from existing institutions. Such a preceptor or governess must possess extensive knowledge, and that superiority of mind which sees the just proportion and value of every acquisition, which is not to be overawed by authority, or dazzled by fashion. Under the eye of such persons, masters will keep precisely their proper places; they will teach all they can teach, without instilling absurd prejudices, or inspiring a spirit of vain rivalship; nor will masters be suffered to continue their lessons when they have nothing more to teach.

Parents who do not think that they have leisure, or feel that they have capacity, to take the entire direction of their children's education upon themselves, will trust this important office to a governess. The inquiry concerning the value of female accomplishments, has been purposely entered into before we could speak of the choice of a governess, because the estimation in which these are held, will very much determine parents in their choice.

If what has been said of the probability of a decline in the public taste for what are usually called accomplishments; of their little utility to the happiness of families and individuals; of the waste of time, and waste of the higher powers of the mind in acquiring them: if what has been observed on any of these points is allowed to be just, we shall have little difficulty in pursuing the same principles further. In the choice of a governess we should not, then, consider her fashionable accomplishments as her best recommendations; these will be only secondary objects. We shall examine with more anxiety, whether she possess a sound, discriminating, and enlarged understanding: whether her mind be free from prejudice; whether she has steadiness of temper to pursue her own plans; and, above all, whether she has that species of integrity which will justify a parent in trusting a child to her care. We shall attend to her conversation, and observe her manners, with scrupulous minuteness. Children are *imitative animals,* and they are peculiarly disposed to imitate the language, manners, and gestures, of those with whom they live, and to whom they look up with admiration. In female education, too much care cannot be taken to form all those habits in morals and in manners, which are distinguishing characteristics of amiable women. These habits must be acquired early, or they will never appear easy or graceful; they will necessarily be formed by those who see none but good models.

We have already pointed out the absolute necessity of union amongst all those who are concerned in a child's education. A governess must either rule, or obey, decidedly. If she do not agree with the child's parents in opinion, she must either know how to convince them by argument, or she must with strict integrity conform her practice to their theories. There are few parents, who will choose to give up the entire care of their children to any governess; therefore, there will probably be some points in which a difference of opinion will arise. A sensible woman will never submit to be treated, as governesses are in some families, like the servant who was asked by his master what business he had to think: nor will a woman of sense or temper insist upon her opinions without producing her reasons. She will thus ensure the respect and the confidence of enlightened parents.

It is surely the interest of parents to treat the person who educates their children, with that perfect equality and kindness, which will conciliate her affection, and which will at the same time preserve her influence and authority over her pupils. And it is with pleasure we observe, that the style of behaviour to governesses, in well bred families, is much changed within these few years. A governess is no longer treated as an upper servant, or as an intermediate being between a servant and a gentlewoman: she is now treated as the friend and companion of the family, and she must, consequently, have warm and permanent interest in its prosperity:

she becomes attached to her pupils from gratitude to their parents, from sympathy, from generosity, as well as from the strict sense of duty.

In fashionable life there is, however, some danger that parents should go into extremes in their behaviour towards their governesses. Those who disdain the idea of assuming superiority of rank and fortune, and who desire to treat the person who educates their children as their equal, act with perfect propriety; but if they make her their companion in all their amusements, they go a step too far, and they defeat their own purposes. If a governess attends the card-table, and the assembly-room; if she is to visit, and be visited, what is to become of her pupils in her absence? They must be left to the care of servants. There are some ladies who will not accept of any invitation, in which the governess of their children is not included. This may be done from a good motive, but, surely, it is unreasonable; for the very use of a governess is to supply the mother's place in her absence. Cannot this be managed better? Cannot the mother and governess both amuse themselves at different times? There would then be perfect equality; the governess would be in the same society, and would be treated with the same respect, without neglecting her duty. The reward which is given to women of abilities, and of unblemished reputation, who devote themselves to the superintendence of the education of young ladies in the higher ranks of life, the daughters of our affluent nobility, ought to be considerably greater than what it is at present: it ought to be such as to excite women to cultivate their talents, and their understandings, with a view to this profession. A profession we call it, for it should be considered as such, as an honourable profession, which a gentlewoman might follow without losing any degree of the estimation in which she is held by what is called *the world*. There is no employment, at present, by which a gentlewoman can maintain herself, without losing something of that respect, something of that rank in society, which neither female fortitude nor male philosophy willingly foregoes. The liberal professions are open to men of small fortunes; by presenting one similar resource to women, we should give a strong motive for their moral and intellectual improvement.

Nor does it seem probable, that they should make a disgraceful or imprudent use of their increasing influence and liberty in this case, because their previous education must previously prepare them properly. The misfortune of women has usually been, to have power trusted to them before they were educated to use it prudently. To say that preceptresses in the higher ranks of life should be liberally rewarded, is but a vague expression; something specific should be mentioned, wherever general utility is the object. Let us observe, that many of the first dignities of the church are bestowed, and properly bestowed, upon men who have educated the highest ranks of our nobility. Those who look with an evil eye upon these promotions, do not fairly estimate the *national* importance of education for the rich and powerful. No provision can be made for women who direct the education of the daughters of our nobility, any ways equivalent to the provision made for preceptors by those who have influence in the state. A pecuniary compensation is in the power of opulent families. Three hundred a year, for twelve or fourteen years, the space of time which a preceptress must probably employ in the education of a young lady, would be a suitable compensation for her care. With this provision she would be enabled, after her pupil's education was completed, either to settle in her own family, or she would, in the decline of life, be happily independent, secure from the temptation of marrying for money. If a few munificent and enlightened individuals set the example of liberally rewarding merit in this situation, many young women will probably appear with talents and good qualities suited to the views of the most sanguine parents. With good sense, and literary tastes, a young woman might instruct herself during the first years of her pupils childhood, and might gradually prepare herself with all the necessary knowledge: according to the principles that have been suggested, there would be no necessity for her being a *mistress of arts*, a performer in music, a paintress, a linguist, or a poetess. A general knowledge of literature is indispensable; and yet further, she must have sufficient taste and judgment to direct the literary talents of her pupils.

With respect to the literary education of the female sex, the arguments on both sides of the question have already been stated, with all the impartiality in our power, in another place. [38] Without obtruding a detail of the same arguments again upon the public, it will be sufficient to profess the distinct opinion, which a longer consideration of the subject has yet more fully confirmed, that it will tend to the happiness of society in general, that women should have their understandings cultivated and enlarged as much as possible; that the happiness of domestic life, the virtues and the powers of pleasing in the female sex, the yet more desirable power of attaching those worthy of their love and esteem, will be increased by the judicious cultivation of the female understanding, more than by all that modern gallantry or ancient chivalry could devise in favour of the sex. Much prudence and ability are requisite to conduct properly a young woman's literary education. Her imagination must not be raised above the taste for necessary occupations, or the numerous small, but not trifling, pleasures of domestic life: her mind must be enlarged, yet the delicacy of her manners must be preserved: her knowledge must be various, and her powers of reasoning unawed by authority; yet she must *habitually* feel that nice sense of propriety, which is at once the guard and the charm of every feminine virtue. By early caution, unremitting, scrupulous caution in the choice of the books which are put into the hands of girls, a mother, or a preceptress, may fully occupy and entertain their pupils, and excite in their minds a *taste* for propriety, as well as a taste for literature. It cannot be necessary to add more than this general idea, that a mother ought to be answerable to her daughter's husband for the books her daughter had read, as well as for the company she had kept.

Those observations, which apply equally to the cultivation of the understanding both of men and of women, we do not here mean to point out; we would speak only of what may be peculiar to female education. From the study of the learned languages, women, by custom, fortunately for them, are exempted: of ancient literature they may, in translations which are acknowledged to be excellent, obtain a sufficient knowledge, without paying too much time and labour for this classic pleasure. Confused notions from fashionable publications, from periodical papers, and comedies, have made their way into common conversation, and thence have assumed an appearance of authority, and have been extremely disadvantageous to female education. Sentiment and ridicule have conspired to represent reason, knowledge, and science, as unsuitable or dangerous to women; yet at the same time wit, and superficial acquirements in literature, have been the object of admiration in society; so that this dangerous inference has been drawn, almost without our perceiving its fallacy, that superficial knowledge is more desirable in women than accurate knowledge. This principle must lead to innumerable errours; it must produce continual contradictions in the course of education: instead of making women more reasonable, and less presuming, it will render them at once arrogant and ignorant; full of pretensions, incapable of application, and unfit to hear themselves convinced. Whatever young women learn, let them be taught accurately; let them know ever so little apparently, they will know much if they have learnt that little *well*. A girl who runs through a course of natural history, hears something about chemistry, has been taught something of botany, and who knows but just enough of these to make her fancy that she is well informed, is in a miserable situation, in danger of becoming ridiculous, and insupportably tiresome to men of sense and science. But let a woman know any one thing completely, and she will have sufficient understanding to learn more, and to apply what she has been taught so as to interest men of generosity and genius in her favour. The knowledge of the general principles of any science, is very different from superficial knowledge of the science; perhaps, from not attending to this distinction, or from not understanding it, many have failed in female education. Some attempt will be made to mark this distinction practically, when we come to speak of the cultivation of the memory, invention, and judgment. No intelligent preceptress will, it is hoped, find any difficulty in the application of the observations they may meet with in the chapters on imagination, sympathy and sensibility, vanity and temper. The masculine pronoun *he*, has been used for grammatical convenience, not at all because we agree with the prejudiced, and uncourteous grammarian, who asserts, "that the masculine is the more worthy gender."

[32] Une virtuose.

[33] V. Storia di quattro fratelli nati ciechi e guariti coll' estrazione delle cateratte.—Di Francesco Buzzi.

[34] V. Zoonomia.

[35] This word is sometimes by mistake spelt *fugal*-man.

[36] Sir Joshua Reynolds.

[37] Condillac.

[38] V. Letters for Literary Ladies.

CHAPTER XXI
MEMORY AND INVENTION

Before we bestow many years of time and pains upon any object, it may be prudent to afford a few minutes previously to ascertain its precise value. Many persons have a vague idea of the great value of memory, and, without analyzing their opinion, they resolve to cultivate the memories of their children as much, and as soon, as possible. So far from having determined the value of this talent, we shall find that it will be difficult to give a popular definition of a good memory. Some people call that a good memory which retains the greatest number of ideas for the longest time. Others prefer a recollective to a retentive memory, and value not so much the number; as the selection, of facts; not so much the mass, or even the antiquity, of accumulated treasure, as the power of producing current specie for immediate use. Memory is sometimes spoken of as if it were a faculty admirable in itself, without any union with the other powers of the mind. Amongst those who allow that memory has no independent claim to regard, there are yet many who believe, that a superior degree of memory is essential to the successful exercise of the higher faculties, such as judgment and invention. The degree in which it is useful to those powers, has not, however, been determined. Those who are governed in their opinions by precedent and authority, can produce many learned names, to prove that memory was held in the highest estimation amongst the great men of antiquity; it was cultivated with much anxiety in their public institutions, and in their private education. But there were many circumstances, which formerly contributed to make a great memory essential to a great man. In civil and military employments, amongst the ancients, it was in a high degree requisite. Generals were expected to know by heart the names of the soldiers in their armies; demagogues, who hoped to please the people, were expected to know the names of all their fellow-citizens. [39] Orators, who did not speak extempore, were obliged to get their long orations by rote. Those who studied science or philosophy, were obliged to cultivate their memory with incessant care, because, if they frequented the schools for instruction, they treasured up the sayings of the masters of different sects, and learned their doctrines only by oral instruction. Manuscripts were frequently got by heart by those who were eager to secure the knowledge they contained, and who had not opportunities of recurring to the originals. It is not surprising, therefore, that memory, to which so much was trusted, should have been held in such high esteem.

At the revival of literature in Europe, before the discovery of the art of printing, it was scarcely possible to make any progress in the literature of the age, without possessing a retentive memory. A man who had read a few manuscripts, and could repeat them, was a wonder, and a treasure: he could travel from place to place, and live by his learning; he was a circulating library to a nation, and the more books he could carry in his head, the better: he was certain of an admiring audience if he could repeat what Aristotle or Saint Jerome had written; and he had far more encouragement to engrave the words of others on his memory, than to invent or judge for himself.

In the twelfth century, above six hundred scholars assembled in the forests of Champagne, to hear the lectures of the learned Abeillard; they made themselves huts of the boughs of trees, and in this new academic grove were satisfied to go almost without the necessaries of life. In the specimens of Abeillard's composition, which are handed down to us, we may discover proofs of his having been vain of a surprising memory; it seems to have been the superior faculty of his mind: his six hundred pupils could carry away with them only so much of his learning as they could get by heart during his course of lectures; and he who had the best memory, must have been best paid for his journey. [40]

The art of printing, by multiplying copies so as to put them within the easy reference of all classes of people, has lowered the value of this species of retentive memory. It is better to refer to the book itself, than to the man who has read the book. Knowledge is now ready classed for use, and it is safely stored up in the great common-place books of public libraries. A man of literature need not incumber his memory with whole passages from the authors he wants to quote; he need only mark down the page, and the words are safe.

Mere erudition does not in these days ensure permanent fame. The names of the Abbé de Longuerue, and of the Florentine librarian Magliabechi, excite no vivid emotions in the minds of those who have heard of them before; and there are many, perhaps not illiterate persons, who would not be ashamed to own that they had never heard of them at all. Yet these men were both of them, but a few years ago, remarkable for extraordinary memory and erudition. When M. de Longuerue was a child, he was such a prodigy of memory and knowledge, that Lewis the fourteenth, passing through the abbé's province, stopped to see and hear him. When he grew up, Paris consulted him as the oracle of learning. His erudition, says d'Alembert, [41] was not only prodigious, but actually terrible. Greek and Hebrew were more familiar to him than his native tongue. His memory was so well furnished with historic facts, with chronological and topographical knowledge, that upon hearing a person assert in conversation, that it would be a difficult task to write a good historical description of France, [42] he asserted, that he could do it from memory, without consulting any books. All he asked, was, to have some maps of France laid before him: these recalled to his mind the history of each province, of all the fiefs of the crown of each city, and even of each distinguished nobleman's seat in the kingdom. He wrote his folio history in a year. It was admired as a great curiosity in manuscript; but when it came to be printed, sundry gross errours appeared: he was obliged to take out several leaves in correcting the press. The edition was very expensive, and the work, at last, would have been rather more acceptable to the public, if the author had not written it from memory. Love of the wonderful must yield to esteem for the useful.

The effect which all this erudition had upon the Abbé de Longuerue's taste, judgment, and imagination, is worth our attention. Some of his opinions speak sufficiently for our purpose. He was of opinion that the English have never done any good, [43] since they renounced the study of Greek and Arabic, for Geometry and Physics. He was of opinion, that two antiquarian books upon Homer, viz. *Antiquitates Homericæ* and *Homeri Gnomologia*, are preferable to Homer himself. He would rather have them, he declared, because with these he had all that was useful in the poet, without being obliged to go through long stories, which put him to sleep. "As for that madman Ariosto," said he, "I sometimes divert myself with him." One odd volume of Racine was the only French book to be found in his library. His erudition died with him, and the world has not profited much by his surprising memory.

The librarian Magliabechi was no less famous than M. de Longuerue for his memory, and he was yet more strongly affected by the mania for books. His appetite for them was so voracious, that he acquired the name of the glutton of literature. [44] Before he died, he had *swallowed* six large rooms full of books. Whether he had time to digest any of them we do not know, but we are sure that he wished it; for the only line of his own composition which he has left for the instruction of posterity, is round a medal. The medal represents him sitting with a book in his hand, and with a great number of books scattered on the floor round him. The candid inscription signifies, that to become learned it is not sufficient to read much, if we read without reflection. The names of Franklin and of Shakespeare are known wherever literature is cultivated, to all who have any pretensions to science or to genius; yet they were neither of them men of extraordinary erudition, nor from their works should we judge that memory was their predominant faculty. It may be said, that a superior degree of memory was essential to the exercise of their judgment and invention; that without having treasured up in his memory a variety of minute observations upon human nature, Shakespeare could never have painted the passions with so bold and just a hand; that if Franklin had not accurately remembered his own philosophical observations, and those of others, he never would have made those discoveries which have immortalized his name. Admitting the justice of these assertions, we see that memory to great men is but a subordinate servant, a treasurer who receives, and is expected to keep faithfully whatever is committed to his care; and not only to preserve faithfully all deposits, but to produce them at the moment they are wanted. There are substances which are said to imbibe and retain the rays of light, and to emit them only in certain situations. As long as they retain the rays, no eye regards them.

It has often been observed, that a recollective and retentive memory are seldom found united. If this were true, and that we had our choice of either, which should we prefer? For the purposes of ostentation, perhaps the one; for utility, the other. A person who could repeat from beginning to end the whole Economy of Human Life, which he had learned in his childhood, might, if we had time to sit still and listen to him, obtain our admiration for his extraordinary retentive memory; but the person who, in daily occurrences, or interesting affairs, recollects at the proper time what is useful to us, obtains from our gratitude something more than vain admiration. To speak accurately, we must remark, that retentive and recollective memories are but relative terms: the recollective memory must be retentive of all that it recollects; the retentive memory cannot show itself till the moment it becomes recollective. But we value either precisely in proportion as they are useful and agreeable.

Just at the time when philosophers were intent upon trying experiments in electricity, Dr. Heberden recollected to have seen, many years before, a small electrical stone, called tourmalin, [45] in the possession of Dr. Sharpe at Cambridge. It was the only one known in England at that time. Dr. Heberden procured it; and several curious experiments were made and verified with it. In this instance, it is obvious that we admire the retentive, local memory of Dr. Heberden, merely because it became recollective and useful. Had the tourmalin never been wanted, it would have been a matter of indifference, whether the direction for it at Dr. Sharpe's at Cambridge, had been remembered or forgotten. There was a man [46] who undertook, in going from Temple Bar to the furthest part of Cheapside and back again, to enumerate at his return every sign on each side of the way in its order, and to repeat them, if it should be required, either backwards or forwards. This he exactly accomplished. As a playful trial of memory, this affords us a moments entertainment; but if we were to be serious upon the subject, we should say it was a pity that the man did not use his extraordinary memory for some better purpose. The late king of Prussia, when he intended to advance Trenck in the army, upon his first introduction, gave him a list of the strangest names which could be picked out, to learn by rote. Trenck learned them quickly, and the king was much pleased with this instance of his memory; but Frederick would certainly never have made such a trial of the abilities of Voltaire.

We cannot always foresee what facts may be useful, and what may be useless to us, otherwise the cultivation of the memory might be conducted by unerring rules. In the common business of life, people regulate their memories by the circumstances in which they happen to be placed. A clerk in a counting-house, by practice, learns to remember the circumstances, affairs, and names of numerous merchants, of his master's customers, the places of their abode, and, perhaps, something of their peculiar humours and manners. A fine lady remembers her visiting list, and, perhaps, the dresses and partners of every couple at a crowded ball; she finds all these particulars a useful supply for daily conversation, she therefore remembers them with care. An amateur, who is ambitious to shine in the society of literary men, collects literary anecdotes, and retails them whenever occasion permits. Men of sense, who cultivate their memories for useful purposes, are not obliged to treasure up heterogeneous facts: by reducing particulars to general principles, and by connecting them with proper associations, they enjoy all the real advantages, whilst they are exempt from the labour of accumulation.

Mr. Stewart has, with so much ability, pointed out the effects of systematic arrangement of writing, reading, and the use of technical contrivances in the cultivation of the memory, that it would be a presumptuous and unnecessary attempt to expatiate in other words upon the same subject. It may not be useless, however, to repeat a few of his observations, because, in considering what further improvement may be made, it is always essential to have fully in our view what is already known.

"Philosophic arrangement assists the memory, by classing under a few principles, a number of apparently dissimilar and unconnected particulars. The habit, for instance, of attending to the connection of cause and effect, presents a multitude of interesting analogies to the minds of men of science, which escape other persons; the vulgar feel no pleasure in contemplating objects that appear remote from common life; and they find it extremely difficult to remember observations and reasonings which are foreign to their customary course of associated ideas. Even literary and ingenious people, when they begin to learn any art or science, usually complain that their memory is not able to retain all the terms and ideas which pour in upon them with perplexing rapidity. In time, this difficulty is conquered, not so much by the strength of the memory, as by the exercise of judgment: they learn to distinguish, and select the material terms, facts and arguments, from those that are subordinate, and they class them under general heads, to relieve the memory from all superfluous labour.

"In all studies, there is some prevalent associating principle, which gradually becomes familiar to our minds, but which we do not immediately discover in our first attempts. In poetry, resemblance; in philosophy, cause and effect; in mathematics, demonstrations continually recur; and, therefore, each is expected by persons who have been used to these respective studies.

"The habit of committing our knowledge to writing, assists the memory, because, in writing, we detain certain ideas long enough in our view to perceive all their relations; we use fixed and abbreviated signs for all our thoughts; with the assistance of these, we can prevent confusion in our reasonings. We can, without fatigue, by the help of words, letters, figures, or algebraic signs, go through a variety of mental processes, and solve many difficult problems, which, without such assistance, must have been too extensive for our capacities.

"If our books be well chosen, and if we read with discrimination and attention, reading will improve the memory, because, as it increases our knowledge, it increases our interest in every new discovery, and in every new combination of ideas."

We agree entirely with Mr. Stewart in his observations upon technical helps to the memory; they are hurtful to the understanding, because they break the general habits of philosophic order in the mind. There is no connection of ideas between the memorial lines, for instance, in Grey's Memoria Technica, the history of the Kings or Emperors, and the dates that we wish to remember. However, it may be advantageous in education to use such contrivances, to assist our pupils in remembering those technical parts of knowledge, which are sometimes valued above their worth in society.

The facts upon which the principles of any science are founded, should never be learnt by rote in a technical manner. But the names and the dates of the reigns of a number of kings and emperors, if they must be remembered by children, should be learnt in the manner which may give them the least trouble. [47]

It is commonly asserted, that our memory is to be improved by exercise: exercise may be of different kinds, and we must determine what sort is best.

Repetition is found to fix words, and sometimes ideas, strongly in the mind; the words of the burden of a song, which we have frequently heard, are easily and long remembered. When we want to get any thing by rote, we repeat it over and over again, till the sounds seem to follow one another habitually, and then we say we have them perfectly by rote. [48] The regular recurrence of sounds, at stated intervals, much assists us. In poetry, the rhymes, the cadence, the alliteration, the peculiar structure of the poet's lines, aids us. All these are mechanical helps to the memory. Repetition seems much more agreeable to some people than to others; but it may be doubted whether a facility and propensity to repetition be favourable to rational memory. Whilst we repeat, we exclude all thought from the mind; we form a habit of saying certain sounds in a certain order; but if this habit be afterwards broken by any trifling external circumstances, we lose all our labour. We have no means of recollecting what we have learned in this manner. Once gone, it is gone for ever. It depends but upon one principle of association. Those who exert ingenuity as well as memory in learning by heart, may not, perhaps, associate sounds with so much expedition, but they will have the power of recollection in a greater degree. They will have more chances in their favour, besides the great power of voluntary exertion: a power which few passive repeaters ever possess. The following lines are easily learned:

"Haste, then, ye spirits; to your charge repair,
The fluttering fan be Zephyretta's care;
The drops to thee, Brillante, we consign,
And, Momentilla, let the watch be thine;
Do thou, Crispissa, tend her favourite lock,
Ariel himself shall be the guard of Shock."

To a person who merely learned the sounds in these lines by rote, without knowing the sense of the words, all the advantage of the appropriated names and offices of the sylphs would be lost. No one, who has any sense of propriety, can call these sylphs by wrong names, or put them out of their places. Momentilla and the watch, Zephyretta and the fan, Crispissa and the lock of hair, Brillante and the diamond drops, are so intimately associated, that they necessarily recur together in the memory. The following celebrated lines on envy, some people will find easy, and others difficult, to learn by heart:

"Envy will merit, as its shade, pursue;
But, like a shadow, proves the substance true:
For envy'd wit, like Sol eclips'd, makes known
Th' opposing body's grossness, not its own.
When first that sun too pow'rful beams displays,

It draws up vapour, which obscures its rays;
But ev'n those clouds at last adorn its way,
Reflect new glories, and augment the day. "

The flow of these lines is not particularly easy; those who trust merely to the power of reiteration in getting them by rote, will find the task difficult; those who seize the ideas, will necessarily recollect their order, and the sense will conduct them to their proper places with certainty: they cannot, for instance, make the clouds adorn the sun's rays before the sun's powerful beams have drawn up the vapours. This fixes the place of the four last lines. The simile of merit and the sun, and envy and the clouds, keeps each idea in its order; if any one escapes, it is easily missed, and easily recalled.

We seldom meet with those who can give us an accurate account of their own thoughts; it is, therefore, difficult to tell the different ways in which different people manage their memory. We judge by the effects frequently, that causes are the same, which sometimes are entirely different. Thus we, in common conversation, should say, that two people had an equally good memory, who could repeat with equal exactness any thing which they had heard or read. But in their methods of remembering, these persons might differ essentially; the one might have exerted much more judgment and ingenuity in the conduct of his memory than the other, and might thus have not only fatigued himself less, but might have improved his understanding, whilst the other learned merely by rote. When Dr. Johnson reported the parliamentary debates for the gentleman's Magazine, his judgment, his habit of attending to the order in which ideas follow one another in reasoning, his previous knowledge of the characters and style of the different speakers, must considerably have assisted his memory. His taste for literary composition must have shown him instantly where any argument or allusion was misplaced. A connecting phrase, or a link in a chain of reasoning, is missed as readily by a person used to writing and argument, as a word in a line of poetry is missed by a poetic ear. If any thing has escaped the memory of persons who remember by general classification, they are not only by their art able to discover that something is missing, but they have a general direction where to find it; they know to what class of ideas it must belong; they can hunt from generals to particulars, till they are sure at last of tracing and detecting the deserter; they have certain signs by which they know the object of which they are in search, and they trust with more certainty to these characteristics, than to the mere vague recollection of having seen it before. We feel disposed to trust the memory of those who can give us some reason for what they remember. If they can prove to us that their assertion could not, consistently with other facts, be false, we admit the assertion into the rank of facts, and their judgment thus goes surety for their memory.

The following advertisement (taken from the star of the 21st September, 1796) may show that experience justifies these theoretic notions:

"Literature.

"A gentleman capable of reporting the debates in parliament, is wanted for a London newspaper. A business of no such great difficulty as is generally imagined by those unacquainted with it. A *tolerable* good style and facility of composition, as well as a facility of writing, together with a good memory (*not an extraordinary one*) are all the necessary requisites. If a gentleman writes short hand, it is an advantage; but memory and composition are more important.

"The advertiser, conceiving that many gentlemen either in London or at the Universities, or in other parts of the kingdom, may think such a situation desirable, takes this public method of enabling them to obtain it. The salary, which will vary according to the talents of the reporter, will at least afford a genteel subsistence, and the business need not interrupt the pursuit of studies necessary for a more important profession. *A gentleman who has never tried parliamentary reporting, will be preferred by the advertiser, because he has observed, that those who have last attempted it, are now the best reporters.*"

In the common mode of education, great exactness of repetition is required from pupils. This seems to be made a matter of too much importance. There are circumstances in life, in which this talent is useful, but its utility, perhaps, we shall find, upon examination, is over-rated.

In giving evidence of words, dates, and facts, in a court of justice, the utmost precision is requisite. The property, lives, and characters of individuals depend upon this precision.

But we must observe, that after long detailed evidence has been given by a number of witnesses, an advocate separates the material from the immaterial circumstances, and the judge in his charge again compresses the arguments of the counsel, so that much of what has been said during the trial, might as well have been omitted. All these superfluous ideas were *remembered* to no purpose. An evidence sometimes, if he be permitted, would tell not only all that he remembers of the circumstances about which he is examined, but also a number of other circumstances, which are casually associated with these in his memory. An able advocate rejects, by a quickness of judgment which appears like intuition, all that is irrelevant to his argument and his cause; and it is by this selection that *his* memory, in the evidence, perhaps, of twenty different people, is able to retain all that is useful. When this heterogeneous mass of evidence is classed by his perspicuous arrangement, his audience feel no difficulty either in understanding or recollecting all which had before appeared confused. Thus the exercise of the judgment saves much of the labour of memory; labour which is not merely unnecessary, but hurtful, to our understanding.

In making observations upon subjects which are new to us, we must be content to use our memory unassisted at first by our reason; we must treasure up the ore and rubbish together, because we cannot immediately distinguish them from each other. But the sooner we can separate them, the better. In the beginning of all experimental sciences, a number of useless particulars are recorded, because they are not known to be useless; when, from comparing these, a few general principles are discovered, the memory is immediately relieved, the judgment and inventive faculty have power and liberty to work, and then a rapid progress and great discoveries are made. It is the misfortune of those who first cultivate new sciences, that their memory is overloaded; but if those who succeed to them, submit to the same senseless drudgery, it is not their misfortune, but their fault. Let us look over the history of those who have made discoveries and inventions, we shall perceive, that it has been by rejecting useless ideas that they have first cleared their way to truth. Dr. Priestley's Histories of Vision and of Electricity, are as useful when we consider them as histories of the human mind, as when we read them as histories of science. Dr. Priestley has published a catalogue of books, [49] from which he gathered his materials. The pains, he tells us, that it cost him to compress and abridge the accounts which ingenious men have given of their own experiments, teach us how much our progress in real knowledge depends upon rejecting all that is superfluous. When Simonides offered to teach Themistocles the art of memory, Themistocles answered, "Rather teach me the art of forgetting; for I find that I remember much that I had better forget, and forget" (*consequently*) "some things which I wish to remember."

When any discovery or invention is completed, we are frequently astonished at its obvious simplicity. The ideas necessary to the discovery, are seldom so numerous as to fatigue our memory. Memory seems to have been useful to inventors only as it presented a few ideas in a certain happy connection, as it presented them faithfully and distinctly to view in the proper moment. If we wish for examples of *the conduct of* the understanding, we need only look into Dr. Franklin's works. He is so free from all affectation, he lays his mind so fairly before us, that he is, perhaps, the best example we can select. Those who are used to look at objects in a microscope, say, that full as much depends upon the object's being well prepared for inspection, as upon the attention of the observer, or the excellence of the glass.

The first thing that strikes us, in looking over Doctor Franklin's works, is the variety of his observations upon different subjects. We might imagine, that a very tenacious and powerful memory was necessary to register all these; but Dr. Franklin informs us, that it was his constant practice to note down every hint as it occurred to him: he urges his friends to do the same; he observes, that there is scarcely a day passes without our hearing or seeing something which, if properly attended to, might lead to useful discoveries. By thus committing his ideas to writing, his mind was left at liberty *to think*. No extraordinary effort of memory was, even upon the greatest occasions, requisite. A friend wrote to him to inquire how he was led to his great discovery of the identity of lightning and electricity; and how he first came to think of drawing down lightning from the clouds. Dr. Franklin replies, that he could not answer better than by giving an extract from the minutes he used to keep of the experiments he made, with memorandums of such as he purposed to make, the reasons for making them, and the observations that rose upon them. By this extract, says Dr. Franklin, you will see that the thought was not so much *an out of the way one*, but that it might have occurred to any electrician. [50]

When the ideas are arranged in clear order, as we see them in this note, the analogy or induction to which Dr. Franklin was led, appears easy. Why, then, had it never been made by any other person? Numbers of ingenious men were at this time intent upon electricity. The ideas which were necessary to this discovery, were not numerous or complicated. We may remark, that one analogy connecting these observations together, they are more easily recollected; and their being written down for a particular purpose, on which Dr. Franklin's mind was intent, must have made it still easier to him to retain them.

The degree of memory he was forced to employ, is thus reduced to a portion in which few people are defective. Now, let us suppose, that Dr. Franklin, at the time he wrote his memorandum, had fully in his recollection every previous experiment that had ever been tried on electricity; and not only these, but the theories, names, ages, and private history, of all the men who had tried these experiments; of what advantage would this have been to him? He must have excluded all these impertinent ideas successively as they rose before him, and he must have selected the fifteen useful observations, which we have mentioned, from this troublesome multitude. The chance in such a selection would have been against him; the time employed in the examination and rejection of all the unnecessary recollections, would have been absolutely wasted.

We must wish that it were in our power, when we make observations upon nature, or when we read the reflections of others, to arrange our thoughts so as to be ready when we want to reason or invent. When cards are dealt to us, we can sort our hand according to the known probabilities of the game, and a new arrangement is easily made when we hear what is trumps.

In collecting and sorting observations, Dr. Franklin particularly excelled; therefore we may safely continue to take him for our example. Wherever he happened to be, in a boat, in a mine, in a printer's shop, in a crowded city, or in the country, in Europe or America, he displays the same activity of observation. When any thing, however trifling, struck him which he could not account for, he never rested till he had traced the effect to its cause. Thus, after having made one remark, he had fresh motive to collect facts, either to confirm or refute an hypothesis; his observations tending consequently to some determinate purpose, they were arranged in the moment they were made, in the most commodious manner, both for his memory and invention; they were arranged either according to their obvious analogies, or their relation to each other as cause and effect. He had two useful methods of judging of the value of his own ideas; he either considered how they could be immediately applied to practical improvements in the arts, or how they could lead to the solution of any of the great problems in science. Here we must again observe, that judgment saved the labour of memory. A person, who sets about to collect facts at random, is little better than a magpie, who picks up and lays by any odd bits of money he can light upon, without knowing their use.

Miscellaneous observations, which are made by those who have no philosophy, may accidentally lead to something useful; but here we admire the good fortune, and not the genius, of the individuals who make such discoveries: these are prizes drawn from the lottery of science, which ought not to seduce us from the paths of sober industry. How long may an observation, fortunately made, continue to be useless to mankind, merely because it has not been reasoned upon! The trifling observation, that a straight stick appears bent in water, was made many hundred years before the reason of that appearance was discovered! The invention of the telescope might have been made by any person who could have pursued this slight observation through all its consequences.

Having now defined, or rather described, what we mean by *a good memory*, we may consider how the memory should be cultivated. In children, as well as in men, the strength of that habit, or perhaps of that power of the mind which associates ideas together, varies considerably. It is probable, that this difference may depend sometimes upon organization. A child who is born with any defect in his eyes, cannot possibly have the same pleasure in objects of sight, which those enjoy who have strong eyes: ideas associated with these external objects, are, therefore, not associated with pleasure, and, consequently, they are not recollected with any sensations of pleasure. An ingenious writer [51] supposes, that all the difference of capacity amongst men ultimately depends on their original power of feeling pleasure or pain, and their consequent different habits of attention.

When there is any defect in a child's organization, we must have recourse to physics, and not to metaphysics; but even among children, who are apparently in the full possession of all their senses, we see very different degrees of vivacity: those who have most vivacity, seldom take delight in repeating their ideas; they are more pleased with novelty than prone to habit. Those children who are deficient in vivacity, are much disposed to the easy indolent pleasure of repetition; it costs them less exertion to say or do the same thing over again, than to attempt any thing new; they are uniformly good subjects to habit, because novelty has no charms to seduce their attention.

The education of the memory in these two classes of children, ought not to be the same. Those who are disposed to repetition, should not be indulged in it, because it will increase their indolence; they should be excited by praise, by example, by sympathy, and by all the strongest motives that we can employ. Their interest in every thing around them must by all means be increased: when they show eagerness about any thing, no matter what it is, we may then exercise their memory upon that subject with some hopes of success. It is of importance that they should succeed in their first trials, otherwise they will be discouraged from repeating their attempts, and they will distrust their own memory in future. The fear of not remembering, will occupy, and agitate, and weaken their minds; they should, therefore, be animated by hope. If they fail, at all events let them not be reproached; the mortification they naturally feel, is sufficient: nor should they be left to dwell upon their disappointment; they should have a fresh and easier trial given to them, that they may recover their own self-complacency as expeditiously as possible. It may be said, that there are children of such a sluggish temperament, that they feel no pleasure in success, and no mortification in perceiving their own mental deficiencies. There are few children of this description; scarcely any, perhaps, whose defects have not been increased by education. Exertion has been made so painful to them, that at length they have sunk into apathy, or submitted in despair to the eternal punishment of shame.

The mistaken notion, that the memory must be exercised only in books, has been often fatal to the pupils of literary people. We remember best those things which interest us most; which are useful to us in conversation; in our daily business or amusement. So do children. On these things we should exercise their memory. Tell a boy who has lost his top, to remember at such a particular time to put you in mind of it, and if he does, that you will give him another, he will probably remember your requests after this, better than you will yourself. Affectionate children will easily extend their recollective memories in the service of their friends and companions. "Put me in mind to give your friend what he asked for, and I will give it to him if you remember it at the right time." It will be best to manage these affairs so that convenience, and not caprice, shall appear to be your motive for the requests. The time and place should be precisely fixed, and something should be chosen which is likely to recall your request at the appointed time. If you say, put me in mind of such a thing the moment the cloth is taken away after dinner; or as soon as candles are brought into the room; or when I go by such a shop in our walk this evening; here are things mentioned which will much assist the young remembrancer: the moment the cloth is taken away, or the candles come, he will recollect, from association, that something is to be done, that *he* has something to do; and presently he will make out what that something is.

A good memory for business depends upon local, well arranged associations. The man of business makes an artificial memory for himself out of the trivial occurrences of the day, and the hours as they pass recall their respective occupations. Children can acquire these habits very early in their education; they are eager to give their companions an account of any thing they have seen or heard; their tutors should become their companions, and encourage them by sympathy to address these narrations to them. Children who forget their lessons in chronology, and their pence tables, can relate with perfect accuracy any circumstances which have interested themselves. This shows that there is no deficiency in their capacity. Every one, who has had any experience of the pleasure of talking, knows how intimately it is connected with the pleasure of being listened to. The auditors, consequently, possess supreme power over narrative childhood, without using any artifice, by simply showing attention to well arranged, and well recollected narratives, and ceasing to attend when the young orator's memory and story become confused, he will naturally be excited to arrange his ideas. The order of *time* is the first and easiest principle of association to help the memory. This, till young people acquire the ideas of cause and effect, will be their favourite mode of arrangement. Things that happen at the same time; things that are said, thoughts that have occurred, at the same time, will recur to the mind together. We may observe, that ill educated people continue through life to remember things by this single association; and, consequently, there is a heterogeneous collection of ideas in their mind, which have no rational connection with each other; crowds which have accidentally met, and are forced to live for ever together.

A vulgar evidence, when he is examined about his memory of a particular fact, gives as a reason for his remembering it, a relation of a number of other circumstances, which he tells you happened at the same time; or he calls to witness any animate or inanimate objects, which he happened to see at the same time. All these things are so joined with the principal fact in his mind, that his remembering them distinctly, seems to him, and he expects will seem to others, demonstration of the truth and accuracy of his principal assertion. When a lawyer tells him he has nothing to do with these ideas, he is immediately at a stand in his narrative; he can recollect nothing, he is sure of nothing; he has no reason to give for his belief, unless he may say that it was Michaelmas-day when such a thing happened, that he had a goose for dinner that day, or that he had a new wig. Those who have more enlarged minds, seldom produce these strange reasons for remembering facts. Indeed, no one can reason clearly, whose memory has these foolish habits; the ill matched ideas are inseparably joined, and hence they imagine there is some natural connection between them. Hence arise those obstinate prejudices which no arguments can vanquish.

To prevent children from arguing ill, we must, therefore, take care, in exercising their memory, to discourage them in this method of proving that they remember one thing by telling us a number of others which happened at the same time; rather let them be excited to bring their reasoning faculty into play in support of their memory. Suppose, for instance, that a child had mislaid his hat, and was trying to recollect where he had put it. He first may recollect, from the association of time, that he had the hat the last time he went out; but when he wants to recollect when that time was, he had better go back, if he can, to his motive for going out; this one idea will bring a number of others in right order into his mind. He went out, suppose, to fetch his kite, which he was afraid would be wet by a shower of rain; then the boy recollects that his hat must have been wet by the same rain, and that when he came in, instead of hanging it up in its usual place, it was put before the fire to be dried. What fire, is the next question, &c.

Such an instance as this may appear very trivial; but children whose minds are well managed about trifles, will retain good habits when they are to think about matters of consequence. By exercising the memory in this manner about things, instead of about books and lessons, we shall not disgust and tire our pupils, nor shall we give the false notion, that all knowledge is acquired by reading.

Long before children read fluently for their own amusement, they like to hear others read aloud to them, because they have then the entertainment without the labour. We may exercise their memory by asking for an account of what they have heard. But let them never be required to repeat in the words of the book, or even to preserve the same arrangement; let them speak in words of their own, and arrange their ideas to their own plan; this will exercise at once their judgment, invention, and memory.

"Try if you can explain to me what I have just been explaining to you," a sensible tutor will frequently say to his pupils; and he will suffer them to explain in a different manner from himself; he will only require them to remember what is essential to the explanation. In such repetitions as these, the mind is active, therefore it will strengthen and improve.

Children are all, more or less, pleased with the perception of resemblances and of analogy. This propensity assists us much in the cultivation of the memory; but it must be managed with discretion, or it will injure the other powers of the understanding. There is, in some minds, a futile love of tracing analogies, which leads to superstition, to false reasoning, and false taste. The quick perception of resemblances is, in other minds, productive of wit, poetic genius, and scientific invention. The difference between these two classes, depends upon this—the one has more judgment, and more the habit of using it, than the other. Children who are pleased by trifling coincidences, by allusions, and similitudes, should be taught with great care to reason: when once they perceive the pleasure of demonstration, they will not be contented with the inaccuracy of common analogies. A tutor is often tempted to teach pupils, who are fond of allusions, by means of them, because he finds that they remember well whatever suits their taste for resemblances. By following the real analogies between different arts and sciences, and making use of the knowledge children have on one subject to illustrate another, we may at once amuse their fancy, and cultivate their memory with advantage. Ideas laid up in this manner, will recur in the same order, and will be ready for further use. When two ideas are remembered by their mutual connection, surely it is best that they should both of them be substantially useful; and not that one should attend merely to answer for the appearance of the other.

As men readily remember those things which are every day useful to them in business, what relates to their amusements, or to their favourite tastes in arts, sciences, or in literature; so children find no difficulty in remembering every thing which mixes daily with their little pleasures. They value knowledge, which is *useful* and *agreeable* to them, as highly as we do; but they consider only the present, and we take the future into our estimate. Children feel no interest in half the things that are committed, with the most solemn recommendations, to the care of their memory. It is in vain to tell them, "You must remember *such a thing*, because it will be useful to you when you grow up to be a man." The child feels like a child, and has no idea of what he may feel when he grows up to be a man. He tries to remember what he is desired, perhaps, because he wishes to please his wiser friends; but if the ideas are remote from his every day business, if nothing recall them but voluntary exertion, and if he be obliged to abstract his little soul from every thing it holds dear, before he can recollect his lessons, they will have no hold upon his memory; he will feel that recollection is too operose, and he will enjoy none of the "pleasures of memory."

To induce children to exercise their memory, we must put them in situations where they may be immediately rewarded for their exertion. We must create an interest in their minds—nothing uninteresting is long remembered. In a large and literary family, it will not be difficult to invent occupations for children which may exercise all their faculties. Even the conversation of such a family, will create in their minds a desire for knowledge; what they hear, will recall to their memory what they read; and if they are encouraged to take a reasonable share in conversation, they will acquire the habit of listening to every thing that others say. By permitting children to talk freely of what they read, we are more likely to improve their memory for books, than by exacting from them formal repetitions of lessons.

Dr. Johnson, who is said to have had an uncommonly good memory, tells us, that when he was a boy, he used, after he had acquired any fresh knowledge from his books, to run and tell it to an old woman, of whom he was very fond. This exercise was so agreeable to him, that it imprinted what he read upon his memory.

La Gaucherie, one of the preceptors of Henry IV. having found that he had to do with a young prince of an impatient mind, and active genius, little suited to sedentary studies, instead of compelling his pupil to read, taught him by means of conversation: anecdotes of heroes, and the wise sayings of ancient philosophers, were thus imprinted upon the mind of this prince. It is said, that Henry IV. applied, in his subsequent life, all the knowledge he had acquired in this manner so happily, that learned men were surprised at his memory. [52]

By these observations, we by no means would insinuate, that application to books is unnecessary. We are sensible that accurate knowledge upon any subject, cannot be acquired by superficial conversation; that it can be obtained only by patient application. But we mean to point out, that an early taste for literature may be excited in children by conversation; and that their memory should be first cultivated in the manner which will give them the least pain. When there is motive for application, and when habits of industry have been gradually acquired, we may securely trust, that our pupils will complete their own education. Nor should we have reason to fear, that those who have a good memory for all other things, should not be able to retain all that is worth remembering in books. Children should never be praised for merely remembering exactly what they read, they should be praised for selecting with good sense what is best worth their attention, and for applying what they remember to useful purposes.

We have observed how much the habit of inventing increases the wish for knowledge, and increases the interest men take in a number of ideas, which are indifferent to uncultivated and indolent people. It is the same with children. Children who invent, exercise their memory with pleasure, from the immediate sense of utility and success. A piece of knowledge, which they lay by in their minds, with the hopes of making use of it in some future invention, they have more motives for remembering, than what they merely learn by rote, because they are commanded to do so by the voice of authority.

(June 19th, 1796.) S— —, a boy of nine years old, of good abilities, was translating Ovid's description of envy. When he came to the Latin word *suffusa*, he pronounced it as if it had been spelled with a single *f* and a double *s*, *sufussa*; he made the same mistake several times: at last his father, to *try* whether it would make him remember the right pronunciation, desired him to repeat *suffusa* forty times. The boy did so. About three hours afterwards, the boy was asked whether he recollected the word which he had repeated forty times. No, he said, he did not; but he remembered that it meant diffused. His father recalled the word to his mind, by asking him what letter it was that he had sounded as if it had been a double letter; he said *s*. And what double letter did you sound as if it had been single? *f*, said the boy. Then, said his father, you have found out that it was a word in which there was a double *ff* and a single *s*, and that it is the Latin for *diffused*. Oh, suffusa, said the boy.

This boy, who had such difficulty in learning a single Latin word, by repeating it forty times, showed in other instances, that he was by no means deficient in recollective memory. On the contrary, though he read very little, and seldom learned any thing by rote, he applied happily any thing that he read or heard in conversation.

(March 31st, 1796.) His father told him, that he had this morning seen a large horn at a gentleman's in the neighbourhood. It was found thirty spades depth below the surface of the earth, in a bog. With the horn was found a carpet, and wrapped up in the carpet a lump of tallow. "Now," said his father, "how could that lump of tallow come there? Or was it tallow, do you think? Or what could it be?"

H—— (a boy of 14, brother to S——) said, he thought it might have been buried by some robbers, after they had committed some robbery; he thought the lump was tallow.

S—— said, "Perhaps some dead body might have been wrapped up in the carpet and buried; and the dead body might have turned into tallow." [53]

"How came you," said his father, "to think of a dead body's turning into tallow?"

"You told me," said the boy, "You read to me, I mean, an account of some dead bodies that had been buried a great many years, which had turned into.tallow."

"Spermaceti," you mean? "Yes."

S—— had heard the account he alluded to above two months before this time. No one in company recollected it except himself, though several had heard it.

Amongst the few things which S—— had learnt by heart, was the Hymn to Adversity. A very slight circumstance may show, that he did not get this poem merely as a tiresome lesson, as children sometimes learn by rote what they do not understand, and which they never recollect except in the arduous moments of formal repetition.

A few days after S—— had learned the Hymn to Adversity, he happened to hear his sister say to a lady, "I observed you pitied me for having had a whitlow on my finger, more than any body else did, because you have had one yourself." S——'s father asked him why he smiled. "Because," said S——, "I was thinking of the *song*, [54] the *hymn* to adversity;

"And from her own she learned to melt at other's wo."

A recollective memory of books appears early in children who are not overwhelmed with them; if the impressions made upon their minds be distinct, they will recur with pleasure to the memory when similar ideas are presented.

July 1796. S—— heard his father read Sir Brook Boothby's excellent epitaph upon Algernon Sidney; the following lines pleased the boy particularly:

"Approach, contemplate this immortal name,
Swear on this shrine to emulate his fame;
To dare, like him, e'en to thy latest breath,
Contemning chains, and poverty, and death."

S——'s father asked him why he liked these lines, and whether they put him in mind of any thing that he had heard before. S—— said, "It puts me in mind of Hamilcar's making his son Hannibal swear to hate the Romans, and love his countrymen eternally. But I like *this* much better. I think it was exceedingly foolish and wrong of Hamilcar to make his son swear always to hate the Romans."

Latin lessons are usually so very disagreeable to boys, that they seldom are pleased with any allusions to them; but by a good management in a tutor, even these lessons may be associated with agreeable ideas. Boys should be encouraged to talk and think about what they learn in Latin, as well as what they read in English; they should be allowed to judge of the characters described in ancient authors, to compare them with our present ideas of excellence, and thus to make some use of their learning. It will then be not merely engraved upon their memory in the form of lessons, it will be mingled with their notions of life and manners; it will occur to them when they converse, and when they act; they will possess the admired talent for classical allusion, as well as all the solid advantages of an unprejudiced judgment. It is not enough that gentlemen should be masters of the learned languages, they must know how to produce their knowledge without pedantry or affectation. The memory may in vain be stored with classical precedents, unless these can be brought into use in speaking or writing without the parade of dull citation, or formal introduction. "Sir," said Dr. Johnson, to some prosing tormentor, "I would rather a man would knock me down, than to begin to talk to me of the Punic wars." A public speaker, who rises in the House of Commons, with pedantry prepense to quote Latin or Greek, is coughed or laughed down; but the beautiful unpremeditated classical allusions of Burke or Sheridan, sometimes conveyed in a single word, seize the imagination irresistibly.

Since we perceive, that memory is chiefly useful as it furnishes materials for invention, and that invention can greatly abridge the mere labour of accumulation, we must examine how the inventive faculty can be properly exercised. The vague precept of, cultivate the memory and invention of young people at the same time, will not inform parents how this is to be accomplished; we trust, therefore, that we may be permitted, contrary to the custom of didactic writers, to illustrate a general precept by a few examples; and we take these examples from real life, because we apprehend, that fictions, however ingenious, will never advance the science of education so much as simple experiments.

No elaborate theory of invention shall here alarm parents. It is a mistake, to suppose that the inventive faculty can be employed only on important subjects; it can be exercised in the most trifling circumstances of domestic life. Scarcely any family can be so unfortunately situated, that they may not employ the ingenuity of their children without violent exertion, or any grand apparatus. Let us only make use of the circumstances which happen every hour. Children are interested in every thing that is going forward. Building, or planting, or conversation, or reading; they attend to every thing, and from every thing might they with a little assistance obtain instruction. Let their useful curiosity be encouraged; let them make a part of the general society of the family, instead of being treated as if they had neither senses nor understanding. When any thing is to be done, let them be asked to invent the best way of doing it. When they see that their invention becomes immediately useful, they will take pleasure in exerting themselves.

June 4th, 1796. A lady, who had been ruling pencil lines for a considerable time, complained of its being a tiresome operation; and she wished that a quick and easy way of doing it could be invented. Somebody present said they had seen pens for ruling music books, which ruled four lines at a time; and it was asked, whether a leaden rake could not be made to rule a sheet of paper at once.

Mr. —— said, that he thought such a pencil would not rule well; and he called to S——, (the same boy we mentioned before) and asked him if he could invent any method of doing the business better. S—— took about a quarter of an hour to consider; and he then described a little machine for ruling a sheet of paper at a single stroke, which his father had executed for him. It succeeded well, and this success was the best reward he could have.

Another day Mr. —— observed, that the maid, whose business it was to empty a bucket of ashes into an ash-hole, never could be persuaded to do it, because the ashes were blown against her face by the wind; and he determined to invent a method which should make it convenient to her to do as she was desired. The maid usually threw the ashes into a heap on the sheltered side of a wall; the thing to be done was, to make her put the bucket through a hole in this wall, and empty the ashes on the other side. This problem was given to all the children and grown up persons in the family. One of the children invented the shelf, which, they said, should be like part of the vane of a winnowing machine which they had lately seen; the manner of placing this vane, another of the children suggested: both these ideas joined together, produced the contrivance which was wanted.

A little model was made in wood of this bucket, which was a pretty toy. The thing itself was executed, and was found useful.

June 8th, 1796. Mr. — — was balancing a pair of scales very exactly, in which he was going to weigh some opium; this led to a conversation upon scales and weighing. Some one said that the dealers in diamonds must have very exact scales, as the difference of a grain makes such a great difference in their value. S— — was very attentive to this conversation. M— —told him, that jewellers always, if they can, buy diamonds when the air is light, and sell them when it is heavy. S— — did not understand the reason of this, till his father explained to him the general principles of hydrostatics, and showed him a few experiments with bodies of different specific gravity: these experiments were distinctly understood by every body present. The boy then observed, that it was not fair of the jewellers to buy and sell in this manner; they should not, said he, use *these* weights. Diamonds should be the weights. Diamonds should be weighed against diamonds.

November, 1795. One day after dinner, the candles had been left for some time without being snuffed; and Mr. — — said he wished candles could be made which would not require snuffing.

Mrs. ******** thought of cutting the wick into several pieces before it was put into the candle, that so, when it burned down to the divisions, the wick might fall off. M— — thought that the wick might be tied tight round at intervals, before it was put into the candle; that when it burned down to the places where it was tied, it would snap off: but Mr. — — objected, that the candle would most likely go out when it had burned down to her knots. It was then proposed to send a stream of oxygene through the candle, instead of a wick. M— — asked if some substance might not be used for wicks which should burn into powder, and fly off or sublime. Mr. — — smiled at this, and said, "*Some substance*; some *kind of air*; some *chemical mixture*! A person ignorant of chemistry always talks of, as an ignorant person in mechanics always says, "Oh, you can do it somehow with *a spring*."

As the company could not immediately discover any way of making candles which should not require to be snuffed, they proceeded to invent ways of putting out a candle at a certain time without hands. The younger part of the company had hopes of solving this problem, and every eye was attentively fixed upon the candle.

"How would you put it out, S— —?" said Mr. — —. S— — said, that if a weight, a very little lighter than the extinguisher, were tied to a string, and if the string were put over a pulley, and if *the* extinguisher were tied to the other end of the string, and the candle put exactly under the extinguisher; the extinguisher would move very, very gently down, and at last put out the candle.

Mr. — — observed, that whilst it was putting out the candle, there would be a disagreeable smell, because the extinguisher would be a considerable time moving *very, very gently down*, over the candle after the candle had begun to go out.

C— — (a girl of twelve years old) spoke next. "I would tie an extinguisher to one end of a thread. I would put this string through a pulley fastened to the ceiling; the other end of this string should be fastened to the middle of another thread, which should be strained between two posts set upright on each side of the candle, so as that the latter string might lean against the candle at any distance you want below the flame. When the candle burns down to this string, it will burn it in two, and the extinguisher will drop upon the candle."

This is the exact description of *the weaver's alarm*, mentioned in the Philosophical Transactions which C— — had never seen or heard of.

Mr. — — now showed us the patent extinguisher, which was much approved of by all the rival inventors.

It is very useful to give children problems which have already been solved, because they can immediately compare their own imperfect ideas with successful inventions, which have actually been brought into real use. We know beforehand what ideas are necessary to complete the invention, and whether the pupil has all the necessary knowledge. Though by the courtesy of poetry, a creative power is ascribed to inventive genius, yet we must be convinced that no genius can invent without materials. Nothing can come of nothing. Invention is nothing more than the new combination of materials. We must judge in general of the ease or difficulty of any invention, either by the number of ideas necessary to be combined, or by the dissimilarity or analogy of those ideas. In giving any problem to children, we should not only consider whether they know all that is necessary upon the subject, but also, whether that knowledge is sufficiently *familiar* to their minds, whether circumstances are likely to recall it, and whether they have a perfectly Clear idea of the thing to be done. By considering all these particulars, we may pretty nearly proportion our questions to the capacity of the pupil; and we may lead his mind on step by step from obvious to intricate inventions.

July 30th, 1796. L— —, who had just returned from Edinburgh, and had taken down in two large volumes, Dr. Black's Lectures, used to read to us part of them, for about a quarter of an hour, every morning after breakfast. He was frequently interrupted (which interruptions he bore with heroic patience) by Mr. — —'s explanations and comments. When he came to the expansive power of steam, and to the description of the different steam engines which have been invented, Mr. — — stopped to ask B— —, C— —, and S— —, to describe the steam engine in their own words. They all described it in such a manner as to show that they clearly understood the principle of the machine. Only the general principle had been explained to them. L— —, after having read the description of Savary's and Newcomen's steam engines, was beginning to read the description of that invented by Mr. Watt; but Mr. — — stopped him, that he might try whether any person present could invent it. Mr. E— — thus stated the difficulty: "In the old steam engine, cold water, you know, is thrown into the cylinder to condense the steam; but in condensing the steam, the cold water at the same time cools the cylinder. Now the cylinder must be heated again, before it can be filled with steam; for till it is heated, it will condense the steam. There is, consequently, a great waste of heat and fuel in the great cylinder. How can you condense the steam without cooling the cylinder?"

S— —. "Let down a cold tin tube into the cylinder when you want to condense the steam, and draw it up again as soon as the steam is condensed; or, if you could put a *cylinder* of ice up the great tube."

Some of the company next asked, if an horizontal plate of cold metal, made to slide up the inside of the cylinder, would condense the steam. The edges of the plate only would touch the cylinder; the surface of the plate might condense the steam.

"But," said Mr. — —"how can you introduce and withdraw it?"

C— — (a girl of 12) then said, "I would put a cold vessel to condense the steam at the top of the cylinder."

Mr. — —. "So as to touch the cylinder, do you mean?"

C— —. "No, not so as to touch the cylinder, but at some distance from it."

Mr. — —. "Then the cold air would rush into the cylinder whilst the steam was passing from the cylinder to your condenser."

C— —. "But I would cover in the cold vessel, and I would cover in the passage to it."

Mr. — —. "I have the pleasure of informing you, that you have invented part of the great Mr. Watt's improvement on the steam engine. You see how it facilitates invention, to begin by stating the difficulty clearly to the mind. This is what every practical inventor does when he invents in mechanics."

L— — (smiling.) "And what *I* always do in inventing a mathematical demonstration."

To the good natured reader we need offer no apology; to the ill natured we dare attempt none, for introducing these detailed views of the first attempts of young invention. They are not exhibited as models, either to do honour to the tutor or his pupils; but simply to show, how the mind may be led from the easiest steps, to what are supposed to be difficult in education. By imagining ourselves to be in the same situation with children, we may guess what things are difficult to them; and if we can recollect the course of our own minds in acquiring knowledge, or in inventing, we may by retracing the same steps instruct others. The order that is frequently followed by authors, in the division and subdivision of their elementary treatises, is not always the best for those who are to learn. Such authors are usually more intent upon proving to the learned that they understand their subject, than upon communicating their knowledge to the ignorant. Parents and tutors must, therefore, supply familiar oral instruction, and those simple, but essential explanations, which books disdain, or neglect to give. And there is this advantage in all instruction given in conversation, that it can be made interesting by a thousand little circumstances, which are below the dignity of didactic writers. Gradually we may proceed from simple to more complicated contrivances. The invention of experiments to determine a theory, or to ascertain the truth of an assertion, must be particularly useful to the understanding. Any person, who has attended to experiments in chemistry and natural philosophy, must know, that invention can be as fully and elegantly displayed upon these subjects as upon any in the fine arts or literature. There is one great advantage in scientific invention; it is not dependent upon capricious taste for its reward. The beauty and elegance of a poem may be disputed by a thousand amateurs; there can be but one opinion about the truth of a discovery in science.

Independent of all ambition, there is considerable pleasure in the pursuit of experimental knowledge. Children especially, before they are yet fools to fame, enjoy this substantial pleasure. Nor are we to suppose that children have not capacities for such pursuits; they are peculiarly suited to their capacity. They love to see experiments tried, and to try them. They show this disposition not only wherever they are encouraged, but wherever they are permitted to show it; and if we compare their method of reasoning with the reasonings of the learned, we shall sometimes be surprised. They have no prejudices, therefore they have the complete use of all their senses; they have few ideas, but those few are distinct; they can be analyzed and compared with ease; children, therefore, judge and invent better, *in proportion to their knowledge*, than most grown up people.

Dr. Hooke observes, that a sensible man, in solving any philosophical problem, should always lean to that side which is opposite to his favourite taste. A chemist is disposed to account for every thing by chemical means; a geometrician is inclined to solve every problem geometrically; and a mechanic accounts for all the phenomena of nature by the laws of mechanism. This undue bias upon the minds of ingenious people, has frequently rendered their talents less useful to mankind. It is the duty of those who educate ingenious children, to guard against this species of scientific insanity.

There are prejudices of another description, which are fatal to inventive genius; some of these are usually found to attend ignorance, and others sometimes adhere to the learned. Ignorant people, if they possess any degree of invention, are so confident in their own abilities, that they will not take the pains to inquire what others have thought or done; they disdain all general principles, and will rather scramble through some by-path of their own striking out, than condescend to be shown the best road by the most enlightened guide. For this reason, self-taught geniuses, as they are called, seldom go beyond a certain point in their own education, and the praise we bestow upon their ingenuity is always accompanied with expressions of regret: "It is a pity that such a genius had not the advantages of a good education."

The learned, on the contrary, who have been bred up in reverence for established opinions, and who have felt in many instances the advantage of general principles, are apt to adhere too pertinaciously to their theories, and hence they neglect or despise new observations. How long did the maxim, that nature abhors a vacuum, content the learned! And how many discoveries were retarded by this single false principle! For a great number of years it was affirmed and believed, that all objects were seen by the intervention of visual rays, proceeding from the eye much in the same manner as we feel any object at a distance from us by the help of a stick. [55] Whilst this absurd analogy satisfied the mind, no discoveries were made in vision, none were attempted. A prepossession often misleads the industry of active genius. Dr. Hooke, in spite of the ridicule which he met with, was firm in his belief, that mankind would discover some method of sailing in the air. Balloons have justified his prediction; but all his own industry in trying experiments upon flying was wasted, because he persisted in following a false analogy to the wings of birds. He made wings of various sorts; till he took it for granted that he *must* learn to fly by mechanical means: had he applied to chemistry, he might have succeeded. It is curious to observe, how nearly he once touched upon the discovery, and yet, misled by his prepossessions, quitted his hold. He observed, that the air cells [56] of fishes are filled with air, which buoys them up in the water; and he supposes that this air is lighter than *common* air. Had he pursued this idea, he might have invented balloons; but he returned with fatal perseverance to his old theory of wings. From such facts, we may learn the power and danger of prejudice in the most ingenious minds; and we shall be careful to preserve our pupils early from its blind dominion.

The best preservation against the presumption to which ignorance is liable, and the best preservative against the self sufficiency to which the learned are subject, is the habit of varying our studies and occupations. Those who have a general view of the whole map of human knowledge, perceive how many unexplored regions are yet to be cultivated by future industry; nor will they implicitly submit to the reports of ignorant voyagers. No imaginary pillars of Hercules, will bound their enterprises. There is no presumption in believing, that much more is possible to science than ever human ingenuity has executed; therefore, young people should not be ridiculed for that sanguine temper which excites to great inventions. They should be ridiculed only when they imagine that they possess the means of doing things to which they are unequal. The fear of this deserved ridicule, will stimulate them to acquire knowledge, and will induce them to estimate cautiously their own powers before they hazard their reputation. We need not fear that this caution should repress their activity of mind; ambition will secure their perseverance, if they are taught that every acquisition is within the reach of unremitting industry. This is not an opinion to be artfully inculcated to serve a *particular* purpose, but it is an opinion drawn from experience; an opinion which men of the highest abilities and integrity, of talents and habits the most dissimilar, have confirmed by their united testimony. Helvetius maintained, that no great man ever formed a great design which he was not also capable of executing.

Even where great perseverance is exercised, the choice of the subjects on which the inventive powers are employed determines, in a great measure, their value: therefore, in the education of ingenious children, we should gradually turn their attention from curious trifles to important objects. Boverick, [57] who made chains "to yoke a flea," must have possessed exquisite patience; besides his chain of two hundred links, with its padlock and key, all weighing together less than the third part of a grain, this indefatigable *minute artificer* was the maker of a landau, which opened and shut by springs: this equipage, with six horses harnessed to it, a coachman sitting on the box, with a dog between his legs, four inside and two outside passengers, besides a postilion riding one of the fore horses, was drawn with all the ease and safety imaginable by a well trained flea! The inventor and executor of this puerile machine, bestowed on it, probably, as much time as would have sufficed to produce Watt's fire engine, or Montgolfier's balloon. It did not, perhaps, cost the Marquis of Worcester more exertion to draw out his celebrated century of inventions; it did not, perhaps, cost Newton more to write those queries which Maclaurin said he could never read without feeling his hair stand on end with admiration.

Brebeuf, a French wit, wrote a hundred and fifty epigrams upon a painted lady; a brother wit, fired with emulation, wrote upon the same subject three hundred more, making in all four hundred and fifty epigrams, each with appropriate turns of their own. Probably, Pope and Parnell did not rack their invention so much, or exercise more industry in completing "The Rape of the Lock," or "The Rise of Woman." These will live for ever; who will read the four hundred and fifty epigrams?

The most effectual methods to discourage in young people the taste for frivolous ingenuity, will be, never to admire these "laborious nothings," to compare them with useful and elegant inventions, and to show that vain curiosities can be but the wonder and amusement of a moment. Children who begin with trifling inventions, may be led from these to general principles; and with their knowledge, their ambition will necessarily increase. It cannot be expected that the most enlarged plan of education could early give an intimate acquaintance with all the sciences; but with their leading principles, their general history, their present state, and their immediate desiderata, [58] young people may, and ought to be, made acquainted. Their own industry will afterwards collect more precise information, and they will never waste their time in vain studies and fruitless inventions. Even if the cultivation of the memory were our grand object, this plan of education will succeed. When the Abbé de Longuerue, whose prodigious memory we have formerly mentioned, was asked by the Marquis d'Argenson, how he managed to arrange and retain in his head every thing that entered it, and to recollect every thing when wanted? The Abbé answered:

"Sir, the elements of every science must be learned whilst we are very young; the first principles of every language; the a b c, as I may say, of every kind of knowledge: this is not difficult in youth, especially as it is not necessary to penetrate far; simple notions are sufficient; when once these are acquired, every thing we read afterwards, finds its proper place."

[39] V. Plutarch. Quintilian.

[40] Berington's History of the Lives of Abeillard and Heloisa, page 173.

[41] Eloge de M. L'Abbé d'Alary.

[42] Marquis d'Argenson's Essays, page 385.

[43] D'Alembert's Eloge de M. d'Alary.

[44] Curiosities of Literature, vol. ii. page 145.

[45] Priestley on Electricity, page 317.

[46] Fuller, author of the Worthies of England. See Curiosities of Literature, vol. i.

[47] V. Chapter on Books, and on Geography.

[48] Dr. Darwin. Zoonomia.

[49] At the end of the History of Vision.

[50] "Nov. 7, 1749. Electrical fluid agrees with lightning in these particulars. 1. Giving light. 2. Colour of the light. 3. Crooked direction. 4. Swift motion. 5. Being conducted by metals. 6. Crack or noise in exploding. 7. Subsisting in water or ice. 8. Rending bodies it passes through. 9. Destroying animals. 10. Melting metals. 11. Firing inflammable substances. 12. Sulphureous smell. The electric fluid is attracted by points. We do not know whether this property is in lightning. But since they agree in all the particulars wherein we can already compare them, is it not probable they agree likewise in this? Let the experiment be made."

Dr. Franklin's Letters, page 322.

[51] Helvetius, "Sur l'Esprit."

[52] See preface to L'Esprit des Romains considéré.

[53] See the account in the Monthly Review.

[54] He had tried to sing it to the tune of "Hope, thou nurse of young desire."

[55] Priestley on Vision, vol. i. page 23.

[56] V. Hooke's Posthumous Works.

[57] Hooke's Mycrographia, p. 62.

CHAPTER XXII
TASTE AND IMAGINATION

Figurative language seems to have confounded the ideas of most writers upon metaphysics. Imagination, Memory, and Reason, have been long introduced to our acquaintance as allegorical personages, and we have insensibly learned to consider them as real beings. The "viewless regions" of the soul, have been portioned out amongst these ideal sovereigns; but disputes have, nevertheless, sometimes arisen concerning the boundaries of intellectual provinces. Amongst the disputed territories, those of Imagination have been most frequently the seat of war; her empire has been subject to continual revolution; her dominions have been, by potent invaders, divided and subdivided. Fancy, [59] Memory, [60] Ideal presence, [61] and Conception, [62] have shared her spoils.

By poets, imagination has been addressed as the great parent of genius, as the arbiter, if not the creator, of our pleasures; by philosophers, her name has been sometimes pronounced with horror; to her fatal delusions, they have ascribed all the crimes and miseries of mankind. Yet, even philosophers have not always agreed in their opinions: whilst some have treated Imagination with contempt, as the irreconcileable enemy of Reason, by others [63] she has been considered with more respect, as Reason's inseparable friend; as the friend who collects and prepares all the arguments upon which Reason decides; as the injured, misrepresented power who is often forced to supply her adversaries with eloquence, who is often called upon to preside at her own trial, and to pronounce her own condemnation.

Imagination is "*the power,*" we are told, of "*forming images:*" the word image, however, does not, strictly speaking, express any thing more than a representation of an object of sight; but the power of imagination extends to objects of all the senses.

"I hear a voice you cannot hear,
Which says I must not stay.
I see a hand you cannot see,
Which beckons me away."

Imagination hears the voice, as well as sees the hand; by an easy license of metaphor, what was originally used to express the operation of our senses, is extended to them all. We do not precisely say, that Imagination, forms *images* of past sounds, or tastes, or smells; but we say that she forms ideas of them; and ideas, we are told, are mental images. It has been suggested by Dr. Darwin, that all these analogies between images and thoughts have, probably, originated in our observing the little pictures painted on the retina of the eye.

It is difficult certainly, if not impossible, to speak of the invisible operations of the mind or body, without expressing ourselves in metaphor of some kind or other; and we are easily misled by allusions to sensible objects, because when we comprehend the allusion, we flatter ourselves that we understand the theory which it is designed to illustrate. Whether we call ideas images in popular language, or vibrations, according to Dr. Hartley's system, or modes of sensation with Condillac, or motions of the sensorium, in the language of Dr. Darwin, may seem a matter of indifference. But even the choices of names is not a matter of indifference to those who wish to argue accurately; when they are obliged to describe their feelings or thoughts by metaphoric expressions, they will prefer the simplest; those with which the fewest extraneous associations are connected. Words which call up a variety of heterogeneous ideas to our minds, are unfit for the purposes of sober reasoning; our attention is distracted by them, and we cannot restrain it to the accurate comparison of simple proportions. We yield to pleasing reverie, instead of exerting painful voluntary attention. Hence it is probably useful in our attempts to reason, especially upon metaphysical subjects, to change from time to time our nomenclature, [64] and to substitute terms which have no relation to our old associations, and which do not affect the prejudices of our education. We are obliged to define with some degree of accuracy the sense of new terms, and we are thus led to compare our old notions with more severity. Our superstitious reverence for mere symbols is also dissipated; symbols are apt to impose even upon those who acknowledge their vanity, and who profess to consider them merely as objects of vulgar worship.

When we call a class of our ideas *images* and pictures, a tribe of associations with painting comes into our mind, and we argue about Imagination as if she were actually a paintress, who has colours at her command, and who, upon some invisible canvass in the soul, portrays the likeness of all earthly and celestial objects. When we continue to pursue the same metaphor in speaking of the moral influence of Imagination, we say that her *colouring* deceives us, that her *pictures* are flattering and false, that she draws objects out of proportion, &c. To what do all these metaphors lead? We make no new discoveries by talking in this manner; we do not learn the cause or the cure of any of the diseases of the mind; we only persuade ourselves that we know something, when we are really ignorant.

We have sedulously avoided entering into any metaphysical disquisitions; but we have examined with care the systems of theoretic writers, that we may be able to avail ourselves of such of their observations as can be reduced to practice in education. With respect to the arts, imagination may be considered practically in two points of view, as it relates to our taste, and as it relates to our talents for the arts. Without being a poet, or an orator, a man may have a sufficient degree of imagination to receive pleasure from the talents of others; he may be a critical judge of the respective merits of orators, poets, and artists. This sensibility to the pleasures of the imagination, when judiciously managed, adds much to the happiness of life, and it must be peculiarly advantageous to those who are precluded by their station in society from the necessity of manual labour. Mental exercise, and mental amusements, are essential to persons in the higher ranks of life, who would escape from the fever of dissipation, or from the lethargy of ennui. The mere physical advantages which wealth can procure, are reducible to the short sum of "*meat, fire, and clothes.*" A nobleman of the highest birth, and with the longest line of ancestry, inherits no intuitive taste, nor can he purchase it from the artist, the painter, or the poet; the possession of the whole Pinelli library could not infuse the slightest portion of literature. Education can alone give the full power to enjoy the real advantages of fortune. To educate the taste and the imagination, it is not necessary to surround the heir of an opulent family with masters and connoisseurs. Let him never hear the jargon of amateurs, let him learn the art "not to admire." But in his earliest childhood cultivate his senses with care, that he may be able to see and hear, to feel and understand, for himself. Visible images he will rapidly collect in his memory; but these must be selected, and his first associations must not be trusted to accident. Encourage him to observe with attention all the works of nature, but show him only the best imitations of art; the first objects that he contemplates with delight, will remain long associated with pleasure in his imagination; you must, therefore, be careful, that these early associations accord with the decisions of those who have determined the national standard of taste. In many instances taste is governed by arbitrary and variable laws; the fashions of dress, of decoration, of manner, change from day to day; therefore no exclusive prejudices should confine your pupil's understanding. Let him know, as far as we know them, the general principles which govern mankind in their admiration of the sublime and beautiful; but at the same time give him that enlarged toleration of mind, which comprehends the possibility of a taste different from our own. Show him, and you need not go further than the Indian skreen, or the Chinese paper in your drawing room, for the illustration, that the sublime and beautiful vary at Pekin, at London, on Westminster bridge, and on the banks of the Ganges. Let your young pupil look over a collection of gems or of ancient medals; it is necessary that his eye should be early accustomed to Grecian beauty, and to all the classic forms of grace. But do not suffer him to become a bigot, though he may be an enthusiast in his admiration of the antique. Short lessons upon this subject may be conveyed in a few words. If a child sees you look at the bottom of a print for the name of the artist, before you will venture to pronounce upon its merits, he will follow your example, and he will judge by the authority of others, and not by his own taste. If he hears you ask, who wrote this poem? Who built this palace? Is this a genuine antique? he will ask the same questions before he ventures to be pleased. If he hears you pronounce with emphasis, that such a thing comes from Italy, and therefore must be in good taste, he will take the same compendious method of decision upon the first convenient occasion.

He will not trouble himself to examine why utility pleases, nor will he analyze his taste, or discover why one proportion or one design pleases him better than another; he will, if by example you teach him prejudice, content himself with repeating the words, proportion, antique, picturesque, &c. without annexing any precise ideas to these words.

Parents, who have not turned their attention to metaphysics, may, perhaps, apprehend, that they have something very abstruse or intricate to learn, before they can instruct their pupils in the principles of taste: but these principles are simple, and two or three entertaining books, of no very alarming size, comprise all that has yet been ascertained upon this subject. Vernet's Théorie des Sentiments Agréables; Hogarth's Analysis of Beauty; an Essay of Hume's on the standard of taste; Burke's Sublime and Beautiful; Lord Kames's Elements of Criticism; Sir Joshua Reynold's Discourses; and Alison on Taste; contain so much instruction, mixed with so much amusement, that we cannot think that it will be a *terrible task* to any parent to peruse them.

These books are above the comprehension of children; but the principles which they contain, can be very early illustrated in conversation. It will be easy, in familiar instances, to show children that the fitness, propriety, or utility of certain forms, recommends them to our approbation: that uniformity, an appearance of order and regularity, are, in some cases, agreeable to us; contrast, in others: that one class of objects pleases us from habit, another from novelty, &c. The general principle that governs taste, in the greatest variety of instances, is the association of ideas, and this, fortunately, can be most easily illustrated.

"I like such a person, because her voice puts me in mind of my mother's. I like this walk, because I was very happy the last time I was here with my sister. I think green is the prettiest of all colours; my father's room is painted green, and it is very cheerful, and I have been very happy in that room; and, besides, the grass is green in spring." Such simple observations as these, come naturally from children; they take notice of the influence of association upon their taste, though, perhaps, they may not extend their observations so as to deduce the general principle according to philosophical forms. We should not lay down for them this or any other principle of taste, as a rule which they are to take for granted; but we should lead them to class their own desultory remarks, and we should excite them to attend to their own feelings, and to ascertain the truth, by experiments upon themselves. We have often observed, that children have been much entertained with comparing the accidental circumstances they have met with, and the unpremeditated expressions used in conversation, with any general maxim. In this point of view, we may render even general maxims serviceable to children, because they will excite to experiment: our pupils will detect their falsehood, or, after sufficient reflection, acknowledge their truth.

Perhaps it may be thought, that this mode of instruction will tend rather to improve the judgment than the taste; but every person of good taste, must have also a good judgment in matters of taste: sometimes the judgment may have been partially exercised upon a particular class of objects, and its accuracy of discrimination may be confined to this one subject; therefore we hastily decide, that, because men of taste may not always be men of universally good judgment, these two powers of the mind are unnecessary to one another. By teaching the philosophy, at the same time that we cultivate the pleasures, of taste, we shall open to our pupils a new world; we shall give them a new sense. The pleasure of every effect will be increased by the perception of its cause; the magic of the scenery will not lose its power to charm, though we are aware of the secret of the enchantment.

We have hitherto spoken of the taste for what is beautiful; a taste for the sublime we should be cautious in cultivating. Obscurity and terror are two of the grand sources of the sublime; analyze the feeling, examine accurately the object which creates the emotion, and you dissipate the illusion, you annihilate the pleasure.

> "What seemed its head, the likeness of a kingly crown had
> on."

The indistinctness of the head and of the kingly crown, makes this a sublime image. Upon the same principle,

"Danger, whose limbs, of giant mould,
No mortal eye can fix'd behold,"

always must appear sublime as long as the passion of fear operates. Would it not, however, be imprudent in education to permit that early propensity to superstitious terrors, and that temporary suspension of the reasoning faculties, which are often essential to our taste for the sublime? When we hear of "Margaret's grimly ghost," or of the "dead still hour of night," a sort of awful tremor seizes us, partly from the effect of early associations, and partly from the solemn tone of the reader. The early associations which we perhaps have formed of terror, with the ideas of apparitions, and winding sheets, and sable shrouds, should be unknown to children. The silent solemn hour of midnight, should not to them be an hour of terror. In the following poetic description of the beldam telling dreadful stories to her infant audience, we hear only of the pleasures of the imagination; we do not recollect how dearly these pleasures must be purchased by their votaries:

"* * * * * * finally by night
The village matron, round the blazing hearth,
Suspends the infant audience with her tales,
Breathing astonishment! of witching rhymes,
And evil spirits; of the death-bed call
Of him who robbed the widow, and devour'd
The orphan's portion; of the unquiet souls
Ris'n from the grave to ease the heavy guilt
Of deeds in life concealed; of shapes that walk
At dead of night, and clank their chains, and wave
The torch of hell around the murd'rer's bed.
At every solemn pause the crowd recoil,
Gazing each other speechless, and congeal'd
With shiv'ring sighs; till, eager for th' event,
Around the beldam all erect they hang,
Each trembling heart with grateful terrors quell'd." [65]

No prudent mother will ever imitate this eloquent village matron, nor will she permit any beldam in the nursery to conjure up these sublime shapes, and to quell the hearts of her children with these grateful terrors. We were once present when a group of speechless children sat listening to the story of Blue-beard, "breathing astonishment." A gentleman who saw the charm beginning to operate, resolved to counteract its dangerous influence. Just at the critical moment, when the fatal key drops from the trembling hands of the imprudent wife, the gentleman interrupted the awful pause of silence that ensued, and requested permission to relate the remainder of the story. Tragi-comedy does not offend the taste of young, so much as of old critics; the transition from grave to gay was happily managed. Blue-beard's wife afforded much diversion, and lost all sympathy the moment she was represented as a curious, tattling, timid, ridiculous woman. The terrors of Blue-beard himself subsided when he was properly introduced to the company; and the denouement of the piece was managed much to the entertainment of the audience; the catastrophe, instead of freezing their young blood, produced general laughter. Ludicrous images, thus presented to the mind which has been prepared for horror, have an instantaneous effect upon the risible muscles: it seems better to use these means of counteracting the terrors of the imagination, than to reason upon the subject whilst the fit is on; reason should be used between the fits. [66] Those who study the minds of children know the nice touches which affect their imagination, and they can, by a few words, change their feelings by the power of association.

Ferdinand Duke of Tuscany was once struck with the picture of a child crying: the painter, [67] who was at work upon the head, wished to give the duke a proof of his skill: by a few judicious strokes, he converted the crying into a laughing face. The duke, when he looked at the child again, was in astonishment: the painter, to show himself master of the human countenance, restored his first touches; and the duke, in a few moments, saw the child weeping again. A preceptor may acquire similar power over the countenance of his pupil if he has studied the oratorical art. By the art of oratory, we do not mean the art of misrepresentation, the art of deception; we mean the art of showing the truth in the strongest light; of exciting virtuous enthusiasm and generous indignation. Warm, glowing eloquence, is not inconsistent with accuracy of reasoning and judgment. When we have expressed our admiration or abhorrence of any action or character, we should afterwards be ready coolly to explain to our pupils the justice of our sentiments: by this due mixture and alternation of eloquence and reasoning, we may cultivate a taste for the moral and sublime, and yet preserve the character from any tincture of extravagant enthusiasm. We cannot expect, that the torrent of passion should never sweep away the land-marks of exact morality; but after its overflowing impetuosity abates, we should take a calm survey of its effects, and we should be able to ascertain the boundaries of right and wrong with geometrical precision.

There is a style of bombast morality affected by some authors, which must be hurtful to young readers. Generosity and honour, courage and sentiment, are the striking qualities which seize and enchant the imagination in romance: these qualities must be joined with justice, prudence, economy, patience, and many humble virtues, to make a character really estimable; but these would spoil the effect, perhaps, of dramatic exhibitions.

Children may with much greater safety see hideous, than gigantic representations of the passions. Richard the Third excites abhorrence; but young Charles de Moor, in "The Robbers," commands our sympathy; even the enormity of his guilt, exempts him from all ordinary modes of trial; we forget the murderer, and see something like a hero. It is curious to observe, that the legislature in Germany, and in England, have found it necessary to interfere as to the representation of Captain Mac Heath and the Robbers; two characters in which the tragic and the comic muse have had powerful effects in exciting imitation. George Barnwell is a hideous representation of the passions, and therefore beneficial.

There are many sublime objects which do not depend upon terror, or at least upon false associations of terror, for their effect; and there are many sublime thoughts, which have no connection with violent passions or false ideas of morality. These are what we should select, if possible, to raise, without inflating, the imagination. The view of the ocean, of the setting or the rising sun, the great and bold scenes of nature, affects the mind with sublime pleasure. All the objects which suggest ideas of vast space, or power, of the infinite duration of time, of the decay of the monuments of ancient grandeur, or of the master-pieces of human art and industry, have power to raise sublime sensations: but we should consider, that they raise this pleasure only by suggesting certain ideas; those who have not the previous ideas, will not feel the pleasure. We should not, therefore, expect that children should admire objects which do not excite any ideas in their minds; we should wait till they have acquired the necessary knowledge, and we should not injudiciously familiarize them with these objects.

Simplicity is a source of the sublime, peculiarly suited to children; accuracy of observation and distinctness of perception, are essential to this species of the sublime. In Percy's collection of ancient ballads, and in the modern poems of the Ayreshire ploughman, we may see many instances of the effect of simplicity. To preserve our pupil's taste from a false love of ornament, he must avoid, either in books or in conversation, all verbose and turgid descriptions, the use of words and epithets which only fill up the measure of a line.

When a child sees any new object, or feels any new sensation, we should assist him with appropriate words to express his thoughts and feelings: when the impression is fresh in his mind, the association, with the precise descriptive epithets, can be made with most certainty. As soon as a child has acquired a sufficient stock of words and ideas, he should be from time to time exercised in description; we should encourage him to give an exact account of his own feelings in his own words. Those parents who have been used to elegant, will not, perhaps, be satisfied with the plain, descriptions of unpractised pupils; but they should not be fastidious; they should rather be content with an epithet too little, than with an epithet too much; and they should compare the child's description with the objects actually described, and not with the poems of Thomson or Gray, or Milton or Shakespeare. If we excite our pupils to copy from the writings of others, they never can have any originality of thought. To show parents what sort of simple descriptions they may reasonably expect from children, we venture to produce the following extempore description of a summer's evening, given by three children of different ages.

July 12th, 1796. Mr. — — was walking out with his family, and he asked his children to describe the evening just as it appeared to them. "There were three bards in Ossian's poems," said he, "who were sent out to see what sort of a night it was; they all gave different descriptions upon their return; you have never any of you read Ossian, but you can give us some description of this evening; try."

B— — (a girl of 14.) "The clouds in the west are bright with the light of the sun which has just set; a thick mist is seen in the east, and the smoke which had been *heaped up* in the day-time, is now spread, and mixes with the mist all round us; the noises are heard more plainly (though there are but few) than in the day-time; and those which are at a distance, sound almost as near as those which are close to us; there is a red mist round the moon."

C— — (a girl of eleven years old.) "The western clouds are pink with the light of the sun which has just set. The moon shines red through the mist. The smoke and mist make it look dark at a distance; but the few objects near us appear plainer. If it was not for the light of the moon, they would not be seen; but the moon is exceedingly bright; it shines upon the house and the windows. Every thing sounds busy at a distance; but what is near us is still."

S— — (a boy between nine and ten years old). "The sun has set behind the hill, and the western clouds are tinged with light. The mist mixes with the smoke, which rises from the heaps of weeds which some poor man is burning to earn bread for his family. The moon through the mist peeps her head, and sometimes she *goes back*, retires into her bower of clouds. The few noises that are heard, are heard very plain—very plainly."

We should observe, that the children who attempted these little descriptions, had not been habituated to the *poetic trade*; these were the only descriptions of an evening which they ever made. It would be hurtful to exercise children frequently in descriptive composition; it would give them the habit of exact observation, it is true, but something more is necessary to the higher species of poetry. Words must be selected which do not represent only, but which suggest, ideas. Minute veracity is essential to some sorts of description; but in a higher style of poetry, only the large features characteristic of the scene must be produced, and all that is subordinate must be suppressed. Sir Joshua Reynolds justly observes, that painters, who aim merely at deception of the eye by exact imitation, are not likely, even in their most successful imitations, to rouse the imagination. The man who mistook the painted fly for a real fly, only brushed, or attempted to brush it, away. The exact representation of such a common object, could not raise any sublime ideas in his mind; and when he perceived the deception, the wonder which he felt at the painter's art, was a sensation no wise connected with poetic enthusiasm.

As soon as young people have collected a variety of ideas, we can proceed a step in the education of their fancy. We should sometimes in conversation, sometimes in writing or in drawing, show them how a few strokes, or a few words, can suggest or combine various ideas. A single expression from Cæsar, charmed a mutinous army to instant submission. Unless the words "*Roman Citizens!*" had suggested more than meets the ear, how could they have produced this wonderful effect? The works of Voltaire and Sterne abound with examples of the skilful use of the language of suggestion: on this the wit of Voltaire, and the humour and pathos of Sterne, securely depend for their success. Thus, corporal Trim's eloquence on the death of his young master, owed its effect upon the whole kitchen, including "the fat scullion, who was scouring a fish-kettle upon her knees," to the well-timed use of the mixed language of action and suggestion.

"'Are we not here now?' continued the corporal (striking the end of his stick perpendicularly upon the floor, so as to give an idea of health and stability) 'and are we not' (dropping his hat upon the ground) 'gone in a moment?'"

"Are we not here now, and gone in a moment?" continues Sterne, who, in this instance, reveals the secret of his own art. "There was nothing in the sentence; it was one of your self-evident truths we have the advantage of hearing every day; and if Trim had not trusted more to his hat than his head, he had made nothing at all of it."

When we point out to our pupils such examples in Sterne, we hope it will not be understood, that we point them out to induce servile imitation. We apprehend, that the imitators of Sterne have failed from not having discovered that the interjections and — — dashes of this author, are not in themselves beauties, but that they affect us by suggesting ideas. To prevent any young writers from the intemperate or absurd use of interjections, we should show them Mr. Horne Tooke's acute remarks upon this mode of embellishment. We do not, however, entirely agree with this author in his abhorrence of interjections. We do not believe that "where speech can be employed they are totally useless; and are always insufficient for the purpose of communicating our thoughts." [68] Even if we class them, as Mr. Tooke himself does, [69] amongst "involuntary convulsions with oral sound," such as groaning, shrieking, &c. yet they may suggest ideas, as well as express animal feelings. Sighing, according to Mr. Tooke, is in the class of interjections, yet the poet acknowledges the superior eloquence of sighs:

"Persuasive words, and *more persuasive* sighs."

"'I wish,' said Uncle Toby, with a deep sigh (after hearing the story of Le Fevre) 'I wish, Trim, I was asleep.'" The sigh here adds great force to the wish, and it does not mark that Uncle Toby, from vehemence of passion, had returned to the brutal state of a savage who has not learnt the use of speech; but, on the contrary, it suggests to the reader, that Uncle Toby was a man of civilized humanity; not one whose compassion was to be excited merely as an animal feeling by the actual *sight* of a fellow-creature in pain, but rather by the description of the sufferer's situation.

In painting, as well as in writing, the language of suggestion affects the mind, and if any of our pupils should wish to excel in this art, they must early attend to this principle. The picture of Agamemnon hiding his face at the sacrifice of his daughter, expresses little to the eye, but much to the imagination. The usual signs of grief and joy make but slight impression; to laugh and to weep are such common expressions of delight or anguish, that they cannot be mistaken, even by the illiterate; but the imagination must be cultivated to enlarge the sphere of sympathy, and to render a more refined language intelligible. It is said that a Milanese artist painted two peasants, and two country-girls, who laughed so heartily, that *no one* could look at them without laughing. [70] This is an instance of sympathy unconnected with imagination. The following is an instance of sympathy excited by imagination. When Porcia was to part from Brutus, just before the breaking out of the civil war, "she endeavoured," says Plutarch, "as well as possible, to conceal the sorrow that oppressed her; but, notwithstanding her magnanimity, a picture betrayed her distress. The subject was the parting of Hector and Andromache. He was represented delivering his son Astyanax into her arms, and the eyes of Andromache were fixed upon him. The resemblance that this picture bore to her own distress, made *Porcia* burst into tears the moment she beheld it." If Porcia had never read Homer, Andromache would not have had this power over her imagination and her sympathy.

The imagination not only heightens the power of sympathy with the emotions of all the passions which a painter would excite, but it is likewise essential to our taste for another class of pleasures. Artists, who like Hogarth would please by humour, wit, and ridicule, must depend upon the imagination of the spectators to supply all the intermediate ideas which they would suggest. The cobweb over the poor box, one of the happiest strokes of satire that Hogarth ever invented, would probably say nothing to the inattentive eye, or the dull imagination. A young person must acquire the language, before he can understand the ideas, of superior minds.

The taste for poetry must be prepared by the culture of the imagination. The united powers of music and poetry could not have triumphed over Alexander, unless his imagination had assisted "the mighty master."

> "With downcast looks the joyless victor sat,
> Revolving in his altered soul
> The various turns of chance below;
> And now and then a sigh he stole,
> And tears began to flow."

The sigh and the tears were the consequences of Alexander's own thoughts, which were only recalled by kindred sounds. We are well aware, that savage nations, or those that are imperfectly civilized, are subject to enthusiasm; but we are inclined to think, that the barbarous clamour with which they proclaim their delight in music and poetry, may deceive us as to the degree in which it is felt: the sensations of cultivated minds may be more exquisite, though they are felt in silence. It has been supposed, that ignorance is extremely susceptible of the pleasures of wonder: but wonder and admiration are different feelings: the admiration which a cultivated mind feels for excellence, of which it can fully judge, is surely a higher species of pleasure, than the brute wonder expressed by "a foolish face of praise." Madame Roland tells us, that once, at a sermon preached by a celebrated Frenchman, she was struck with the earnest attention painted in the countenance of a young woman who was looking up at the preacher. At length the fair enthusiast exclaimed, "My God, how he perspires!" A different sort of admiration was felt by Cæsar, when the scroll dropped from his hand whilst he listened to an oration of Cicero's.

There are an infinite variety of associations, by which the orator has power to rouse the imagination of a person of cultivated understanding; there are comparatively few, by which he can amuse the fancy of illiterate auditors. It is not that they have less imagination than others; they have equally the power of raising vivid images; but there are few images which can be recalled to them: the combinations of their ideas are confined to a small number, and words have no poetic or literary associations in their minds: even amongst children, this difference between the power we have over the cultivated and uncultivated mind, early appears. A laurel leaf is to the eye of an illiterate boy nothing more than a shrub with a shining, pale-green, pointed leaf: recall the idea of that shrub by the most exact description, it will affect him with no peculiar pleasure: but associate early in a boy's mind the ideas of glory, of poetry, of olympic crowns, of Daphne and Apollo; by some of these latent associations the orator may afterwards raise his enthusiasm. We shall not here repeat what has been said [71] upon the choice of literature for young people, but shall once more warn parents to let their pupils read only the best authors, if they wish them to have a fine imagination, or a delicate taste. When their minds are awake and warm, show them excellence; let them hear oratory only when they can feel it; if the impression be vivid, no matter how transient the touch. Ideas which have once struck the imagination, can be recalled by the magic of a word, with all their original, all their associated force. Do not fatigue the eye and ear of your vivacious pupil with the monotonous sounds and confused images of vulgar poetry. Do not make him repeat the finest passages of Shakespeare and Milton; the effect is lost by repetition; the words, the ideas are profaned. Let your pupils hear eloquence from eloquent lips, and they will own its power. But let a drawling, unimpassioned reader, read a play of Shakespeare's, or an oration of Demosthenes, and if your pupil is not out of patience, he will never taste the charms of eloquence. If he feels a fine sentiment, or a sublime idea, pause, leave his mind full, leave his imagination elevated. Five minutes afterwards, perhaps, your pupil's attention is turned to something else, and the sublime idea seems to be forgotten: but do not fear; the idea is not obliterated; it is latent in his memory; it will appear at a proper time, perhaps a month, perhaps twenty years afterwards. Ideas may remain long useless, and almost forgotten in the mind, and may be called forth by some corresponding association from their torpid state.

Young people, who wish to make themselves orators or eloquent writers, should acquire the habit of attending first to the general impression made upon their own minds by oratory, and afterwards to the cause which produced the effect; hence they will obtain command over the minds of others, by using the knowledge they have acquired of their own. The habit of considering every new idea, or new fact, as a subject for allusion, may also be useful to the young orator. A change from time to time in the nature of his studies, will enlarge and invigorate his imagination. Gibbon says, that, after the publication of his first volume of the Roman history, he gave himself a short holyday. "I indulged my curiosity in some studies of a very different nature: a course of anatomy, which was demonstrated by Dr. Hunter, and some lessons of chemistry, which were delivered by Dr. Higgins. The principles of these sciences, and a taste for books of natural history, contributed to multiply my ideas and images; and the anatomist and chemist may sometimes track me in their own snow."

Different degrees of enthusiasm are requisite in different professions; but we are inclined to think, that the imagination might with advantage be cultivated to a much higher degree than is commonly allowed in young men intended for public advocates. We have seen several examples of the advantage of a general taste for the belles lettres in eminent lawyers; [72] and we have lately seen an ingenious treatise called Deinology, or instructions for a Young Barrister, which confirms our opinion upon this subject. An orator, by the judicious preparation of the minds of his audience, may increase the effect of his best arguments. A Grecian painter, [73] before he would produce a picture which he had finished, representing a martial enterprise, ordered martial music to be played, to raise the enthusiasm of the assembled spectators; when their imagination was sufficiently elevated, he uncovered the picture, and it was beheld with sympathetic transports of applause.

It is usually thought, that persons of extraordinary imagination are deficient in judgment: by proper education, this evil might be prevented. We may observe that persons, who have acquired particular facility in certain exercises of the imagination, can, by voluntary exertion, either excite or suppress certain trains of ideas on which their enthusiasm depends. An actor, who storms and raves whilst he is upon the stage, appears with a mild and peaceable demeanor a moment afterwards behind the scenes. A poet, in his inspired moments, repeats his own verses in his garret with all the emphasis and fervour of enthusiasm; but when he comes down to dine with a mixed convivial company, his poetic fury subsides, a new train of ideas takes place in his imagination. As long as he has sufficient command over himself to lay aside his enthusiasm in company, he is considered as a reasonable, sensible man, and the more imagination he displays in his poems, the better. The same exercise of fancy, which we admire in one case, we ridicule in another. The enthusiasm which characterizes the man of genius, borders upon insanity.

When Voltaire was teaching mademoiselle Clairon, the celebrated actress, to perform an impassioned part in one of his tragedies, she objected to the violence of his enthusiasm. "Mais, monsieur, on me prendroit pour une possedée!" [74] "Eh, mademoiselle," replied the philosophic bard, "il faut être un possedé pour réussir en aucun art."

The degree of enthusiasm, which makes the painter and poet set, what to more idle, or more busy mortals, appears an imaginary value upon their respective arts, supports the artist under the pressure of disappointment and neglect, stimulates his exertions, and renders him almost insensible to labour and fatigue. Military heroes, or those who are *"insane with ambition,"* [75] endure all the real miseries of life, and brave the terrors of death, under the invigorating influence of an extravagant imagination. Cure them of their enthusiasm, and they are no longer heroes. We must, therefore, decide in education, what species of characters we would produce, before we can determine what degree, or what habits of imagination, are desirable.

"Je suis le Dieu de la danse!" [76] exclaimed Vestris; and probably Alexander the Great did not feel more pride in his Apotheosis. Had any cynical philosopher undertaken to cure Vestris of his vanity, it would not have been a charitable action. Vestris might, perhaps, by force of reasoning, have been brought to acknowledge that a dancing-master was not a divinity, but this conviction would not have increased his felicity; on the contrary, he would have become wretched in proportion as he became rational. The felicity of enthusiasts depends upon their being absolutely incapable of reasoning, or of listening to reason upon certain subjects; provided they are resolute in repeating their own train of thoughts without comparing them with that of others, they may defy the malice of wisdom, and in happy ignorance may enjoy perpetual delirium.

Parents, who value the happiness of their children, will consider exactly what chance there is of their enjoying unmolested any partial enthusiasm; they will consider, that by early excitations, it is very easy to raise any species of ambition in the minds of their pupils. The various species of enthusiasm necessary to make a poet, a painter, an orator, or a military hero, may be inspired, without doubt, by education. How far these are connected with happiness, is another question. Whatever be the object which he pursues, we must, as much as possible, ensure our pupil's success. Those who have been excited to exertion by enthusiasm, if they do not obtain the reward or admiration which they had been taught to expect, sink into helpless despondency. Whether their object has been great or small, if it has been their favourite object, and they fail of its attainment, their mortification and subsequent languor are unavoidable. The wisest of monarchs exclaimed, that all was vanity and vexation of spirit; he did not, perhaps, feel more weary of the world than the poor juggler felt, who, after educating his hands to the astonishing dexterity of throwing up into the air, and catching as they fell, six eggs successively, without breaking them, received from the emperor, before whom he performed, six eggs to reward the labour of his life!

This poor man's ambition appears obviously absurd; and we are under no immediate apprehension, that parents should inspire their children with the enthusiasm necessary to the profession of a juggler: but, unless some precautions are taken, the objects which excite the ambition of numbers, may be placed so as to deceive the eye and imagination of children; and they may labour through life in pursuit of phantoms. If children early hear their parents express violent admiration for riches, rank, power, or fame, they catch a species of enthusiasm for these things, before they can estimate justly their value; from the countenance and manner, they draw very important conclusions. "Felicity is painted on your countenance," is a polite phrase of salutation in China. The taste for looking happy, is not confined to the Chinese: the rich and great, [77] by every artifice of luxury, endeavour to impress the spectator with the idea of their superior felicity. From experience we know, that the external signs of delight are not always sincere, and that the apparatus of luxury is not necessary to happiness. Children who live with persons of good sense, learn to separate the ideas of happiness and a coach and six; but young people who see their fathers, mothers, and preceptors, all smitten with sudden admiration at the sight of a fine phaeton, or a fine gentleman, are immediately infected with the same absurd enthusiasm. These parents do not suspect, that they are perverting the imagination of their children, when they call them with foolish eagerness to the windows to look at a fine equipage, a splendid cavalcade, or a military procession; they perhaps summon a boy, who is intended for a merchant, or a lawyer, to hear "the spirit stirring drum;" and they are afterwards surprised, if he says, when he is fifteen or sixteen, that, "*if his father pleases*, he had rather go into the army, than go to the bar." The mother is alarmed, perhaps, about the same time, by an unaccountable predilection in her daughter's fancy for a red coat, and totally forgets having called the child to the window to look at the smart cockades, and to hear the tune of "See the conquering hero comes."

"Hear you me, Jessica," says Shylock to his daughter, "lock up my doors; and when you hear the drum, and the vile squeaking of the wry-necked fife, clamber not you up into the casements then."

Shylock's exhortations were vain; Jessica had arrived at years of discretion, and it was too late to forbid her clambering into the casements; the precautions should have been taken sooner; the epithets vile squeaking and wry-necked fife, could not alter the lady's taste: and Shylock should have known how peremptory prohibitions and exaggerated expressions of aversion operate upon the female imagination; he was imprudent in the extreme of his caution. We should let children see things as they really are, and we should not prejudice them either by our exclamations of rapture, or by our affected disgust. If they are familiarized with show, they will not be caught by it; if they see the whole of whatever is to be seen, their imagination will not paint things more delightful than they really are. For these reasons, we think that young people should not be restrained, though they may be guided in their tastes; we should supply them with all the information in which they are deficient, and leave them to form their own judgments.

Without making it a matter of favour, or of extraordinary consequence, parents can take their children to see public exhibitions, or to partake of any amusements which are really agreeable; they can, at the same time, avoid mixing factitious with real pleasure. If, for instance, we have an opportunity of taking a boy to a good play, or a girl to a ball, let them enjoy the full pleasure of the amusement, but do not let us excite their imagination by great preparations, or by anticipating remarks: "Oh, you'll be very happy to-morrow, for you're to go to the play. You must look well to-night, for you are going to the ball. Were you never at a ball? Did you never see a play before? Oh, *then* you'll be delighted, I'm sure!" The children often look much more sensible, and sometimes more composed, in the midst of these foolish exclamations, than their parents. "Est ce que je m'amuse, maman?" said a little girl of six years old, the first time she was taken to the playhouse.

Besides the influence of opinion, there are a number of other circumstances to be considered in cultivating the imagination; there are many other circumstances which must be attended to, and different precautions are necessary, to regulate properly the imagination of children of different dispositions, or temperaments. The disposition to associate ideas, varies in strength and quickness in opposite temperaments: the natural vivacity or dulness of the senses, the habit of observing external objects, the power of voluntary exertion, and the propensity to reverie, must all be considered before we can adapt a plan of education exactly to the pupil's advantage. A wise preceptor will counteract, as much as possible, all those defects to which a child may appear most liable, and will cultivate his imagination so as to prevent the errours to which he is most exposed by natural, or what we call natural, disposition.

Some children appear to feel sensations of pleasure or pain with more energy than others; they take more delight in feeling than in reflection; they have neither much leisure nor much inclination for the intellectual exertions of comparison or deliberation. Great care should be taken to encourage children of this temper to describe and to compare their sensations. By their descriptions we shall judge what motives we ought to employ to govern them, and if we can teach them to compare their feelings, we shall induce that voluntary exertion of mind in which they are naturally defective. We cannot compare or judge of our sensations without voluntary exertion. When we deliberate, we repeat our ideas deliberately; and this is an exercise peculiarly useful to those who feel quickly.

When any pleasure makes too great an impression upon these children of vivid sensations, we should repeat the pleasure frequently, till it begins to fatigue; or we should contrast it, and bring it into direct comparison with some other species of pleasure. For instance, suppose a boy had appeared highly delighted with seeing a game at cards, and that we were apprehensive he might, from this early association, acquire a taste for gaming, we might either repeat the amusement till the playing at cards began to weary the boy, or we might take him immediately after playing at cards to an interesting comedy; probably, the amusement he would receive at the playhouse, would be greater than that which he had enjoyed at the card-table; and as these two species of pleasure would immediately succeed to each other, the child could scarcely avoid comparing them. Is it necessary to repeat, that all this should be done without any artifice? The child should know the meaning of our conduct, and then he will never set himself in opposition to our management.

If it is not convenient, or possible, to dull the charm of novelty by repetition, or to contrast a new pleasure with some other superior amusement, there is another expedient which may be useful; we may call the power of association to our assistance: this power is sometimes a full match for the most lively sensations. For instance, suppose a boy of strong feelings had been offended by some trifle, and expressed sensations of hatred against the offender obviously too violent for the occasion; to bring the angry boy's imagination to a temperate state, we might recall some circumstance of his former affection for the offender; or the general idea, that it is amiable and noble to command our passion, and to forgive those who have injured us. At the sight of his mother, with whom he had many agreeable associations, the imagination of Coriolanus raised up instantly a train of ideas connected with the love of his family, and of his country, and immediately the violence of his sensations of anger were subdued.

Brutus, after his friend Cassius has apologized to him for his "rash humour," by saying, "that it was hereditary from his mother," promises that the next time Cassius is over-earnest with "his Brutus, he will think his mother chides, and leave him so;" that is to say, Brutus promises to recollect an association of ideas, which shall enable him to bear with his friend's ill humour.

Children, who associate ideas very strongly and with rapidity, [78] must be educated with continual attention. With children of this class, the slightest circumstances are of consequence; they may at first appear to be easily managed, because they will remember pertinaciously any reproof, any reward or punishment; and, from association, they will scrupulously avoid or follow what has, in any one instance, been joined with pain or pleasure in their imagination: but unfortunately, accidental events will influence them, as well as the rewards and punishments of their preceptors; and a variety of associations will be formed, which may secretly govern them long before their existence is suspected. We shall be surprised to find, that even where there is apparently no hope, or fear, or passion, to disturb their judgment, they cannot reason, or understand reasoning. On studying them more closely, we shall discover the cause of this seeming imbecility. A multitude of associated ideas occur to them upon whatever subject we attempt to reason, which distract their attention, and make them change the terms of every proposition with incessant variety. Their pleasures are chiefly secondary reflected pleasures, and they do not judge by their actual sensations so much as by their associations. They like and dislike without being able to assign any sufficient cause for their preference or aversion. They make a choice frequently without appearing to deliberate; and if you, by persuading them to a more detailed examination of the objects, convince them, that according to the common standard of good and evil, they have made a foolish choice, they will still seem puzzled and uncertain; and, if you leave them at liberty, will persist in their original determination. By this criterion we may decide, that they are influenced by some secret false association of ideas; and, instead of arguing with them upon the obvious folly of their present choice, we should endeavour to make them trace back their ideas, and discover the association by which they are governed. In some cases this may be out of their power, because the original association may have been totally forgotten, and yet those connected with it may continue to act: but even when we cannot succeed in any particular instance in detecting the cause of the errour, we shall do the pupils material service by exciting them to observe their own minds. A tutor, who carefully remarks the circumstances in which a child expresses uncommon grief or joy, hope or fear, may obtain complete knowledge of his associations, and may accurately distinguish the proximate and remote causes of all his pupil's desires and aversions. He will then have absolute command over the child's mind, and he should upon no account trust his pupil to the direction of any other person. Another tutor, though perhaps of equal ability, could not be equally secure of success; the child would probably be suspected of cunning, caprice, or obstinacy, because the causes of his tastes and judgments could not be discovered by his new preceptor.

It often happens, that those who feel pleasure and pain most strongly, are likewise most disposed to form strong associations of ideas. [79] Children of this character are never stupid, but often prejudiced and passionate: they can readily assign a reason for their preference or aversion; they recollect distinctly the original sensations of pleasure or pain, on which their associations depend; they do not, like Mr. Transfer in Zelucco, like or dislike persons and things, because they have *been used to them*, but because they have received some injury or benefit from them. Such children are apt to make great mistakes in reasoning, from their registering of coincidences hastily; they do not wait to repeat their experiments, but if they have in one instance observed two things to happen at the same time, they expect that they will always recur together. If one event precedes or follows another accidentally, they believe it to be the cause or effect of its concomitant, and this belief is not to be shaken in their minds by ridicule or argument. They are, consequently, inclined both to superstition and enthusiasm, according as their hopes and fears predominate. They are likewise subject to absurd antipathies—antipathies which verge towards insanity.

Dr. Darwin relates a strong instance of antipathy in a child from association. The child, on tasting the gristle of sturgeon, asked what gristle was? and was answered, that gristle was like the division of a man's nose. The child, disgusted at this idea, for twenty years afterwards could never be persuaded to taste sturgeon. [80]

Zimmermann assures us, that he was an eye-witness of a singular antipathy, which we may be permitted to describe in his own words:

"Happening to be in company with some English gentlemen, all of them men of distinction, the conversation fell upon antipathies. Many of the company denied their reality, and considered them as idle stories, but I assured them that they were truly a disease. Mr. William Matthews, son to the governor of Barbadoes, was of my opinion, because he himself had an antipathy to spiders. The rest of the company laughed at him. I undertook to prove to them that this antipathy *was really an impression on his soul, resulting from the determination of a mechanical effect*. (We do not pretend to know what Dr. Zimmermann means by this.) Lord John Murray undertook to shape some black wax into the appearance of a spider, with a view to observe whether the antipathy would take place at the simple figure of the insect. He then withdrew for a moment, and came in again with the wax in his hand, which he kept shut. Mr. Matthews, who in other respects was a very amiable and moderate man, immediately conceiving that his friend really had a spider in his hand, clapped his hand to his sword with extreme fury, and running back towards the partition, cried out most horribly. All the muscles of his face were swelled, his eyes were rolling in their sockets, and his body was immoveable. We were all exceedingly alarmed, and immediately ran to his assistance, took his sword from him, and assured him that what he conceived to be a spider, was nothing more than a bit of wax, which he might see upon the table.

"He remained some time in this spasmodic state; but at length he began to recover, and to deplore the horrible passion from which he still suffered. His pulse was very strong and quick, and his whole body was covered with a cold perspiration. After taking an anodyne draft, he resumed his usual tranquillity.

"We are not to wonder at this antipathy," continues Zimmermann; "the spiders at Barbadoes are very large, and of an hideous figure. Mr. Matthews was born there, and his antipathy was therefore to be accounted for. Some of the company undertook to make a little waxen spider in his presence. He saw this done with great tranquillity, but he could not be persuaded to touch it, though he was by no means a timorous man in other respects. Nor would he follow my advice to endeavour to conquer this antipathy by first drawing parts of spiders of different sorts, and after a time whole spiders, till at length he might be able to look at portions of real spiders, and thus gradually accustom himself to whole ones, at first dead, and then living ones." [81]

Dr. Zimmermann's method of cure, appears rather more ingenious, than his way of accounting for the disease. Are all the natives of Barbadoes subject to convulsions at the sight of the large spiders in that island? or why does Mr. William Matthews' having been born there account so satisfactorily for his antipathy?

The cure of these unreasonable fears of harmless animals, like all other antipathies, would, perhaps, be easily effected, if it were judiciously attempted early in life. The epithets which we use in speaking of animals, and our expressions of countenance, have great influence on the minds of children. If we, as Dr. Darwin advises, call the spider *the ingenious spider*, and the frog *the harmless frog*, and if we look at them with complacency, instead of aversion, children, from sympathy, will imitate our manner, and from curiosity will attend to the animals, to discover whether the commendatory epithets we bestow upon them, are just.

It is comparatively of little consequence to conquer antipathies which have trifling objects. An individual can go through life very well without eating sturgeon, or touching spiders; but when we consider the influence of the same disposition to associate false ideas too strongly in more important instances, we shall perceive the necessity of correcting it by education.

Locke tells us of a young man, who, having been accustomed to see an old trunk in the room with him when he learned to dance, associated his dancing exertions so strongly with the sight of this trunk, that he could not succeed by any voluntary efforts in its absence. We have, in our remarks upon attention, [82] pointed out the great inconveniences to which those are exposed who acquire associated habits of intellectual exertion; who cannot speak, or write, or think, without certain habitual aids to their memory or imagination. We must further observe, that incessant vigilance is necessary in the moral education of children disposed to form strong associations; they are liable to sudden and absurd dislikes or predilections, with respect to persons, as well as things; they are subject to caprice in their affections and temper, and liable to a variety of mental infirmities, which, in different degrees, we call passion or madness. Locke tells us, that he knew a man who, after having been restored to health by a painful operation, had so strongly associated the idea and figure of the operator with the agony he had endured, that though he acknowledged the obligation, and felt gratitude towards this friend who had saved him, he never afterwards could bear to see his benefactor. There are some people who associate so readily and incorrigibly the idea of any pain or insult they have received from another, with his person and character, that they can never afterwards forget or forgive. They are hence disposed to all the intemperance of hatred and revenge; to the chronic malice of a Jago, or the acute pangs of an Achilles. Homer, in his speech of Achilles to Agamemnon's mediating ambassadors, has drawn a strong and natural picture of the progress of anger. It is worth studying as a lesson in metaphysics. Whenever association suggests to the mind of Achilles the injury he has received, he loses his reason, and the orator works himself up from argument to declamation, and from declamation to desperate resolution, through a close linked connection of ideas and sensations.

The insanities of ambition, avarice, and vanity, originate in early mistaken associations. A feather, or a crown, or an alderman's chain, or a cardinal's hat, or a purse of yellow counters, are unluckily associated in the minds of some men with the idea of happiness, and, without staying to deliberate, these unfortunate persons hunt through life the phantasms of a disordered imagination. Whilst we pity, we are amused by the blindness and blunders of those whose mistakes can affect no one's felicity but their own; but any delusions which prompt their victims to actions inimical to their fellow-creatures, are the objects not unusually of pity, but of indignation, of private aversion and public punishment. We smile at the avaricious insanity of the miser, who dresses himself in the cast-off Wig of a beggar, and pulls a crushed pancake from his pocket for his own and for his friend's dinner. [83] We smile at the insane vanity of the pauper, who dressed himself in a many-coloured paper star, assumed the title of Duke of Baubleshire, and as such required homage from every passenger. [84] But are we inclined to smile at the outrageous vanity of the man who styled himself the son of Jupiter, and who murdered his best friend for refusing him divine honours? Are we disposed to pity the slave-merchant, who, urged by the maniacal desire for gold, hears unmoved the groans of his fellow-creatures, the execrations of mankind, and that "small still voice," which haunts those who are stained with blood.

The moral insanities which strike us with horror, compassion, or ridicule, however they may differ in their effects, have frequently one common origin; an early false association of ideas. Persons who mistake in measuring their own feelings, or who neglect to compare their ideas, and to balance contending wishes, scarcely merit the name of *rational* creatures. The man, who does not deliberate, is lost.

We have endeavoured, though well aware of the difficulty of the subject, to point out some of the precautions that should be used in governing the imagination of young people of different dispositions. We should add, that in all cases the pupils attention to his own mind will be of more consequence, than the utmost vigilance of the most able preceptor; the sooner he is made acquainted with his own character, and the sooner he can be excited to govern himself by reason, or to attempt the cure of his own defects, the better.

There is one habit of the imagination, to which we have not yet adverted, the habit of reverie. In reverie we are so intent upon a particular train of ideas, that we are unconscious of all external objects, and we exert but little voluntary power. It is true that some persons in castle-building both reason and invent, and therefore must exert some degree of volition; even in the wildest reverie, there may be traced some species of consistency, some connection amongst the ideas; but this is simply the result of the association of ideas. Inventive castle-builders are rather nearer the state of insanity than of reverie; they reason well upon false principles; their airy fabrics are often both in good taste and in good proportion; nothing is wanting to them but a foundation. On the contrary, nothing can be more silly than the reveries of silly people; they are not only defective in consistency, but they want all the unities; they are not extravagant, but they are stupid; they consist usually of a listless reiteration of uninteresting ideas; the whole pleasure enjoyed by those addicted to them consists in the facility of repetition.

It is a mistaken notion, that only people of ardent imaginations are disposed to reverie; the most indolent and stupid persons waste their existence in this indulgence; they do not act always in consequence of their dreams, therefore we do not detect their folly. Young people of active minds, when they have not sufficient occupation, necessarily indulge in reverie; and, by degrees, this wild exercise of their invention and imagination becomes so delightful to them, that they prefer it to all sober employments.

Mr. Williams, in his Lectures upon Education, gives an account of a boy singularly addicted to reverie. The desire of invisibility had seized his mind, and for several years he had indulged his fancy with imagining all the pleasures that he should command, and all the feats that he could perform, if he were in possession of Gyges's ring. The reader should, however, be informed, that this castle-builder was not a youth of strict veracity; his confession upon this occasion, as upon others, might not have been sincere. We only state the story from Mr. Williams.

To prevent children from acquiring a taste for reverie, let them have various occupations both of mind and body. Let us not direct their imagination to extraordinary future pleasures, but let us suffer them to enjoy the present. Anticipation is a species of reverie; and children, who have promises of future pleasures frequently made to them, live in a continual state of anticipation.

To cure the habit of reverie when it has once been formed, we must take different methods with different tempers. With those who indulge in the *stupid reverie*, we should employ strong excitations, and present to the senses a rapid succession of objects, which will completely engage without fatiguing them. This mode must not be followed with children of different dispositions, else we should increase, instead of curing, the disease. The most likely method to break this habit in children of great quickness or sensibility, is to set them to some employment which is wholly new to them, and which will consequently exercise and exhaust all their faculties, so that they shall have no life left for castle-building. Monotonous occupations, such as copying, drawing, or writing, playing on the harpsichord, &c. are not, *if habit has made them easy* to the pupil, fit for our purpose. We may all perceive, that in such occupations, the powers of the mind are left unexercised. We can frequently read aloud with tolerable emphasis for a considerable time together, and at the same time think upon some subject foreign to the book we hold in our hands.

The most difficult exercises of the mind, such as invention, or strict reasoning, are those alone which are sufficient to subjugate and chain down the imagination of some active spirits. To such laborious exercises they should be excited by the encouraging voice of praise and affection. Imaginative children will be more disposed to invent than to reason, but they cannot perfect any invention without reasoning; there will, therefore, be a mixture of what they like and dislike in the exercise of invention, and the habit of reasoning will, perhaps, gradually become agreeable to them, if it be thus dexterously united with the pleasures of the imagination.

So much has already been written by various authors upon the pleasures and the dangers of imagination, that we could scarcely hope to add any thing new to what they have produced: but we have endeavoured to arrange the observations which appeared most applicable to practical education; we have pointed out how the principles of taste may be early taught without injury to the general understanding, and how the imagination should be prepared for the higher pleasures of eloquence and poetry. We have attempted to define the boundaries between the enthusiasm of genius, and its extravagance; and to show some of the precautions which may be used, to prevent the moral defects to which persons of ardent imagination are usually subject. The degree in which the imagination should be cultivated must, we have observed, be determined by the views which parents may have for their children, by their situations in society, and by the professions for which they are destined. Under the government of a sober judgment, the powers of the imagination must be advantageous in every situation; but their value to society, and to the individuals by whom they are possessed, depends ultimately upon the manner in which they are managed. A magician, under the control of a philosopher, would perform not only great, but useful, wonders. The homely proverb, which has been applied to fire, may with equal truth be applied to imagination: "It is a good servant, but a bad master."

[58] Priestley has ably given the desiderata of electricity, vision, &c.

[59] Wharton's Ode to Fancy.

[60] Gerard.

[61] Lord Kames.

[62] Professor Stewart.

[63] V. An excellent essay of Mr. Barnes's on Imagination. Manchester Society, vol. i.

[64] It is to be hoped that the foreign philosophers, who, it is said, are now employed in drawing up a new metaphysical nomenclature, will avail themselves of the

extensive knowledge, and original genius of the author of Zoonomia.

[65] Akenside.

[66]

"Know there are words and spells which can control,
Between the fits, the fever of the soul.
"Pope.

[67] Peter of Cortona.

[68] V. Epea Pteroenta, p. 88.

[69] Chapter on Grammar.

[70] V. Camper's Works, p. 126.

[71] V. Chapter on Books.

[72] Lord Mansfield, Hussey Burgh, &c.

[73] Theon.

[74] "But, Sir, I shall be taken for one possessed!"

"Well, Ma'am, you must be *like one possessed*, if you would succeed in any art."

[75] Dr. Darwin.

[76] "I am the god of dancing!"

[77] V. Smith's Moral Theory.

[78] Temperament of increased association. Zoonomia.

[79] V. Zoonomia. Temperament of increased sensibility and association joined.

[80] Zoonomia, vol. ii.

[81] Monthly Review of Zimmermann on Experience in Physic. March 1783, p. 211.

[82] V. Chapter on Attention.

[83] Elwes. See his Life.

[84] There is an account of this poor man's death in the Star, 1796.

CHAPTER XXIII
ON WIT AND JUDGMENT

It has been shown, that the powers of memory, invention and imagination, ought to be rendered subservient to judgment: it has been shown, that reasoning and judgment abridge the labours of memory, and are necessary to regulate the highest flights of imagination. We shall consider the power of reasoning in another point of view, as being essential to our conduct in life. The object of reasoning is to adapt means to an end, to attain the command of effects by the discovery of the causes on which they depend.

Until children have acquired some knowledge of effects, they cannot inquire into causes. Observation must precede reasoning; and as judgment is nothing more than the perception of the result of comparison, we should never urge our pupils to judge, until they have acquired some portion of experience.

To teach children to compare objects exactly, we should place the things to be examined distinctly before them. Every thing that is superfluous, should be taken away, and a sufficient motive should be given to excite the pupil's attention. We need not here repeat the advice that has formerly been given [85] respecting the choice of proper motives to excite and fix attention; or the precautions necessary to prevent the pain of fatigue, and of unsuccessful application. If comparison be early rendered a task to children, they will dislike and avoid this exercise of the mind, and they will consequently show an inaptitude to reason: if comparing objects be made interesting and amusing to our pupils, they will soon become expert in discovering resemblances and differences; and thus they will be prepared for reasoning.

Rousseau has judiciously advised, that *the senses* of children should be cultivated with the utmost care. In proportion to the distinctness of their perceptions, will be the accuracy of their memory, and, probably, also the precision of their judgment. A child, who sees imperfectly, cannot reason justly about the objects of sight, because he has not sufficient data. A child, who does not hear distinctly, cannot judge well of sounds; and, if we could suppose the sense of touch to be twice as accurate in one child as in another, we might conclude, that the judgment of these children must differ in a similar proportion. The defects in organization are not within the power of the preceptor; but we may observe, that inattention, and want of exercise, are frequently the causes of what appear to be natural defects; and, on the contrary, increased attention and cultivation sometimes produce that quickness of eye and ear, and that consequent readiness of judgment, which we are apt to attribute to natural superiority of organization or capacity. Even amongst children, we may early observe a considerable difference between the quickness of their senses and of their reasoning upon subjects where they have had experience, and upon those on which they have not been exercised.

The first exercises for the judgment of children should, as Rousseau recommends, relate to visible and tangible substances. Let them compare the size and shape of different objects; let them frequently try what they can lift; what they can reach; at what distance they can see objects; at what distance they can hear sounds: by these exercises they will learn to judge of distances and weight; and they may learn to judge of the solid contents of bodies of different shapes, by comparing the observations of their sense of feeling and of sight. The measure of hollow bodies can be easily taken by pouring liquids into them, and then comparing the quantities of the liquids that fill vessels of different shapes. This is a very simple method of exercising the judgment of children; and, if they are allowed to try these little experiments for themselves, the amusement will fix the facts in their memory, and will associate pleasure with the habits of comparison. Rousseau rewards Emilius with cakes when he judges rightly; success, we think, is a better reward. Rousseau was himself childishly fond of cakes and cream.

The step which immediately follows comparison, is deduction. The cat is larger than the kitten; then a hole through which the cat can go, must be larger than a hole through which the kitten can go. Long before a child can put this reasoning into words, he is capable of forming the conclusion, and we need not be in haste to make him announce it in mode and figure. We may see by the various methods which young children employ to reach what is above them, to drag, to push, to lift different bodies, that they reason; that is to say, that they adapt means to an end, before they can explain their own designs in words. Look at a child building a house of cards; he dexterously balances every card as he floors the edifice; he raises story over story, and shows us that he has some design in view, though he would be utterly incapable of describing his intentions previously in words. We have formerly [86] endeavoured to show how the vocabulary of our pupils may be gradually enlarged, exactly in proportion to their real knowledge.

A great deal depends upon our attention to this proportion; if children have not a sufficient number of words to make their thoughts intelligible, we cannot assist them to reason by our conversation, we cannot communicate to them the result of our experience; they will have a great deal of useless labour in comparing objects, because they will not be able to understand the evidence of others, as they do not understand their language; and at last, the reasonings which they carry on in their own minds will be confused for want of signs to keep them distinct. On the contrary, if their vocabulary exceed their ideas, if they are taught a variety of words to which they connect no accurate meaning, it is impossible that they should express their thoughts with precision. As this is one of the most common errours in education, we shall dwell upon it more particularly.

We have pointed out the mischief which is done to the understanding of children by the nonsensical conversation of common acquaintance. [87] "Should you like to be a king? What are you to be? Are you to be a bishop, or a judge? Had you rather be a general, or an admiral, my little dear?" are some of the questions which every one has probably heard proposed to children of five or six years old. Children who have not learned by rote the expected answers to such interrogatories, stand in amazed silence upon these occasions; or else answer at random, having no possible means of forming any judgment upon such subjects. We have often thought, in listening to the conversations of grown up people with children, that the children reasoned infinitely better than their opponents. People, who are not interested in the education of children, do not care what arguments they use, what absurdities they utter in talking to them; they usually talk to them of things which are totally above their comprehension; and they instil errour and prejudice, without the smallest degree of compunction; indeed, without in the least knowing what they are about. We earnestly repeat our advice to parents, to keep their children as much as possible from such conversation: children will never reason, if they are allowed to hear or to talk nonsense.

When we say, that children should not be suffered to talk nonsense, we should observe, that unless they have been in the habit of hearing foolish conversation, they very seldom talk nonsense. They may express themselves in a manner which we do not understand, or they may make mistakes from not accurately comprehending the words of others; but in these cases, we should not reprove or silence them; we should patiently endeavour to find out their hidden meaning. If we rebuke or ridicule them, we shall intimidate them, and either lessen their confidence in themselves or in us. In the one case, we prevent them from thinking; in the other, we deter them from communicating their thoughts; and thus we preclude ourselves from the possibility of assisting them in reasoning. To show parents the nature of the mistakes which children make from their imperfect knowledge of words, we shall give a few examples from real life.

S— —, at five years old, when he heard some one speak of *bay* horses, said, he supposed that the bay horses must be the best horses. Upon cross-questioning him, it appeared that he was led to this conclusion by the analogy between the sound of the words *bay* and *obey*. A few days previous to this, his father had told him that spirited horses were always the most ready to obey.

These erroneous analogies between the sound of words and their sense, frequently mislead children in reasoning; we should, therefore, encourage children to explain themselves fully, that we may rectify their errours.

When S— — was between four and five years old, a lady who had taken him upon her lap playfully, put her hands before his eyes, and (we believe) asked if he liked to be blinded. S— — said no; and he looked very thoughtful. After a pause, he added, "Smellie says, that children like better to be blinded than to have their legs tied." (S— — had read this in Smellie two or three days before.)

Father. "Are you of Smellie's opinion?"

S— — hesitated.

Father. "Would you rather be blinded, or have your legs tied?"

S— —. "I would rather have my legs tied not quite tight."

Father. "Do you know what is meant by *blinded*?"

S— —. "Having their eyes put out."

Father. "How do you mean?"

S— —. "To put something into the eye to make the blood burst out; and then the blood would come all over it, and cover it, and stick to it, and hinder them from seeing—I don't know how."

It is obvious, that whilst this boy's imagination pictured to him a bloody orb when he heard the word *blinded*, he was perfectly right in his reasoning in preferring to have his legs tied; but he did not judge of the proposition meant to be laid before him; he judged of another which he had formed for himself. His father explained to him, that Smellie meant blindfolded, instead of blinded; a handkerchief was then tied round the boy's head, so as to hinder him from seeing, and he was made perfectly to understand the meaning of the word *blindfolded*.

In such trifles as these, it may appear of little consequence to rectify the verbal errours of children; but exactly the same species of mistake, will prevent them from reasoning accurately in matters of consequence. It will not cost us much more trouble to detect these mistakes when the causes of them are yet recent; but it will give us infinite trouble to retrace thoughts which have passed in infancy. When prejudices, or the habits of reasoning inaccurately, have been formed, we cannot easily discover or remedy the remote trifling origin of the evil.

When children begin to inquire about causes, they are not able to distinguish between coincidence and causation: we formerly observed the effect which this ignorance produces upon their temper; we must now observe its effect upon their understanding. A little reflection upon our own minds, will prevent us from feeling that stupid amazement, or from expressing that insulting contempt which the natural thoughts of children sometimes excite in persons who have frequently less understanding than their pupils. What account can we give of the connection between cause and effect? How is the idea, that one thing is the cause of another, first produced in our minds? All that we know is, that amongst human events, those which precede, are, in some cases, supposed to produce what follow. When we have observed, in several instances, that one event constantly precedes another, we believe, and expect, that these events will in future recur together. Before children have had experience, it is scarcely possible that they should distinguish between fortuitous circumstances and causation; accidental coincidences of time, and juxta-position, continually lead them into errour. We should not accuse children of reasoning ill; we should not imagine that they are defective in judgment, when they make mistakes from deficient experience; we should only endeavour to make them delay to decide until they have repeated their experiments; and, at all events, we should encourage them to lay open their minds to us, that we may assist them by our superior knowledge.

This spring, little W — — (three years old) was looking at a man who was mowing the grass before the door. It had been raining, and when the sun shone, the vapour began to rise from the grass. "Does the man mowing *make* the smoke rise from the grass?" said the little boy. He was not laughed at for this simple question. The man's mowing immediately preceded the rising of the vapour; the child had never observed a man mowing before, and it was absolutely impossible that he could tell what effects might be produced by it; he very naturally imagined, that the event which immediately preceded the rising of the vapour, was the cause of its rise; the sun was at a distance; the scythe was near the grass. The little boy showed by the tone of his inquiry, that he was in the philosophic state of doubt; had he been ridiculed for his question; had he been told that he talked nonsense, he would not, upon another occasion, have told us his thoughts, and he certainly could not have improved in reasoning.

The way to improve children in their judgment with respect to causation, is to increase their knowledge, and to lead them to try experiments by which they may discover what circumstances are essential to the production of any given effect; and what are merely accessory, unimportant concomitants of the event. [88]

A child who, for the first time, sees blue and red paints mixed together to produce purple, could not be certain that the pallet on which these colours were mixed, the spatula with which they were tempered, were not necessary circumstances. In many cases, the vessels in which things are mixed are essential; therefore, a sensible child would repeat the experiment exactly in the same manner in which he had seen it succeed. This exactness should not be suffered to become indolent imitation, or superstitious adherence to particular forms. Children should be excited to add or deduct particulars in trying experiments, and to observe the effects of these changes. In "Chemistry," and "Mechanics," we have pointed out a variety of occupations, in which the judgment of children may be exercised upon the immediate objects of their senses.

It is natural, perhaps, that we should expect our pupils to show surprise at those things which excite surprise in our minds; but we should consider that almost every thing is new to children; and, therefore, there is scarcely any gradation in their astonishment. A child of three or four years old, would be as much amused, and, probably, as much surprised, by seeing a paper kite fly, as he could by beholding the ascent of a balloon. We should not attribute this to stupidity, or want of judgment, but simply to ignorance.

A few days ago, W—— (three years old) who was learning his letters, was let sow an *o* in the garden with mustard seed. W—— was much pleased with the operation. When the green plants appeared above ground, it was expected that W—— would be much surprised at seeing the exact shape of his *o*. He was taken to look at it; but he showed no surprise, no sort of emotion.

We have advised that the judgment of children should be exercised upon the objects of their senses. It is scarcely possible that they should reason upon the subjects which are sometimes proposed to them: with respect to manners and society, they have had no experience, consequently they can form no judgments. By imprudently endeavouring to turn the attention of children to conversation that is unsuited to them, people may give the *appearance* of early intelligence, and a certain readiness of repartee and fluency of expression; but these are transient advantages. Smart, witty children, amuse the circle for a few hours, and are forgotten: and we may observe, that almost all children who are praised and admired for sprightliness and wit, reason absurdly, and continue ignorant. Wit and judgment depend upon different opposite habits of the mind. Wit searches for remote resemblances between objects or thoughts apparently dissimilar. Judgment compares the objects placed before it, in order to find out their differences, rather than their resemblances. The comparisons of judgment may be slow: those of wit must be rapid. The same power of attention in children, may produce either wit or judgment. Parents must decide in which faculty, or rather, in which of these habits of the mind, they wish their pupils to excel; and they must conduct their education accordingly. Those who are desirous to make their pupils witty, must sacrifice some portion of their judgment to the acquisition of the talent for wit; they must allow their children to talk frequently at random. Amongst a multitude of hazarded observations, a happy hit is now and then made: for these happy hits, children who are to be made wits should be praised; and they must acquire sufficient courage to speak from a cursory view of things; therefore the mistakes they make from superficial examination must not be pointed out to them; their attention must be turned to the comic, rather than to the serious side of objects; they must study the different meanings and powers of words; they should hear witty conversation, read epigrams, and comedies; and in all company they should be exercised before numbers in smart dialogue and repartee.

When we mention the methods of educating a child to be witty, we at the same time point out the dangers of this education; and it is but just to warn parents against expecting inconsistent qualities from their pupils. Those who steadily prefer the solid advantages of judgment, to the transient brilliancy of wit, should not be mortified when they see their children, perhaps, deficient at nine or ten years old in the showy talents for general conversation; they must bear to see their pupils appear slow; they must bear the contrast of flippant gayety and sober simplicity; they must pursue exactly an opposite course to that which has been recommended for the education of wits; they must never praise their pupils for hazarding observations; they must cautiously point out any mistakes that are made from a precipitate survey of objects; they should not harden their pupils against that feeling of shame, which arises in the mind from the perception of having uttered an absurdity; they should never encourage their pupils to play upon words; and their admiration of wit should never be vehemently or enthusiastically expressed.

We shall give a few examples to convince parents, that children, whose reasoning powers have been cultivated, are rather slow in comprehending and in admiring wit. They require to have it explained, they want to settle the exact justice and morality of the repartee, before they will admire it.

(November 20th, 1796.) To day at dinner the conversation happened to turn upon wit. Somebody mentioned the well known reply of the hackney coachman to Pope. S— —, a boy of nine years old, listened attentively, but did not seem to understand it; his father endeavoured to explain it to him. "Pope was a little ill made man; his favourite exclamation was, 'God mend me!' Now, when he was in a passion with the hackney coachman, he cried as usual, 'God mend me!' 'Mend *you*, sir?' said the coachman; 'it would be easier to make a new one.' Do you understand this now, S— —?"

S— — looked dull upon it, and, after some minutes consideration, said, "Yes, Pope was ill made; the man meant it would be better to make a new one than to mend him." S— — did not yet seem to taste the wit; he took the answer literally, and understood it soberly.

Immediately afterwards, the officer's famous reply to Pope was told to S— —. About ten days after this conversation, S— — said to his sister, "I wonder, M— —, that people don't oftener laugh at crooked people; like the officer who called Pope a note of interrogation."

M— —. "It would be ill natured to laugh at them."

S— —. "But you all praised that man for saying *that* about Pope. You did not think him ill natured."

Mr. — —. "No, because Pope had been impertinent to him."

S— —. "How?"

M— —. "Don't you remember, that when the officer said that a note of interrogation would make the passage clear, Pope turned round, and looking at him with great contempt, asked if he knew what a note of interrogation was?"

S— —. "Yes, I remember that; but I do not think that was very impertinent, because Pope might not know whether the man knew it or not."

Mr. — —. "Very true: but then you see, that Pope took it for granted that the officer was extremely ignorant; a boy who is just learning to read knows what a note of interrogation is."

S— — (thoughtfully.) "Yes, it *was* rude of Pope; but then the man was an officer, and therefore, it was very likely that he might be ignorant; you know you said that officers were often very ignorant."

Mr. ——. "I said *often*; but not *always.* Young men, I told you, who are tired of books, and ambitious of a red coat, often go into the army to save themselves the trouble of acquiring the knowledge necessary for other professions. A man cannot be a good lawyer, or a good physician, without having acquired a great deal of knowledge; but an officer need have little knowledge to know how to stand to be shot at. But though it may be true in general, that officers are often ignorant, it is not necessary that they should be so; a man in a red coat may have as much knowledge as a man in a black, or a blue one; therefore no sensible person should decide that a man is ignorant merely because he is an officer, as Pope did."

S——. "No, to be sure. I understand now."

M——. "But I thought, S——, you understood this before."

Mr. ——. "He is very right not to let it pass without understanding it thoroughly. You are very right, S——, not to swallow things whole; chew them well."

S—— looked as if he was still chewing.

M——. "What are you thinking of S——?"

S——. "Of the man's laughing at Pope for being crooked."

Mr. ——. "If Pope had not said any thing rude to that man, the man would have done very wrong to have laughed at him. If the officer had walked into a coffee-house, and pointing at Pope, had said, 'there's a little crooked thing like a note of interrogation,' people might have been pleased with his wit in seeing that resemblance, but they would have disliked his ill nature; and those who knew Mr. Pope, would probably have answered, 'Yes Sir, but that crooked little man is one of the most witty men in England; he is the great poet, Mr. Pope.' But when Mr. Pope had insulted the officer, the case was altered. Now, if the officer had simply answered, when he was asked what a note of interrogation was, 'a little crooked thing;' and if he had looked at Pope from head to foot as he spoke these words, every body's attention would have been turned upon Pope's figure; but then the officer would have reproached him only for his personal defects: by saying, 'a little crooked thing *that asks questions,*' the officer reproved Pope for his impertinence. Pope had just asked him a question, and every body perceived the double application of the answer. It was an exact description of a note of interrogation, and of Mr. Pope. It is this sort of partial resemblance quickly pointed out between things, which at first appear very unlike, that surprises and pleases people, and they call it wit."

How difficult it is to explain wit to a child! and how much more difficult to fix its value and morality! About a month after this conversation had passed, S—— returned to the charge: his mind had not been completely settled about *wit*.

(January 9th, 1796.) "So, S——, you don't yet understand wit, I see," said M—— to him, when he looked very grave at something that was said to him in jest. S—— immediately asked, "What *is* wit?"

M—— answered (laughing) "Wit is the folly of grown up people."

Mr. ——. "How can you give the boy such an answer? Come to me, my dear, and I'll try if I can give you a better. There are two kinds of wit, one which depends upon words, and another which depends upon thoughts. I will give you an instance of wit depending upon words:

> "Hear yonder beggar, how he cries,
> I am so lame I cannot rise!
> If he tells truth, he lies."

"Do you understand that?"

S——. "No! If he tells truth, he lies! No, he can't both tell truth and tell a lie at the same time; that's impossible."

Mr. ——. "Then there is something in the words which you don't understand: in the *common* sense of the words, they contradict each other; but try if you can find out any uncommon sense—any word which can be understood in two senses."

S—— muttered the words, "If he tells truth, he lies," and looked indignant, but presently said, "Oh, now I understand; the beggar was lying down; he lies, means he lies down, not he tells a lie."

The perception of the double meaning of the words, did not seem to please this boy; on the contrary, it seemed to provoke him; and he appeared to think that he had wasted his time upon the discovery.

Mr. ——. "Now I will give you an instance of wit that depends upon the ideas, rather than on the words. A man of very bad character had told falsehoods of another, who then made these two lines;

> "Lie on, whilst my revenge shall be,
> To tell the very truth of thee."

S—— approved of this immediately, and heartily, and recollected the only epigram he knew by rote, one which he had heard in conversation two or three months before this time. It was made upon a tall, stupid man, who had challenged another to make an epigram extempore upon him.

Unlike to Robinson shall be my song;
It shall be witty, and it shan't be long.

At the time S— — first heard this epigram, he had been as slow in comprehending it as possible; but after it had been thoroughly explained, it pleased him, and remained fixed in his memory.

Mr. — — observed, that this epigram contained wit both in words and in ideas: and he gave S— —one other example. "There were two contractors; I mean people who make a bargain with government, or with those who govern the country, to supply them with certain things at a certain price; there were two contractors, one of whom was employed to supply government with corn; the other agreed to supply government with rum. Now, you know, corn may be called grain, and rum may be called spirit. Both these contractors cheated in their bargain; both their names were the same; and the following epigram was made on them:

"Both of a name, lo! two contractors come;
One cheats in corn, and t'other cheats in rum.
Which is the greater, if you can, explain,
A rogue in spirit, or a rogue in grain?"

"*Spirit*," continued Mr. — —, "has another sense, you know—will, intention, soul; he has the spirit of a rogue; she has the spirit of contradiction. And grain has also another meaning; the grain of this table, the grain of your coat. Dyed in grain, means dyed into the substance of the material, so that the dye can't be washed out. A rogue in grain, means a man whose habit of cheating is fixed in his mind: and it is difficult to determine which is the worst, a man who has the wish, or a man who has the habit, of doing wrong. At first it seems as if you were only asked which was the worst, to cheat in selling grain, or in selling spirit; but the concealed meaning, makes the question both sense and wit."

These detailed examples, we fear, may appear tiresome; but we knew not how, without them, to explain ourselves fully. We should add, for the consolation of those who admire wit, and we are amongst the number ourselves, that it is much more likely that wit should be engrafted upon judgment, than that judgment should be engrafted upon wit. The boy whom we have just mentioned, who was so slow in comprehending the nature of wit, was asked whether he could think of any answer that Pope might have made to the officer who called him a note of interrogation.

S— —. "Is there any note which means *answer*?"

Mr. — —. "I don't know what you mean."

S——. "Any note which means answer, as - - - - like the note of interrogation, which shows that a question is asked?"

Mr. ——. "No; but if there were, what then?"

S——. "Pope might have called the man that note."

S—— could not exactly explain his idea; somebody who was present said, that if he had been in Pope's place, he would have called the officer a note of admiration. S—— would have made this answer, if he had been familiarly acquainted with the *name* of the note of admiration. His judgment taught him how to set about looking for a proper answer; but it could not lead him to the exact place for want of experience.

We hope that we have, in the chapter on books, fully explained the danger of accustoming children to read what they do not understand. Poetry, they cannot early comprehend; and even if they do understand it, they cannot improve their reasoning faculty by poetic studies. The analogies of poetry, and of reasoning, are very different. "The muse," says an excellent judge upon this subject, "would make but an indifferent school-mistress." We include under the head poetry, all books in which declamation and eloquence are substituted for reasoning. We should accustom our pupils to judge strictly of the reasoning which they meet with in books; no names of high authority should ever preclude an author's arguments from examination.

The following passage from St. Pierre's Etudes de la Nature, was read to two boys: H——, 14 years old; S——, 10 years old.

"Hurtful insects, present (the same) oppositions and signs of destruction; the gnat, thirsty of human blood, announces himself to our sight by the white spots with which his brown body is speckled; and by the shrill sound of his wings, which interrupts the calm of the groves, he announces himself to our ear as well as to our eye. The carnivorous wasp is streaked like the tiger, with bands of black over a yellow ground."

H—— and S—— both at once exclaimed, that these spots in the gnat, and streaks in the wasp, had nothing to do with their stinging us. "The buzzing of the gnat," said S——, "would, I think, be a very agreeable sound to us, if we did not know that the gnat would sting, and that it was coming near us; and, as to the wasp, I remember stopping one day upon the stairs to look at the beautiful black and yellow body of a wasp. I did not think of danger, nor of its stinging me then, and I did not know that it was like the tiger. After I had been stung by a wasp, I did not think a wasp such a beautiful animal. I think it is very often from our knowing that animals can hurt us, that we think them ugly. We might as well say," continued S——, pointing to a crocus which was near him, "we might as well say, that a man who has a yellow face has the same disposition as that crocus, or that the crocus is in every thing like the man, because it is yellow."

Cicero's "curious consolation for deafness" is properly noticed by Mr. Hume. It was read to S—— a few days ago, to try whether he could detect the sophistry: he was not previously told what was thought of it by others.

"How many languages are there," says Cicero, "which you do not understand! The Punic, Spanish, Gallic, Egyptian, &c. With regard to all these, you are as if you were deaf, and yet you are indifferent about the matter. Is it then so great a misfortune to be deaf to one language more?"

"I don't think," said S——, "that was at all a good way to console the man, because it was putting him in mind that he was more deaf than he thought he was. He did not think of those languages, perhaps, till he was put in mind that he could not hear them."

In stating any question to a child, we should avoid letting our own opinion be known, lest we lead or intimidate his mind. We should also avoid all appearance of anxiety, all impatience for the answer; our pupil's mind should be in a calm state when he is to judge: if we turn his sympathetic attention to our hopes and fears, we agitate him, and he will judge by our countenances rather than by comparing the objects or propositions which are laid before him. Some people, in arguing with children, teach them to be disingenuous by the uncandid manner in which they proceed; they show a desire for victory, rather than for truth; they state the arguments only on their own side of the question, and they will not allow the force of those which are brought against them. Children are thus piqued, instead of being convinced, and in their turn they become zealots in support of their own opinions; they hunt only for arguments in their own favour, and they are mortified when a good reason is brought on the opposite side of the question to that on which they happen to have enlisted. To prevent this, we should never argue, or suffer others to argue for victory with our pupils; we should not praise them for their cleverness in finding out arguments in support of their own opinion; but we should praise their candour and good sense when they perceive and acknowledge the force of their opponent's arguments. They should not be exercised as advocates, but as judges; they should be encouraged to keep their minds impartial, to sum up the reasons which they have heard, and to form their opinion from these without regard to what they may have originally asserted. We should never triumph over children for changing their opinion. "I thought you were on *my* side of the question; or, I thought you were on the other side of the question just now!" is sometimes tauntingly said to an ingenuous child, who changes his opinion when he hears a new argument. You think it a proof of his want of judgment, that he changes his opinion in this manner; that he vibrates continually from side to side: let him vibrate, presently he will be fixed. Do you think it a proof that your scales are bad, because they vibrate with every additional weight that is added to either side?

Idle people sometimes amuse themselves with trying the judgment of children, by telling them improbable, extravagant stories, and then ask the simple listeners whether they believe what has been told them. The readiness of belief in children will always be proportioned to their experience of the veracity of those with whom they converse; consequently children, who live with those who speak truth to them, will scarcely ever be inclined to doubt the veracity of strangers. Such trials of the judgment of our pupils should never be permitted. Why should the example of lying be set before the honest minds of children, who are far from silly when they show simplicity? They guide themselves by the best rules, by which even a philosopher in similar circumstances could guide himself. The things asserted are extraordinary, but the children believe them, because they have never had any experience of the falsehood of human testimony.

The Socratic mode of reasoning is frequently practised upon children. People arrange questions artfully, so as to bring them to whatever conclusion they please. In this mode of reasoning, much depends upon getting the first move; the child has very little chance of having it, his preceptor usually begins first with a peremptory voice, "Now answer me this question!" The pupil, who knows that the interrogatories are put with a design to entrap him, is immediately alarmed, and instead of giving a direct, candid answer to the question, is always looking forward to the possible consequences of his reply; or he is considering how he may evade the snare that is laid for him. Under these circumstances he is in imminent danger of learning the shuffling habits of cunning; he has little chance of learning the nature of open, manly investigation.

Preceptors, who imagine that it is necessary to put on very grave faces, and to use much learned apparatus in teaching the art of reasoning, are not nearly so likely to succeed as those who have the happy art of encouraging children to lay open their minds freely, and who can make every pleasing trifle an exercise for the understanding. If it be playfully pointed out to a child that he reasons ill, he smiles and corrects himself; but you run the hazard of making him positive in errour, if you reprove or ridicule him with severity. It is better to seize the subjects that accidentally arise in conversation, than formally to prepare subjects for discussion.

"The king's stag hounds," (says Mr. White of Selborne, in his entertaining observations on quadrupeds, [89]) "the king's stag hounds came down to Alton, attended by a huntsman and six yeoman prickers with horns, to try for the stag that has haunted Hartley-wood and its environs for so long a time. Many hundreds of people, horse and foot, attended the dogs to see the deer unharboured; but though the huntsman drew Hartley-wood, and Long-coppice, and Shrub-wood, and Temple-hangers, and in their way back, Hartley, and Wardleham-hangers, yet no stag could be found.

"The royal pack, *accustomed to have the deer turned out before them, never drew the coverts with any address and spirit*," &c.

Children, who are accustomed to have the game started and turned out before them by their preceptors, may, perhaps, like the royal pack, lose their wonted address and spirit, and may be disgracefully *at a fault* in the public chase. Preceptors should not help their pupils out in argument, they should excite them to explain and support their own observations.

Many ladies show in general conversation the powers of easy raillery joined to reasoning, unincumbered with pedantry. If they would employ these talents in the education of their children, they would probably be as well repaid for their exertions, as they can possibly be by the polite, but transient applause of the visiters to whom they usually devote their powers of entertaining. A little praise or blame, a smile from a mother, or a frown, a moments attention, or a look of cold neglect, have the happy, or the fatal power of repressing or of exciting the energy of a child, of directing his understanding to useful or pernicious purposes. Scarcely a day passes in which children do not make some attempt to reason about the little events which interest them, and, upon these occasions, a mother, who joins in conversation with her children, may instruct them in the art of reasoning without the parade of logical disquisitions.

Mr. Locke has done mankind an essential service, by the candid manner in which he has spoken of some of the learned forms of argumentation. A great proportion of society, he observes, are unacquainted with these forms, and have not heard the name of Aristotle; yet, without the aid of syllogisms, they can reason sufficiently well for all the useful purposes of life, often much better than those who have been disciplined in the schools. It would indeed "be putting one man sadly over the head of another," to confine the reasoning faculty to the disciples of Aristotle, to any sect or system, or to any forms of disputation. Mr. Locke has very clearly shown, that syllogisms do not assist the mind in the perception of the agreement or disagreement of ideas; but, on the contrary, that they invert the natural order in which the thoughts should be placed, and in which they must be placed, before we can draw a just conclusion. To children who are not familiarized with scholastic terms, the sound of harsh words, and quaint language, unlike any thing that they hear in common conversation, is alone sufficient to alarm their imagination with some confused apprehension of difficulty. In this state of alarm they are seldom sufficiently masters of themselves, either to deny or to acknowledge an adept's major, minor, or conclusion. Even those who are most expert in syllogistical reasoning, do not often apply it to the common affairs of life, in which reasoning is just as much wanted as it is in the abstract questions of philosophy; and many argue, and conduct themselves with great prudence and precision, who might, perhaps, be caught on the horns of a dilemma; or who would infallibly fall victims to *the crocodile*.

Young people should not be ignorant, however, of these boasted forms of argumentation; and it may, as they advance in the knowledge of words, be a useful exercise to resist the attacks of sophistry. No ingenious person would wish to teach a child to employ them. As defensive weapons, it is necessary, that young people should have the command of logical terms; as offensive weapons, these should never be used. They should know the evolutions, and be able to perform the exercise of a logician, according to the custom of the times, according to the usage of different nations; but they should not attach any undue importance to this technical art: they should not trust to it in the day of battle.

We have seen syllogisms, crocodiles, enthymemas, sorites, &c. explained and tried upon a boy of nine or ten years old in playful conversation, so that he became accustomed to the terms without learning to be pedantic in the abuse of them; and his quickness in reasoning was increased by exercise in detecting puerile sophisms; such as that of *the Cretans*—Gorgias and his bargain about the winning of his first cause. In the following sorites [90] of Themistocles—"My son commands his mother; his mother commands me; I command the Athenians; the Athenians command Greece; Greece commands Europe; Europe commands the whole earth; therefore my son commands the whole earth"—the sophism depends upon the inaccurate use of the *commands*, which is employed in different senses in the different propositions. This errour was without difficulty detected by S—— at ten years old; and we make no doubt that any unprejudiced boy of the same age, would immediately point out the fallacy without hesitation; but we do not feel quite sure that a boy exercised in logic, who had been taught to admire and reverence the ancient figures of rhetoric, would with equal readiness detect the sophism. Perhaps it may seem surprising, that the same boy, who judged so well of this sorites of Themistocles, should a few months before have been easily entrapped by the following simple dilemma.

M——. "We should avoid what gives us pain."

S— —. "Yes, to be sure."

M— —. "Whatever burns us, gives us pain."

S— —. "Yes, that it does!"

M— —. "We should then avoid whatever burns us."

To this conclusion S— — heartily assented, for he had but just recovered from the pain of a burn.

M— —. "Fire burns us."

S— —. "Yes, I know that."

M— —. "We should then avoid fire."

S— —. "Yes."

This hasty *yes* was extorted from the boy by the mode of interrogatory; but he soon perceived his mistake.

M— —. "We should avoid fire. What when we are very cold?"

S— —. "Oh, no: I meant to say, that we should avoid a certain degree of fire. We should not go *too* near the fire. We should not go *so* near as to burn ourselves."

Children who have but little experience, frequently admit assertions to be true in general, which are only true in particular instances; and this is often attributed to their want of judgment: it should be attributed to their want of experience. Experience, and nothing else, can rectify these mistakes: if we attempt to correct them by words, we shall merely teach our pupils to argue about terms, not to reason. Some of the questions and themes which are given to boys may afford us instances of this injudicious education. "Is eloquence advantageous, or hurtful to a state?" What a vast range of ideas, what variety of experience in men and things should a person possess, who is to discuss this question! Yet it is often discussed by unfortunate scholars of eleven or twelve years old. "What is the greatest good?" The answer expected by a preceptor to this question, obviously is, virtue; and, if a boy can, in decent language, write a page or two about *pleasure's* being a transient, and virtue a permanent good, his master flatters himself that he has early taught him to reason philosophically. But what ideas does the youth annex to the words pleasure and virtue? Or does he annex any? If he annex no idea to the words, he is merely talking about sounds.

All reasoning ultimately refers to matters of fact: to judge whether any piece of reasoning is within the comprehension of a child, we must consider whether the facts to which it refers are within his experience. The more we increase his knowledge of facts, the more we should exercise him in reasoning upon them; but we should teach him to examine carefully before he admits any thing to be a fact, or any assertion to be true. Experiment, as to substances, is the test of truth; and attention to his own feelings, as to matters of feeling. Comparison of the evidence of others with the general laws of nature, which he has learned from his own observation, is another mode of obtaining an accurate knowledge of facts. M. Condillac, in his Art of Reasoning, maintains, that the evidence of reason depends solely upon our perception of the *identity*, or, to use a less formidable word, *sameness*, of one proposition with another. "A demonstration," he says, "is only a chain of propositions, in which the same ideas, passing from one to the other, differ only because they are differently expressed; the evidence of any reasoning consists solely in its identity."

M. Condillac [91] exemplifies this doctrine by translating this proposition, "The measure of every triangle is the product of its height by half its base," into self-evident, or, as he calls them, identical propositions. The whole ultimately referring to the ideas which we have obtained by our senses of a triangle; of its base, of measure, height, and number. If a child had not previously acquired any one of these ideas, it would be in vain to explain one term by another, or to translate one phrase or proposition into another; they might be identical, but they would not be self-evident propositions to the pupil; and no conclusion, except what relates merely to words, could be formed from such reasoning. The moral which we should draw from Condillac's observations for Practical Education must be, that clear ideas should first be acquired by the exercise of the senses, and that afterwards, when we reason about things in words, we should use few and accurate terms, that we may have as little trouble as possible in changing or translating one phrase or proposition into another.

Children, if they are not overawed by authority, if they are encouraged in the habit of observing their own sensations, and if they are taught precision in the use of the words by which they describe them, will probably reason accurately where their own feelings are concerned.

In appreciating the testimony of others, and in judging of chances and probability, we must not expect our pupils to proceed very rapidly. There is more danger that they should overrate, than that they should undervalue, the evidence of others; because, as we formerly stated, we take it for granted, that they have had little experience of falsehood. We should, to preserve them from credulity, excite them in all cases where it can be obtained, never to rest satisfied without the strongest species of evidence, that of their own senses. If a child says, "I am sure of such a thing," we should immediately examine into his reasons for believing it. "Mr. A. or Mr. B. told me so," is not a sufficient cause of belief, unless the child has had long experience of A. and B.'s truth and accuracy; and, at all events, the indolent habit of relying upon the assertions of others, instead of verifying them, should not be indulged.

It would be waste of time to repeat those experiments, of the truth of which the uniform experience of our lives has convinced us: we run no hazard, for instance, in believing any one who simply asserts, that they have seen an apple fall from a tree; this assertion agrees with the great natural *law of gravity*, or, in other words, with the uniform experience of mankind: but if any body told us, that they had seen an apple hanging self-poised in the air, we should reasonably suspect the truth of their observation, or of their evidence. This is the first rule which we can most readily teach our pupils in judging of evidence. We are not speaking of children from four to six years old, for every thing is almost equally extraordinary to them; but, when children are about ten or eleven, they have acquired a sufficient variety of facts to form comparisons, and to judge to a certain degree of the probability of any new fact that is related. In reading and in conversation we should now exercise them in forming judgments, where we know that they have the means of comparison. "Do you believe such a thing to be true? and why do you believe it? Can you account for such a thing?" are questions we should often ask at this period of their education. On hearing extraordinary facts, some children will not be satisfied with vague assertions; others content themselves with saying, "It is so, I read it in a book." We should have little hopes of those who swallow every thing they read in a book; we are always pleased to see a child hesitate and doubt, and require positive proof before he believes. The taste for the marvellous, is strong in ignorant minds; the wish to account for every new appearance, characterizes the cultivated pupil.

A lady told a boy of nine years old (S——) the following story, which she had just met with in "The Curiosities of Literature." An officer, who was confined in the Bastille, used to amuse himself by playing on the flute: one day he observed, that a number of spiders came down from their webs, and hung round him as if listening to his music; a number of mice also came from their holes, and retired as soon as he stopped. The officer had a great dislike to mice; he procured a cat from the keeper of the prison, and when the mice were entranced by his music, he let the cat out amongst them.

S—— was much displeased by this man's treacherous conduct towards the poor mice, and his indignation for some moments suspended his reasoning faculty; but, when S—— had sufficiently expressed his indignation against the officer in the affair of the mice, he began to question the truth of the story; and he said, that he did not think it was certain, that the mice and spiders came to listen to the music. "I do not know about the mice," said he, "but I think, perhaps, when the officer played upon the flute, he set the air in motion, and shook the cobwebs, so as to disturb the spiders." We do not, nor did the child think, that this was a satisfactory account of the matter; but we mention it as an instance of the love of investigation, which we wish to encourage.

The difficulty of judging concerning the truth of evidence increases, when we take moral causes into the account. If we had any suspicion, that a man who told us that he had seen an apple fall from a tree, had himself pulled the apple down and stolen it, we should set the probability of his telling a falsehood, and his motive for doing so, against his evidence; and though according to the natural physical course of things, there would be no improbability in his story, yet there might arise improbability from his character for dishonesty; and thus we should feel ourselves in doubt concerning the fact. But if two people agreed in the same testimony, our doubt would vanish; the dishonest man's doubtful evidence would be corroborated, and we should believe, notwithstanding his general character, in the truth of his assertion in this instance. We could make the matter infinitely more complicated, but what has been said will be sufficient to suggest to preceptors the difficulty which their young and inexperienced pupils must feel, in forming judgments of facts where physical and moral probabilities are in direct opposition to each other.

We wish that a writer equal to such a task would write trials for children as exercises for their judgment; beginning with the simplest, and proceeding gradually to the more complicated cases in which moral reasonings can be used. We do not mean, that it would be advisable to initiate young readers in the technical forms of law; but the general principles of justice, upon which all law is founded, might, we think, be advantageously exemplified. Such trials would entertain children extremely. There is a slight attempt at this kind of composition, we mean in a little trial in Evenings at Home; and we have seen children read it with great avidity. Cyrus's judgment about the two coats, and the ingenious story of the olive merchant's cause, rejudged by the sensible child in the Arabian Tales, have been found highly interesting to a young audience.

We should prefer truth to fiction: if we could select any instances from real life, any trials suited to the capacity of young people, they would be preferable to any which the most ingenious writer could invent for our purpose. A gentleman who has taken his two sons, one of them ten, and the other fifteen years old, to hear trials at his county assizes, found by the account which the boys gave of what they had heard, that they had been interested, and that they were capable of understanding the business.

Allowance must be made at first for the bustle and noise of a public place, and for the variety of objects which distract the attention.

Much of the readiness of forming judgments depends upon the power of discarding and obliterating from our mind all the superfluous circumstances; it may be useful to exercise our pupils, by telling them now and then stories in the confused manner in which they are sometimes related by puzzled witnesses; let them reduce the heterogeneous circumstances to order, make a clear statement of the case for themselves, and try if they can point out the facts on which the decision principally rests. This is not merely education for a lawyer; the powers of reasoning and judgment, when we have been exercised in this manner, may be turned to any art or profession. We should, if we were to try the judgment of children, observe, whether in unusual circumstances they can apply their former principles, and compare the new objects that are placed before them without perplexity. We have sometimes found, that on subjects entirely new to them, children, who have been used to reason, can lay aside the circumstances that are not essential, and form a distinct judgment for themselves, independently of the opinion of others.

Last winter the entertaining life of the celebrated miser Mr. Elwes was read aloud in a family, in which there were a number of children. Mr. Elwes, once, as he was *walking* home on a dark night, in London, ran against a chair pole and bruised both his shins. His friends sent for a surgeon. Elwes was alarmed at the idea of expense, and he laid the surgeon the amount of his bill, that the leg which he took under his own protection would get well sooner than that which was put under the surgeon's care; at the same time Mr. Elwes promised to put nothing to the leg of which he took charge. Mr. Elwes favourite leg got well sooner than that which the surgeon had undertaken to cure, and Mr. Elwes won his wager. In a note upon this transaction his biographer says, "This wager would have been a bubble bet if it had been brought before the Jockey-club, because Mr. Elwes, though he promised to put nothing to the leg under his own protection, took Velnos' vegetable sirup during the time of its cure."

C— — (a girl of twelve years old) observed when this anecdote was read, that "still the wager was a fair wager, because *the medicine* which Mr. Elwes took, if it was of any use, must have been of use to both legs; therefore the surgeon and Mr. Elwes had equal advantage from it." C— — had never heard of the Jockey-club, or of bubble bets before, and she used the word *medicine*, because she forgot the name of Velnos' vegetable sirup.

We have observed, [92] that works of criticism are unfit for children, and teach them rather to remember what others say of authors, than to judge of the books themselves impartially: but, when we object to works of criticism, we do not mean to object to criticism; we think it an excellent exercise for the judgment, and we have ourselves been so well corrected, and so kindly assisted by the observations of young critics, that we cannot doubt their capacity. This book has been read to a jury of young critics, who gave their utmost attention to it for about half an hour at a sitting, and many amendments have been made from their suggestions. In the chapter on obstinacy, for instance, when we were asserting, that children sometimes forget their old bad habits, and do not consider these as a part of themselves, there was this allusion.

"As the snake, when he casts his skin, leaves the slough behind him, and winds on his way in new and beautiful colours."

The moment this sentence was read, it was objected to by the audience. Mr. — — objected to the word slough, as an ill sounding, disagreeable word, and which conveyed at first to the eye the idea of a wet boggy place; such as the slough of Despond. At last S— —, who had been pondering over the affair in silence, exclaimed, "But I think there's another fault in the allusion; do not snakes cast their skins every year? Then these *new and beautiful colours*, which are the good habits, must be thrown aside and forgotten the next time; but that should not be."

This criticism appeared conclusive even to the author, and the sentence was immediately expunged.

When young people have acquired a command of language, we must be careful lest their fluency and their ready use of synonymous expressions should lessen the accuracy of their reasoning, Mr. Horne Tooke has ably shown the connection between the study of language and the art of reasoning. It is not necessary to make our pupils profound grammarians, or etymologists, but attention to the origin, abbreviations, and various meanings of words, will assist them not only to speak, but to think and argue with precision. This is not a study of abstract speculation, but of practical, daily utility; half the disputes, and much of the misery of the world, originate and perpetuate themselves by the inaccurate use of words. One party uses a word in *this* sense, the opposite party uses the same word in another sense; all their reasonings appear absurd to each other; and, instead of explaining them, they quarrel. This is not the case merely in *philosophical* disputes between authors, but it happens continually in the busy, active scenes of life. Even whilst we were writing this passage, in the newspaper of to-day, we met with an instance that is sufficiently striking.

"The accusation against me," says Sir Sidney Smith, in his excellent letter to Pichegru, expostulating upon his unmerited confinement, "brought forward by *your* justice of the peace, was, that I was the enemy of the republic. You know, general, that with military men, the word *enemy* has merely a technical signification, without expressing the least character of hatred. You will readily admit this principle, the *result* of which is, that I ought not to be persecuted for the injury I have been enabled to do whilst I carried arms against you."

Here the argument between two generals, one of whom is pleading for his liberty, if not for his life, turns upon the meaning and construction of a single word. Accuracy of reasoning, and some knowledge of language, may, it appears, be of essential service in all professions.

It is not only necessary to attend to the exact meaning which is avowedly affixed to any terms used in argument, but is also useful to attend to the thoughts which are often suggested to the disputants by certain words. Thus, the words happiness and beauty, suggest, in conversation, very different ideas to different men; and in arguing, concerning these, they could never come to a conclusion. Even persons who agree in the same definition of a word, frequently do not sufficiently attend to the ideas which the word suggests; to the association of thoughts and emotions which it excites; and, consequently, they cannot strictly abide by their own definition, nor can they discover where the errour lies. We have observed, [93] that the imagination is powerfully affected by words that suggest long trains of ideas; our reasonings are influenced in the same manner, and the elliptical figures of speech are used in reasoning as well as in poetry.

"I would do so and so, if I were Alexander."

"And so would I, if I were Parmenio;"

is a short reply, which suggests a number of ideas, and a train of reasoning. To those who cannot supply the intermediate ideas, the answer would not appear either sublime or rational. Young people, when they appear to admire any compressed reasoning, should be encouraged to show that they can supply the thoughts and reasons that are not expressed. Vivacious children, will be disgusted, however, if they are required to detail upon the subject; [94] all that is necessary, is to be sure that they actually comprehend what they admire.

Sometimes a question that appears simple, involves the consideration of others which are difficult. Whenever a preceptor cannot go to the bottom of the business, he will do wisely to say so at once to his pupil, instead of attempting a superficial or evasive reply. For instance, if a child was to hear that the Dutch burn and destroy quantities of spice, the produce of their India islands, he would probably express some surprise, and perhaps some indignation. If a preceptor were to say, "The Dutch have a right to do what they please with what is their own, and the spice is their own," his pupil would not yet be satisfied; he would probably say, "Yes, they have a right to do what they please with what is their own; but why should they destroy what is useful?" The preceptor might answer, if he chose to make a foolish answer, "The Dutch follow their own interest in burning the spice; they sell what remains at a higher price; the market would be overstocked if they did not burn some of their spice." Even supposing the child to understand the terms, this would not be a satisfactory answer; nor could a satisfactory answer be given, without discussing the nature of commerce, and the *justice* of monopolies. Where one question in this manner involves another, we should postpone the discussion, if it cannot be completely made; the road may be just pointed out, and the pupil's curiosity may be excited to future inquiry. It is even better to be ignorant, than to have superficial knowledge.

A philosopher, who himself excelled in accuracy of reasoning, recommends the study of mathematics, to improve the acuteness and precision of the reasoning faculty. [95] To study any thing accurately, will have an excellent effect upon the mind; and we may afterwards direct the judgment to whatever purposes we please. It has often been remarked, as a reproach upon men of science and literature, that those who judge extremely well of books, and of abstract philosophical questions, do not show the same judgment in the active business of life: a man, undoubtedly, may be a good mathematician, a good critic, an excellent writer, and may yet not show, or rather not employ, much judgment in his conduct: his powers of reasoning cannot be deficient; the habit of employing those powers in conducting himself, he should have been taught by early education. Moral reasoning, and the habit of acting in consequence of the conviction of the judgment, we call prudence; a virtue of so much consequence to all the other virtues; a virtue of so much consequence to ourselves and to our friends, that it surely merits a whole chapter to itself in Practical Education.

[85] V. Chapter on Attention.

[86] V. Tasks.

[87] Chapter on Acquaintance.

[88] V. Stewart.

[89] A Naturalist's Calendar, by the late Rev. Gilbert White, M. A. published by Dr. Aikin, printed for B. and J. White, Fleet Street.

[90] V. Deinology; where there are many entertaining examples of the figures of rhetoric.

[91] Une dèmonstration est donc une suite de propositions, ou les mêmes idées passant de l'une à l'autre, ne différent que parce qu'elles sont énonceès différement; et l'évidence d'un raisonnement consiste uniquement dans l'identité. V. Art de Raisonner, p. 2.

[92] V. Chapter on Books.

[93] V. Chapter on Imagination.

[94] V. Attention.

[95] Locke. Essay on the Conduct of the Human Understanding.

CHAPTER XXIV
ON PRUDENCE AND ECONOMY

Voltaire says, that the king of Prussia always wrote with one kind of enthusiasm, and acted with another. It often happens, that men judge with one degree of understanding, and conduct themselves with another; [96] hence the common-place remarks on the difference between theory and practice; hence the observation, that it is easy to be prudent for other people, but extremely difficult to be prudent for ourselves. Prudence is a virtue compounded of judgment and resolution: we do not here speak of that narrow species of prudence, which is more properly called worldly wisdom; but we mean that enlarged, comprehensive wisdom, which, after taking a calm view of the objects of happiness, steadily prefers the greatest portion of felicity. This is not a selfish virtue; for, according to our definition, benevolence, as one of the greatest sources of our pleasures, must be included in the truly prudent man's estimate. Two things are necessary to make any person prudent, the power to judge, and the habit of acting in consequence of his conviction. We have, in the preceding chapter, as far as we were able, suggested the best methods of cultivating the powers of reasoning in our pupils; we must consider now how these can be applied immediately to their conduct, and associated with habits of action.

Instead of deciding always for our young pupils, we should early accustom them to choose for themselves about every trifle which is interesting to childhood: if they choose wisely, they should enjoy the natural reward of their prudence; and if they decide rashly, they should be suffered to feel the consequence of their own errour. Experience, it is said, makes even fools wise; and the sooner we can give experience, the sooner we shall teach wisdom. But we must not substitute belief upon trust for belief upon conviction. When a little boy says, "I did not eat any more custard, because mamma told me that the custard would make me sick," he is only obedient, he is not prudent; he submits to his mother's judgment, he does not use his own. When obedience is out of the question, children sometimes follow the opinions of others; of this we formerly gave an instance (v. Toys) in the poor boy, who chose a gilt coach, because his mamma *"and every body said it was the prettiest,"* whilst he really preferred the useful cart: we should never prejudice them either by our *wisdom* or our folly.

A sensible little boy of four years old had seen somebody *telling fortunes* in the grounds of coffee; but when he had a cup of coffee given to him, he drank it all, saying, "Coffee is better than fortune!"

When their attention is not turned to divine what the spectators think and feel, children will have leisure to consult their own minds, and to compare their own feelings. As this has been already spoken of, [97] we shall not dwell upon it; we only mention it as a necessary precaution in teaching prudence.

Some parents may perhaps fear, that, if they were to allow children to choose upon every trifling occasion for themselves, they would become wilful and troublesome: this certainly will be the effect, if we make them think that there is a pleasure in the exercise of free-will, independently of any good that may be obtained by judicious choice. "Now, my dear, you shall have *your* choice! You shall choose for *yourself*! You shall have your *free* choice!" are expressions that may be pronounced in such a tone, and with such an emphasis to a child, as immediately to excite a species of triumphant ecstasy from the mere idea of having his *own* free choice. By a different accent and emphasis we may repress the ideas of triumph, and, without intimidating the pupil, we may turn his mind to the difficulties, rather than the glory of being in a situation to decide for himself.

We must not be surprised at the early imprudence of children; their mistakes, when they first are allowed to make a choice, are inevitable; all their sensations are new to them, consequently they cannot judge of what they shall like or dislike. If some of Lord Macartney's suite had, on his return from the late embassy to China, brought home some plant whose smell was perfectly unknown to Europeans, would it have been possible for the greatest philosopher in England to have decided, if he had been asked, whether he should like the unknown perfume? Children, for the first five or six years of their lives, are in the situation of this philosopher, relatively to external objects. We should never reproachfully say to a child, "You asked to smell such a thing; you asked to see such a thing; and now you have had your wish, you don't like them!" How can the child possibly judge of what he shall like or dislike, before he has tried? Let him try experiments upon his own feelings; the more accurate knowledge he acquires, the sooner he will be enabled to choose *prudently.* You may expedite his progress by exciting him to compare each new sensation with those to which he is already familiarized; this will counteract that love of novelty which is often found dangerous to prudence; if the mind is employed in comparing, it cannot be dazzled by new objects.

Children often imagine, that what they like for the present minute, they shall continue to like for ever; they have not learnt from experiment, that the most agreeable sensations fatigue, if they are prolonged or frequently repeated; they have not learnt, that all violent stimuli are followed by weariness or ennui. The sensible preceptor will not insist upon his pupil's knowing these things by inspiration, nor will he expect that his assertions or prophecies should be implicitly believed; he will wait till the child *feels*, and at that moment he will excite his pupil to observe his own feelings. "You thought that you should never be tired of smelling that rose, or of looking at that picture; now you perceive that you *are* tired: remember this; it may be of use to you another time." If this be said in a friendly manner, it will not pique the child to defend his past choice, but it will direct his future judgment.

Young people are often reproached for their imprudence in preferring a small present pleasure to a large distant advantage: this errour also arises from inexperience, not from want of judgment, or deficiency in strength of mind. When that which has been the future, has in its turn become present, children begin to have some idea of the nature of time, and they can then form some comparisons between the value of present and future pleasures. This is a very slow process; old people calculate and depend upon the distant future more than the young, not always from their increased wisdom or prudence, but merely from their increased experience, and consequent belief that the future will in time arrive. It is imprudent in old people to depend upon the future; if they were to reason upon the chance of their lives, they ought not to be secure of its arrival; yet habit in this instance, as in many others, is more powerful than reason: in all the plans of elderly people, there is seldom any errour from impatience as to the future; there often appear gross errours in their security as to its arrival. If these opposite habits could be mixed in the minds of the old and of the young, it would be for their mutual advantage.

It is not possible to *infuse* experience into the mind; our pupils must feel for themselves: but, by teaching them to observe their own feelings, we may abridge their labour; a few lessons will teach a great deal when they are properly applied. To teach children to calculate and compare their present and future pleasures, we may begin by fixing short intervals of time for our experiments; an hour, a day, a week, perhaps, are periods of time to which their imagination will easily extend; they can measure and compare their feelings within these spaces of time, and we may lead them to observe their own errours in not providing for the future. "Now Friday is come; last

Monday you thought Friday would never come. If you had not cut away all your pencil last week, you would have had some left to draw with to-day. Another time you will manage better."

We should also lead them to compare their ideas of any given pleasure, before and after the period of its arrival. "You thought last summer that you should like making snow balls in winter, better than making hay in summer. Now you have made snow-balls to-day; and you remember what you felt when you were making hay last summer; do you like the snow-ball pleasure, or the hay-making pleasure the best?" V. Berquin's Quatre saisons.

If our pupils, when they have any choice to make, prefer a small present gratification to a great future pleasure, we should not, at the moment of their decision, reproach their imprudence, but we should *steadily make them abide by their choice*; and when the time arrives at which the greater pleasure might have been enjoyed, we should remark the circumstance, but not with a tone of reproach, for it is their affair, not ours. "You preferred having a sheet of paper the moment you wanted it last week, to the having a quire of paper this week." "Oh, but," says the child, "I wanted a sheet of paper very much then, but I did not consider how soon this week would come—I wish I had chosen the quire." "Then remember what you feel now, and you will be able to choose better upon another occasion." We should always refer to the pupils' own feelings, and look forward to their future advantage. The reason why so few young people attend to advice, is, that their preceptors do not bring it actually home to their feelings: it is useless to reproach for past imprudence; the child sees the errour as plainly as we do; all that can be done, is to make it a lesson for the future.

To a geometrician, the words *by proposition 1st.* stand for a whole demonstration: if he recollects that he has once gone over the demonstration, he is satisfied of its truth; and, without verifying it again, he makes use of it in making out the demonstration of a new proposition. In moral reasoning, we proceed in the same manner; we recollect the result of our past experiments, and we refer to this moral demonstration in solving a new problem. In time, by frequent practice, this operation is performed so rapidly by the mind, that we scarcely perceive it, and yet it guides our actions. A man, in walking across the room, keeps out of the way of the tables and chairs, without perceiving that he reasons about the matter; a sober man avoids hard drinking, because he knows it to be hurtful to his health; but he does not, every time he refuses to drink, go over the whole train of reasoning which first decided his determination. A modern philosopher, [98] calls this rapid species of reasoning "intuitive analogy;" applied to the business of life, the French call it tact. Sensible people have this tact in higher perfection than others; and prudent people govern themselves by it more regularly than others. By the methods which we have recommended, we hope it may be successfully cultivated in early education.

Rousseau, in expressing his contempt for those who make *habit* their only guide of action, goes, as he is apt to do in the heat of declamation, into the errour opposite to that which he ridicules. "The only habit," cries he, "that I wish my Emilius to have, is the habit of having no habits." Emilius would have been a strange being, had he literally accomplished his preceptor's wish. To go up stairs, would have been a most operose, and to go down stairs, a most tremendous, affair to Emilius, for he was to have no habits: between every step of the stairs, new deliberations must take place, and fresh decisions of the judgment and will ensue. In his moral judgments, Emilius would have had as much useless labour. Habit surely is necessary, even to those who make reason the ultimate judge of their affairs. Reason is not to be appealed to upon every trivial occasion, to rejudge the same cause a million of times. Must a man, every time he draws a straight line, repeat to himself, "a right line is that which lieth evenly between its points?" Must he rehearse the propositions of Euclid, instead of availing himself of their practical use?

"Christian, can'st thou raise a perpendicular upon a straight line?" is the apostrophe with which the cross-legged emperor of Barbary, seated on his throne of rough deal boards, accosts every *learned* stranger who frequents his court. In the course of his reign, probably, his Barbaric majesty may have reiterated the demonstration of this favourite proposition, which he learned from a French surgeon about five hundred times; but his majesty's understanding is not materially improved by these recitals; his geometrical learning is confined, we are told, to this single proposition.

It would have been scarcely worth while to have singled out for combat this paradox of Rousseau's, concerning habit, if it had not presented itself in the formidable form of an antithesis. A false maxim, conveyed in an antithesis, is dangerous, because it is easily remembered and repeated, and it quickly passes current in conversation.

But to return to our subject, of which we have *imprudently* lost sight. Imprudence does not always arise from our neglect of our past experience, or from our forgetting to take the future into our calculations, but from false associations, or from passion. Objects often appear different to one man, from what they do to the rest of the world: this man may reason well upon what the majority of reasonable people agree to call false appearances; he may follow strictly the conviction of his own understanding, and yet the world will say that he acts very imprudently. To the taste or smell of those who are in a fever, objects not only appear, but really are, to the patients different from what they appear to persons in sound health: in the same manner to the imagination, objects have really a different value in moments of enthusiasm, from what they have in our cooler hours, and we scarcely can believe that our view of objects will ever vary. It is in vain to oppose reason to false associations; we must endeavour to combat one set of associations by another, and to alter the situation, and consequently, the views, [99] of the mistaken person. Suppose, for instance, that a child had been in a coach and six upon some *pleasant* excursion (it is an improbable thing, but we may suppose any thing:) suppose a child had enjoyed, from some accidental circumstances, an extraordinary degree of pleasure in a coach and six, he might afterwards long to be in a similar vehicle, from a mistaken notion, that it could confer happiness. Here we should not oppose the force of reasoning to a false association, but we should counteract the former association. Give the child an equal quantity of amusement when he is not in a coach and six, and then he will form fresh pleasurable associations with other objects which may balance his first prepossession. If you oppose reason ineffectually to passion or taste, you bring the voice and power of reason into discredit with your pupil. When you have changed his view of things, you may then reason with him, and show him the cause of his former mistake.

In the excellent fable of the shield that was gold on one side and silver on the other, the two disputants never could have agreed until they changed places.—When you have, in several instances, proved by experiment, that you judge more prudently than your pupil, he will be strongly inclined to listen to your counsels, and then your experience will be of real use to him; he will argue from it with safety and satisfaction. When, after recovering from fits of passion or enthusiasm, you have, upon several occasions, convinced him that your admonitions would have prevented him from the pain of repentance, he will recollect this when he again feels the first rise of passion in his mind; and he may, in that lucid moment, avail himself of your calm reason, and thus avoid the excesses of extravagant passions. That unfortunate French monarch, [100] who was liable to temporary fits of frenzy, learned to foresee his approaching malady, and often requested his friends to disarm him, lest he should injure any of his attendants.

In a malady which precludes the use of reason, it was possible for this humane patient to foresee the probable mischief he might do to his fellow-creatures, and to take prudent measures against his own violence; and may not we expect, that those who are early accustomed to attend to their own feelings, may prepare against the extravagance of their own passions, and avail themselves of the regulating advice of their temperate friends?

In the education of girls, we must teach them much more caution than is necessary to boys: their prudence must be more the result of reasoning than of experiment; they *must* trust to the experience of others; they cannot always have recourse to what *ought to be*; they must adapt themselves to what is. They cannot rectify the material mistakes in their conduct, [101] Timidity, a certain tardiness of decision, and reluctance to act in public situations, are not considered as defects in a woman's character: her pausing prudence does not, to a man of discernment, denote imbecility; but appears to him the graceful, auspicious characteristic of female virtue. There is always more probability that women should endanger their own happiness by precipitation, than by forbearance.—Promptitude of choice, is seldom expected from the female sex; they should avail themselves of the leisure that is permitted to them for reflection. "Begin nothing of which you have not well considered the end," was the piece of advice for which the Eastern Sultan [102] paid a purse of gold, the price set upon it by a sage. The monarch did not repent of his purchase. This maxim should be engraved upon the memory of our female pupils, by the repeated lessons of education. We should, even in trifles, avoid every circumstance which can tend to make girls venturesome; which can encourage them to trust their good fortune, instead of relying on their own prudence. Marmontel's tale, entitled *"Heureusement,"* is a witty, but surely not a *moral*, tale. Girls should be discouraged from hazarding opinions in general conversation; but amongst their friends, they should be excited to reason with accuracy and with temper. [103] It is really a part of a woman's prudence to have command of temper; if she has it not, her wit and sense will not have their just value in domestic life. Calphurnia, a Roman lady, used to plead her own causes before the senate, and we are informed, that she became "so troublesome and confident, that the judges decreed that thenceforward no woman should be suffered to plead." Did not this lady make an imprudent use of her talents?

In the choice of friends, and on all matters of taste, young women should be excited to reason about their own feelings. "There is no reasoning about taste," is a pernicious maxim: if there were more reasoning, there would be less disputation upon this subject. If women questioned their own minds, or allowed their friends to question them, concerning the reasons of their "preferences and aversions," there would not, probably, be so many love matches, and so few love marriages. It is in vain to expect, that young women should begin to reason miraculously at the very moment that reason is wanted in the guidance of their conduct. We should also observe, that women are called upon for the exertion of their prudence at an age when young men are scarcely supposed to possess that virtue; therefore, women should be more early, and more carefully, educated for the purpose. The important decisions of woman's life, are often made before she is twenty: a man does not come upon the theatre of public life, where most of his prudence is shown, till he is much older.

Economy is, in women, an essential domestic virtue. Some women have a foolish love of expensive baubles; a taste which a very little care, probably, in their early education, might have prevented. We are told, that when a collection of three hundred and fifty pounds was made for the celebrated Cuzzona, to save her from absolute want, she immediately laid out two hundred pounds of the money in the purchase of a *shell cap*, which was then in fashion. [104] Prudent mothers, will avoid showing any admiration of pretty trinkets before their young daughters; and they will oppose the ideas of utility and durability to the mere caprice of fashion, which creates a taste for beauty, as it were, by proclamation. "Such a thing is pretty, but it is of no use. Such a thing is pretty, but it will soon wear out"—a mother may say; and she should prove the truth of her assertions to her pupils.

Economy is usually confined to the management of money, but it may be shown on many other occasions: economy may be exercised in taking care of whatever belongs to us; children should have the care of their own clothes, and if they are negligent of what is in their charge, this negligence should not be repaired by servants or friends, they should feel the real natural consequences of their own neglect, but no other punishment should be inflicted; and they should be left to make their own reflections upon their errours and misfortunes, undisturbed by the reproaches of their friends, or by the prosing moral of a governess or preceptor. We recommend, for we must descend to these trifles, that girls should be supplied with an independent stock of all the little things which are in daily use; housewives, and pocket books well stored with useful implements; and there should be no lending [105] and borrowing amongst children. It will be but just to provide our pupils with convenient places for the preservation and arrangement of their little goods. Order is necessary to economy; and we cannot more certainly create a taste for order, than by showing early its advantages in practice as well as in theory. The aversion to *old* things, should, if possible, be prevented in children: we should not express contempt for *old* things, but we should treat them with increased reverence, and exult in their having arrived under our protection to such a creditable age. "I have had such a hat so long, therefore it does not signify what becomes of it!" is the speech of a *promising* little spendthrift. "I have taken care of my hat, it has lasted so long; and I hope I shall make it last longer," is the exultation of a young economist, in which his prudent friends should sympathize.

"Waste not, want not," is an excellent motto in an English nobleman's kitchen. [106] The most opulent parents ought not to be ashamed to adopt it in the economic education of their children: early habits of care, and an early aversion and contempt for the selfish spirit of wasteful extravagance, may preserve the fortunes, and, what is of far more importance, the integrity and peace of mind of noble families.

We have said, that economy cannot be exercised without children's having the management of money. Whilst our pupils are young, if they are educated at home, they cannot have much real occasion for money; all the necessaries of life are provided for them; and if they have money to spend, it must be probably laid out on superfluities. This is a bad beginning. Money should be represented to our pupils as what it really is, the conventional sign of the value of commodities: before children are acquainted with the real and comparative value of any of these commodities, it is surely imprudent to trust them with money. As to the idea that children may be charitable and generous in the disposal of money, we have expressed our sentiments fully upon this subject already. [107] We are, however, sensible that when children are sent to any school, it is advisable to supply them with pocket-money enough to put them upon an equal footing with their companions; otherwise, we might run the hazard of inducing worse faults than extravagance—meanness, or envy.

Young people who are educated at home should, as much as possible, be educated to take a family interest in all the domestic expenses. Parental reserve in money matters is extremely impolitic; as Mr. Locke judiciously observes, that a father, who wraps his affairs up in mystery, and who "views his son with jealous eyes," as a person who is to begin *to live* when he dies, *must* make him an enemy by treating him as such. A frank simplicity and cordial dependence upon the integrity and upon the sympathy of their children, will ensure to parents their disinterested friendship. Ignorance is always more to be dreaded than knowledge. Young people, who are absolutely ignorant of affairs, who have no idea of the relative expense of different modes of living, and of the various wants of a family, are apt to be extremely unreasonable in the imaginary disposal of their parent's fortune; they confine their view merely to their own expenses. "I *only* spend such a sum," they say, "and surely that is nothing to my father's income." They consider only the absolute amount of what they spend; they cannot compare it with the number of other expenses which are necessary for the rest of the family: they do not know these, therefore they cannot perceive the proportion which it is reasonable that their expenditure should bear to the whole. Mrs. D'Arblay, in one of her excellent novels, has given a striking picture of the ignorance in which young women sometimes leave their father's house, and begin to manage in life for themselves, without knowing any thing of the *powers* of money. Camilla's imprudence must chiefly be ascribed to her ignorance. Young women should be accustomed to keep the family accounts, and their arithmetic should not be merely a speculative science; they should learn the price of all necessaries, and of all luxuries; they should learn what luxuries are suited to their fortune and rank, what degree of expense in dress is essential to a regularly neat appearance, and what must be the increased expense and temptations of fashion in different situations; they should not be suffered to imagine that they can resist these temptations more than others, if they get into company above their rank, nor should they have any indistinct idea, that by some wonderful economical operations they can make a given sum of money go further than others can do. The steadiness of calculation will prevent all these vain notions; and young women, when they see in stubborn figures what must be the consequence of getting into situations where they must be tempted to exceed their means, will probably begin by avoiding, instead of braving, the danger.

Most parents think that their sons are more disposed to extravagance than their daughters; the sons are usually exposed to greater temptations. Young men excite one another to expense, and to a certain carelessness of economy, which assumes the name of spirit, while it often forfeits all pretensions to justice. A prudent father will never, from any false notions of forming his son early to *good* company, introduce him to associates whose only merit is their rank or their fortune. Such companions will lead a weak young man into every species of extravagance, and then desert and ridicule him in the hour of distress. If a young man has a taste for literature, and for rational society, his economy will be secured, simply because his pleasures will not be expensive, nor will they be dependent upon the caprice of fashionable associates. The intermediate state between that of a school-boy and a man, is the dangerous period in which taste for expense is often acquired, before the means of gratifying it are obtained. Boys listen with anxiety to the conversation of those who are a few years older than themselves. From this conversation they gather *information* respecting the ways of the world, which, though often erroneous, they tenaciously believe to be accurate: it is in vain that their older friends may assure them that such and such frivolous expenses are not necessary to the well-being of a man in society; they adhere to the opinion of the younger counsel; they conclude that every thing has changed since their parents were young, that they must not govern themselves by antiquated notions, but by the scheme of economy which happens to be the fashion of the day. During this boyish state, parents should be particularly attentive to the company which their sons keep; and they should frequently in conversation with sensible, but not with morose or old fashioned people, lead to the subject of economy, and openly discuss and settle the most essential points. At the same time a father should not intimidate his son with the idea that nothing but rigid economy can win his parental favour; his parental favour should not be a mercenary object; he should rather show his son, that he is aware of the great temptations to which a young man is exposed in going first into the world: he should show him, both that he is disposed to place confidence in him, and that he yet knows the fallibility of youthful prudence. If he expect from his son unerring prudence, he expects too much, and he will, perhaps, create an apprehension of his displeasure, which may chill and repress all ingenuous confidence. In all his childish, and in all his youthful distresses, a son should be habitually inclined to turn to his father as to his most indulgent friend. "Apply to me if ever you get into any difficulties, and you will always find me your *most indulgent friend*," were the words of a father to a child of twelve years old, pronounced with such encouraging benevolence, that they were never forgotten by the person to whom they were addressed.

Before a young man goes into the world, it will be a great advantage to him to have some share in the management of his father's affairs; by laying out money for another person, he will acquire habits of care, which will be useful to him afterwards in his own affairs. A father, who is building, or improving grounds, who is carrying on works of any sort, can easily allot some portion of the business to his son, as an exercise for his judgment and prudence. He should hear and see the estimates of workmen, and he should, as soon as he has collected the necessary facts, form estimates of his own, before he hears the calculation of others: this power of estimating will be of great advantage to gentlemen: it will circumscribe their wishes, and it will protect them against the low frauds of designing workmen.

It may seem trivial, but we cannot forbear to advise young people to read the news-papers of the day regularly: they will keep up by these means with the current of affairs, and they will exercise their judgment upon interesting business, and large objects. The sooner boys acquire the sort of knowledge necessary for the conversation of sensible men, the better; they will be the less exposed to feel false shame. False shame, the constant attendant upon ignorance, often leads young men into imprudent expenses; when, upon any occasion, they do not know by any certain calculation to what any expense may amount, they are ashamed to inquire minutely. From another sort of weakness, they are ashamed to resist the example or importunity of numbers; against this weakness, the strong desire of preserving the good opinion of estimable friends, is the best preservative. The taste for the esteem of superior characters, cures the mind of fondness for vulgar applause.

We have, in the very first chapter of this book, spoken of the danger of the passion for gaming, and the precautions that we have recommended in early education will, it is hoped, prevent the disorder from appearing in our pupils as they grow up. Occupations for the understanding, and objects for the affections, will preclude all desire for the violent stimulus of the gaming table. It may be said, that many men of superior abilities, and of generous social tempers, become gamesters. They do so, because they have exhausted other pleasures, and they have been accustomed to strong excitements. Such excitements do not become necessary to happiness, till they have been made habitual.

There was an excellent Essay on Projects, published some years ago by an anonymous writer, which we think would make a great impression upon any young persons of good sense. We do not wish to repress the generous enterprising ardour of youth, or to confine the ideas to the narrow circle of which self must be the centre. Calculation will show what can be done, and how it can be done; and thus the individual, without injury to himself, may, if he wish it, speculate extensively for the good of his fellow creatures.

It is scarcely possible, that the mean passion of avarice should exist in the mind of any young person who has been tolerably well educated; but too much pains cannot be taken to preserve that domestic felicity, which arises from entire confidence and satisfaction amongst the individuals of a family with regard to property. Exactness in accounts and in business relative to property, far from being unnecessary amongst friends and relations, are, we think, peculiarly agreeable, and essential to the continuance of frank intimacy. We should, whilst our pupils are young, teach them a love for exactness about property; a respect for the rights of others, rather than a tenacious anxiety about their own. When young people are of a proper age to manage money and property of their own, let them know precisely what they can annually spend; in whatever form they receive an income, let that income be certain: if presents of pocket money or of dress are from time to time made to them, this creates expectation and uncertainty in their minds. All persons who have a fluctuating revenue, are disposed to be imprudent and extravagant. It is remarkable, that the West-Indian planters, whose property is a kind of lottery, are extravagantly disposed to speculation; in the hopes of a favourable season, they live from year to year in unbounded profusion. It is curious to observe, that the propensity to extravagance exists in those who enjoy the greatest affluence, and in those who have felt the greatest distress. Those who have little to lose, are reckless about that little; and any uncertainty as to the tenure of property, or as to the rewards of industry, immediately operates, not only to depress activity, but to destroy prudence. "Prudence," says Mr. Edwards, "is a term that has no place in the negro vocabulary; instead of trusting to what are called the *ground provisions*, which are safe from the hurricanes, the negroes, in the cultivation of their *own* lands, trust more to plantain-groves, corn, and other vegetables that are liable to be destroyed by storms. When they earn a little money, they immediately gratify their palate with salted meats and other provisions, which are to them delicacies. The idea of accumulating, and of being economic in order to accumulate, is unknown to these poor slaves, who hold their lands by the most uncertain of all tenures," [108] We are told, that the *provision ground*, the creation of the negro's industry, and the hope of his life, is sold by public auction to pay his master's debts. Is it wonderful that the term prudence should be unknown in the negro vocabulary?

The very poorest class of people in London, who feel despair, and who merely live to bear the evil of the day, are, it is said, very little disposed to be prudent. In a late publication, Mr. Colquhoun's "Treatise on the Police of the Metropolis," he tells us, that the "chief consumption of oysters, crabs, lobsters, pickled salmon, &c. when first in season, and when the prices are high, is by the *lowest* classes of the people. The middle ranks, and those immediately under them, abstain generally from such indulgences until the prices are moderate." [109]

Perhaps it may be thought, that the consumption of oysters, crabs, and pickled salmon, in London, or the management of the negro's *provision ground* in Jamaica, has little to do with a practical essay upon economy and prudence; but we hope, that we may be permitted to use these far fetched illustrations, to show that the same causes act upon the mind independently of climate: they are mentioned here to show, that the little *revenue* of young people ought to be fixed and certain.

When we recommend economy and prudence to our pupils, we must, at the same time, keep their hearts open to the pleasures of generosity; economy and prudence will put it in the power of the generous to give.

> "The worth of everything
> Is as much money as 'twill bring,"

will never be the venal maxim of those who understand the nature of philosophic prudence. The worth of money is to be estimated by the number of real pleasures which it can procure: there are many which are not to be bought by gold; [110] these will never lose their pre-eminent value with persons who have been educated both to reason and to feel.

[96] Here lies the mutton eating king;
Whose promise none relied on;
Who never *said* a foolish thing,
And never did a wise one.
Epitaph on Charles 2d.

[97] V. Taste and Imagination.

[98] Darwin's Zoonomia.

[99] Chapter on Imagination.

[100] Charles VI.

[101] "No penance can absolve their guilty fame,
Nor tears, that wash out sin, can wash out shame."

[102] V. Persian Tales.

[103] V. Chapter on Temper.

[104] Mrs. Piozzi's English Synonymy, vol. i. p. 359.

[105] V. Toys.

[106] Lord Scarsdale's. Keddleston.

[107] V. Chapter on Sympathy and Sensibility.

[108] V. Edwards' History of the West Indies.

[109] V. a note in the Treatise on the Police of the Metropolis.

CHAPTER XXV
SUMMARY

"The general principle," that we should associate pleasure with whatever we wish that our pupils should pursue, and pain with whatever we wish that they should avoid, forms, our readers will perceive, the basis of our plan of education. This maxim, applied to the cultivation of the understanding, or of the affections, will, we apprehend, be equally successful; virtues, as well as abilities, or what is popularly called genius, we believe to be the result of education, not the gift of nature. A fond mother will tremble at the idea, that so much depends upon her own care in the early education of her children; but, even though she may be inexperienced in the art, she may be persuaded that patience and perseverance will ensure her success: even from her timidity we may prophesy favourably; for, in education, to know the danger, is often to avoid it. The first steps require rather caution and gentle kindness, than any difficult or laborious exertions: the female sex are, from their situation, their manners, and talents, peculiarly suited to the superintendence of the early years of childhood. We have, therefore, in the first chapters of the preceding work, endeavoured to adapt our remarks principally to female readers, and we shall think ourselves happy, if any anxious mother feels their practical utility.

In the chapters on Toys, Tasks, and Attention, we have attempted to show how the instruction and amusements of children may be so managed as to coincide with each other. *Play*, we have observed, is only a change of occupation; and toys, to be permanently agreeable to children, must afford them continued employment. We have declared war against *tasks*, or rather against the train of melancholy, which, associated with this word, usually render it odious to the ears of the disgusted scholar. By kind patience, and well timed, distinct, and above all, by short lessons, a young child may be initiated in the mysteries of learning, and in the first principles of knowledge, without fatigue, or punishment, or tears. No matter how little be learned in a given time, provided the pupil be not disgusted; provided the wish to improve be excited, and the habits of attention be acquired. Attention we consider as the faculty of the mind which is essential to the cultivation of all its other powers.

It is essential to success in what are called accomplishments, or talents, as well as to our progress in the laborious arts or abstract sciences. Believing so much to depend upon this faculty or habit, we have taken particular pains to explain the practical methods by which it may be improved. The general maxims, that the attention of young people should at first be exercised but for very short periods; that they should never be urged to the point of fatigue; that pleasure, especially the great pleasure of success, should be associated with the exertions of the pupil; are applicable to children of all tempers. The care which has been recommended, in the use of words, to convey uniformly distinct ideas, will, it is hoped, be found advantageous. We have, without entering into the speculative question concerning the original differences of temper and genius, offered such observations as we thought might be useful in cultivating the attention of vivacious, and indolent children; whether their idleness or indolence proceed from nature, or from mistaken modes of instruction, we have been anxious to point out means of curing their defects; and, from our successful experience with pupils apparently of opposite dispositions, we have ventured to assert with some confidence, that no parent should despair of correcting a child's defects; that no preceptor should despair of producing in his pupil the species of abilities which his education steadily tends to form. These are encouraging hopes, but not flattering promises. Having just opened these bright views to parents, we have paused to warn them, that all their expectations, all their cares, will be in vain, unless they have sufficient prudence and strength of mind to follow a certain mode of conduct with respect to servants, and with respect to common acquaintance. More failures in private education have been occasioned by the interference of servants and acquaintance, than from any other cause. It is impossible, we repeat it in the strongest terms, it is impossible that parents can be successful in the education of their children at home, unless they have steadiness enough to resist all interference from visiters and acquaintance, who from thoughtless kindness, or a busy desire to administer advice, are apt to counteract the views of a preceptor; and who often, in a few minutes, undo the work of years. When our pupils have formed their habits, and have reason and experience sufficient to guide them, let them be left as free as air; let them choose their friends and acquaintance; let them see the greatest variety of characters, and hear the greatest variety of conversation and opinions: but whilst they are children, whilst they are destitute of the means to judge, their parents or preceptors must supply their deficient reason; and authority, without violence, should direct them to their happiness. They must see, that all who are concerned in their education, agree in the means of governing them; in all their commands and prohibitions, in the distribution of praise and blame, of reward and punishment, there must be unanimity. Where there does not exist this unanimity in families; where parents have not sufficient firmness to prevent the interference of acquaintance, and sufficient prudence to keep children *from all private communication with servants*, we earnestly advise that the children be sent to some public seminary of education. We have taken some pains to detail the methods by which all hurtful communication between children and servants, in a well regulated family, may be avoided, and we have asserted, from the experience of above twenty years, that these methods have been found not only practicable, but easy.

In the chapters on Obedience, Temper and Truth, the general principle, that pleasure should excite to exertion and virtue, and that pain should be connected with whatever we wish our pupils to avoid, is applied to practice with a minuteness of detail which we knew not how to avoid. Obedience we have considered as a relative, rather than as a positive, virtue: before children are able to conduct themselves, their obedience must be rendered habitual: obedience alters its nature as the pupil becomes more and more rational; and the only method to secure the obedience, the willing, enlightened obedience of rational beings, is to convince them by experience, that it tends to their happiness. Truth depends upon example more than precept; and we have endeavoured to impress it on the minds of all who are concerned in education, that the first thing necessary to teach their pupils to love truth, is in their whole conduct to respect it themselves. We have reprobated the artifices sometimes used by preceptors towards their pupils; we have shown that all confidence is destroyed by these deceptions. May they never more be attempted! May parents unite in honest detestation of these practices! Children are not fools, and they are not to be governed like fools. Parents who adhere to the firm principle of truth, may be certain of the respect and confidence of their children. Children who never see the example of falsehood, will grow up with a simplicity of character, with an habitual love of truth, that must surprise preceptors who have seen the propensity to deceit which early appears in children who have had the misfortune to live with servants, or with persons who have the habits of meanness and cunning. We have advised, that children, before their habits are formed, should never be exposed to temptations to deceive; that no questions should be asked them which hazard their young integrity; that as they grow older, they should gradually be trusted; and that they should be placed in situations where they may feel the advantages both of speaking truth, and of obtaining a character for integrity. The perception of the utility of this virtue to the individual, and to society, will confirm the habitual reverence in which our pupils have been taught to hold it. As young people become reasonable, the nature of their habits and of their education should be explained to them, and their virtues, from being virtues of custom, should be rendered virtues of choice and reason. It is easier to confirm good habits by the conviction of the understanding, than to induce habits in consequence of that conviction. This principle we have pursued in the chapter on Rewards and Punishments; we have not considered punishment as vengeance or retaliation, but as *pain inflicted with the reasonable hope of procuring some future advantage to the delinquent, or to society.* The smallest possible quantity of pain that can effect this purpose, we suppose, must, with all just and humane persons, be the measure of punishment. This notion of punishment, both for the sake of the preceptor and the pupil, should be clearly explained as early as it can be made intelligible. As to rewards, we do not wish that they should be bribes; they should stimulate, without weakening the mind. The consequences which naturally follow every species of good conduct, are the proper and best rewards that we can devise; children whose understandings are cultivated, and whose tempers are not spoiled, will be easily made happy without the petty bribes which are administered daily to ill educated, ignorant, over stimulated, and, consequently, wretched and ill humoured children. Far from making childhood a state of continual penance, restraint, and misery, we wish that it should be made a state of uniform happiness; that parents and preceptors should treat their pupils with as much equality and kindness as the improving reason of children justifies. The views of children should be extended to their future advantage, [111] and they should consider childhood as a part of their existence, not as a certain number of years which must be passed over before they can enjoy any of the pleasures of life, before they can enjoy any of the privileges of *grown up people.* Preceptors should not accustom their pupils to what they call indulgence, but should give them the utmost degree of present pleasure which is consistent with their future advantage. Would it not be folly and cruelty to give present pleasure at the expense of a much larger portion of future pain? When children acquire experience and reason, they rejudge the conduct of those who have educated them; and their confidence and their gratitude will be in exact proportion to the wisdom and justice with which they have been governed.

It was necessary to explain at large these ideas of rewards and punishments, that we might clearly see our way in the progress of education. After having determined, that our object is to obtain for our pupils the greatest possible portion of felicity; after having observed, that no happiness can be enjoyed in society without the social virtues, without the *useful* and the *agreeable* qualities; our view naturally turns to the means of forming these virtues, of ensuring these essential qualities. On our sympathy with our fellow creatures depend many of our social virtues; from our ambition to excel our competitors, arise many of our most *useful* and *agreeable* actions.

We have considered these principles of action as they depend on each other, and as they are afterwards separated. Sympathy and sensibility, uninformed by reason, cannot be proper guides to action. We have endeavoured to show how sympathy may be improved into virtue. Children should not see the deformed expression of the malevolent passions in the countenance of those who live with them: before the habits are formed, before sympathy has any rule to guide itself, it is necessarily determined by example. Benevolence and affectionate kindness from parents to children, first inspire the pleasing emotions of love and gratitude. Sympathy is not able to contend with passion or appetite: we should therefore avoid placing children in painful competition with one another. We love those from whom we receive pleasure. To make children fond of each other, we must make them the cause of pleasure to each other; we must place them in situations where no passion or appetite crosses their natural sympathy. We have spoken of the difference between transient, convivial sympathy, and that higher species of sympathy which, connected with esteem, constitutes friendship. We have exhorted parents not to exhaust imprudently the sensibility of their children; not to lavish caresses upon their infancy, and cruelly to withdraw their kindness when their children have learned to expect the daily stimulus of affection. The idea of exercising sensibility we have endeavoured to explain, and to show, that if we require premature gratitude and generosity from young people, we shall only teach them affectation and hypocrisy. We have slightly touched on the dangers of excessive female sensibility, and have suggested, that useful, active employments, and the cultivation of the reasoning faculty, render sympathy and sensibility more respectable, and not less graceful.

In treating of vanity, pride, and ambition, we have been more indulgent to vanity than our *proud* readers will approve. We hope, however, not to be misunderstood; we hope that we shall not appear to be admirers of that mean and ridiculous foible, which is anxiously concealed by all who have any desire to obtain esteem. We cannot, however, avoid thinking it is a contradiction to inspire young people with a wish to excel, and at the same time to insist upon their repressing all expressions of satisfaction if they succeed. The desire to obtain the good opinion of others, is a strong motive to exertion: this desire cannot be discriminative in children before they have any knowledge of the comparative value of different qualities, and before they can estimate the consequent value of the applause of different individuals. We have endeavoured to show how, from appealing at first to the opinions of others, children may be led to form judgments of their own actions, and to appeal to their own minds for approbation. The sense of duty and independent self-complacency may gradually be substituted in the place of weak, ignorant vanity. There is not much danger that young people, whose understandings are improved, and who mix gradually with society, should not be able to repress those offensive expressions of vanity or pride, which are disagreeable to the feelings of the "impartial spectators." We should rather let the vanity of children find its own level, than attempt any artificial adjustments; they will learn propriety of manners from observation and experience; we should have patience with their early uncivilized presumption, lest we, by premature restraints, check the energy of the mind, and induce the cold, feeble vice of hypocrisy. In their own family, among the friends whom they ought to love and esteem, let children, with simple, unreserved vivacity, express the good opinion they have of themselves. It is infinitely better that they should be allowed this necessary expansion of self-complacency in the company of their superiors, than that it should be repressed by the cold hand of authority, and afterwards be displayed in the company of inferiors and sycophants. We have endeavoured to distinguish between the proper and improper use of praise as a motive in education: we have considered it as a stimulus which, like all other excitements, is serviceable or pernicious, according to the degree in which it is used, and the circumstances in which it is applied.

Whilst we have thus been examining the general means of educating the heart and the understanding, we have avoided entering minutely into the technical methods of obtaining certain parts of knowledge. It was essential, in the first place, to show, how the desire of knowledge was to be excited; what acquirements are most desirable, and how they are to be most easily obtained, are the next considerations. In the chapter on Books— Classical Literature and Grammar—Arithmetic and Geometry—Geography and Astronomy—Mechanics and Chemistry—we have attempted to show, how a taste for literature may early be infused into the minds of children, and how the rudiments of science, and some general principles of knowledge, may be acquired, without disgusting the pupil, or fatiguing him by unceasing application. We have, in speaking of the choice of books for children, suggested the general principles, by which a selection may be safely made; and by minute, but we hope not invidious, criticism, we have illustrated our principles so as to make them practically useful.

The examination of M. Condillac's Cours d'Etude was meant to illustrate our own sentiments, more than to attack a particular system. Far from intending to depreciate this author, we think most highly of his abilities; but we thought it necessary to point out some practical errours in his mode of instruction. Without examples from real life, we should have wandered, as many others of far superior abilities have already wandered, in the shadowy land of theory.

In our chapters on Grammar, Arithmetic, Mechanics, Chemistry, &c. all that we have attempted has been to recall to preceptors the difficulties which they once experienced, and to trace those early footsteps which time insensibly obliterates. How few possess, like Faruknaz in the Persian tale, the happy art of transfusing their own souls into the bosoms of others!

We shall not pity the reader whom we have dragged through Garretson's Exercises, if we can save one trembling little pilgrim from that "slough of despond." We hope that the patient, quiet mode of teaching classical literature, which we have found to succeed in a few instances, may be found equally successful in others; we are not conscious of having exaggerated, and we sincerely wish that some intelligent, benevolent parents may verify our experiments upon their own children.

The great difficulty which has been found in attempts to instruct children in science, has, we apprehend, arisen from the theoretic manner in which preceptors have proceeded. The knowledge that cannot be immediately applied to use, has no interest for children, has no hold upon their memories; they may learn the principles of mechanics, or geometry, or chemistry; but if they have no means of applying their knowledge, it is quickly forgotten, and nothing but the disgust connected with the recollection of useless labour remains in the pupil's mind. It has been our object, in treating of these subjects, to show how they may be made interesting to young people; and for this purpose we should point out to them, in the daily, active business of life, the practical use of scientific knowledge. Their senses should be exercised in experiments, and these experiments should be simple, distinct, and applicable to some object in which our pupils are immediately interested. We are not solicitous about the quantity of knowledge that is obtained at any given age, but we are extremely anxious that the desire to learn should continually increase, and that whatever is taught should be taught with that perspicuity, which improves the general understanding. If the first principles of science are once clearly understood, there is no danger that the pupil should not, at any subsequent period of his life, improve his practical skill, and increase his knowledge to whatever degree he thinks proper.

We have hitherto proceeded without discussing the comparative advantages of public or private education. Whether children are to be educated at home, or to be sent to public seminaries, the same course of education, during the first years of their lives, should be pursued; and the preparatory care of parents is essential to the success of the public preceptor. We have admitted the necessity of public schools, and, in the present state of society, we acknowledge that many parents have it not in their power properly to superintend the private education of a family. We have earnestly advised parents not to attempt private education without first calculating the difficulties of the undertaking; we have pointed out that, by co-operating with the public instructer, parents may assist in the formation of their children's characters, without undertaking the sole management of their classical instruction. A private education, upon a calm survey of the advantages of both systems, we prefer, because more is in the power of the private than of the public instructer. One uniform course of experience may be preserved, and no examples, but those which we wish to have followed, need be seen by those children who are brought up at home. When we give our opinion in favour of private education, we hope that all we have said on servants and on acquaintance will be full in the reader's recollection. No private education, we repeat it, can succeed without perfect unanimity, consistency, and steadiness, amongst all the individuals in the family.

We have recommended to parents the highest liberality as the highest prudence, in rewarding the care of enlightened preceptors. Ye great and opulent parents, condescend to make your children happy: provide for yourselves the cordial of domestic affection against "that sickness of long life—old age."

In what we have said of governesses, masters, and the value of female accomplishments, we have considered not only what is the fashion of to-day, but rather what is likely to be the fashion of ten or twenty years hence. Mothers will look back, and observe how much the system of female education has altered within their own memory; and they will see, with "the prophetic eye of taste," what may probably be the fashion of another spring— another race. [112] We have endeavoured to substitute the words *domestic happiness* instead of the present terms, "success in the world—fortunate establishments," &c. This will lead, perhaps, at first, to some confusion in the minds of those who have been long used to the old terms: but the new vocabulary has its advantages; the young and unprejudiced will, perhaps, perceive them, and maternal tenderness will calculate with more precision, but not with less eagerness, the chances of happiness according to the new and old tables of interest.

Sectary-metaphysicians, if any of this description should ever deign to open a book that has a *practical* title, will, we fear, be disappointed in our chapters on Memory—Imagination and Judgment. They will not find us the partisans of any system, and they will probably close the volume with supercilious contempt. We endeavour to console ourselves by the hope, that men of sense and candour will be more indulgent, and will view with more complacency an attempt to collect from all metaphysical writers, those observations, which can be immediately of practical use in education. Without any pompous pretensions, we have given a sketch of what we have been able to understand and ascertain of the history of the mind. On some subjects, the wisest of our readers will at least give us credit for knowing that we are ignorant.

We do not set that high value upon Memory, which some preceptors are inclined to do. From all that we have observed, we believe that few people are naturally deficient in this faculty; though in many it may have been so injudiciously cultivated as to induce the spectators to conclude, that there was some original defect in the retentive power. The recollective power is less cultivated than it ought to be, by the usual modes of education: and this is one reason why so few pupils rise above mediocrity. They lay up treasures for moths to corrupt; they acquire a quantity of knowledge, they learn a multitude of words by rote, and they cannot produce a single fact, or a single idea, in the moment when it is wanted: they collect, but they cannot combine. We have suggested the means of cultivating the inventive faculty at the same time that we store the memory; we have shown, that on the order in which ideas are presented to the mind, depends the order in which they will recur to the memory; and we have given examples from the histories of great men and little children, of the reciprocal assistance which the memory and the inventive powers afford each other.

In speaking of Taste, it has been our wish to avoid prejudice and affectation. We have advised that children should early be informed, that the principles of taste depend upon casual, arbitrary, variable associations. This will prevent our pupils from falling into the vulgar errour of being amazed and *scandalized* at the tastes of other times and other nations. The beauties of nature and the productions of art, which are found to be most generally pleasing, we should associate with pleasure in the mind: but we ought not to expect that children should admire those works of imagination which suggest, instead of expressing, ideas. Until children have acquired the language, until they have all the necessary trains of ideas, many of the finest strokes of genius in oratory, poetry, and painting, must to them be absolutely unintelligible.

In a moral point of view, we have treated of the false associations which have early influence upon the imagination, and produce the furious passions and miserable vices. The false associations which first inspire the young and innocent mind with the love of wealth, of power, or what is falsely called pleasure, are pointed out; and some practical hints are offered to parents, which it is hoped may tend to preserve their children from these moral insanities.

We do not think that persons who are much used to children, will quarrel with us for what we have said of early prodigies of wit. People, who merely talk to children for the amusement of the moment, may admire their "lively nonsense," and will probably think the simplicity of mind that we prefer, is downright stupidity. The habit of reasoning is seldom learned by children who are much taken notice of for their sprightly repartees; but we have observed that children, after they have learned to reason, as they grow up and become acquainted with the manners and customs of the world, are by no means deficient in talents for conversation, and in that species of wit which depends upon the perception of analogy between ideas, rather than a play upon words. At all events, we would rather that our pupils should be without the brilliancy of wit, than the solid and essential power of judgment.

To cultivate the judgment of children, we must begin by teaching them accurately to examine and compare such external objects as are immediately obvious to their senses; when they begin to argue, we must be careful to make them explain their terms and abide by them. In books and conversation, they must avoid all bad reasoning, nor should they ever be encouraged in the quibbling habit of arguing for victory.

Prudence we consider as compounded of judgment and resolution. When we teach children to reflect upon and compare their own feelings, when we frequently give them their *choice* in things that are interesting to them, we educate them to be prudent. We cannot teach this virtue until children have had some experience; as far as their experience goes, their prudence may be exercised. Those who reflect upon their own feelings, and find out exactly what it is that makes them happy, are taught wisdom by a very few distinct lessons. Even fools, it is said, grow wise by experience, but it is not until they grow old under her rigid discipline.

Economy is usually understood to mean prudence in the management of money; we have used this word in a more enlarged sense. Children, we have observed, may be economic of any thing that is trusted to their charge; until they have some use for money, they need not be troubled or tempted with it: if all the necessaries and conveniences of life are provided for them, they must spend whatever is given to them as pocket money, in superfluities. This habituates them early to extravagance. We do not apprehend that young people should be entrusted with money, till they have been some time used to manage the money business of others. They may be taught to keep the accounts of a family, from which they will learn the price and value of different commodities. All this, our readers will perceive, is nothing more than the application of the different reasoning powers to different objects.

We have thus slightly given a summary of the chapters in the preceding work, to recall the whole in a connected view to the mind; a few simple principles run through the different parts; all the purposes of practical education tend to one distinct object; to render our pupils good and wise, that they may enjoy the greatest possible share of happiness at present and in future.

Parental care and anxiety, the hours devoted to the instruction of a family, will not be thrown away; if parents have the patience to wait for their reward, that reward will far surpass their most sanguine expectations: they will find in their children agreeable companions, sincere and affectionate friends. Whether they live in retirement, or in the busy world, they will feel their interest in life increase, their pleasures multiplied by sympathy with their beloved pupils; they will have a happy home. How much is comprised in that single expression! The gratitude of their pupils will continually recall to their minds the delightful reflection, that the felicity of their whole family is their work; that the virtues and talents of their children are the necessary consequences of good education.

> [110] "Turn from the glittering bribe your scornful eye,
> Nor sell for gold what gold can never buy."
> *Johnson's London.*

> [111] Emilius.

> [112] "Another spring, another race supplies." Pope's
> Homer.

NOTES,

CONTAINING CONVERSATIONS AND ANECDOTES OF CHILDREN

Several years ago a mother, [113] who had a large family to educate, and who had turned her attention with much solicitude to the subject of education, resolved to write notes from day to day of all the trifling things which mark the progress of the mind in childhood. She was of opinion, that the art of education should be considered as an experimental science, and that many authors of great abilities had mistaken their road by following theory instead of practice. The title of *"Practical Education"* was chosen by this lady, and prefixed to a little book for children, which she began, but did not live to finish. The few notes which remain of her writing, are preserved, not merely out of respect to her memory, but because it is thought that they may be useful. Her plan of keeping a register of the remarks of children, has at intervals been pursued in her family; a number of these anecdotes have been interspersed in this work; a few, which did not seem immediately to suit the didactic nature of any of our chapters, remain, and with much hesitation and diffidence are offered to the public. We have selected such anecdotes as may in some measure illustrate the principles that we have endeavoured to establish; and we hope, that from these trifling, but genuine conversations of children and parents, the reader will distinctly perceive the difference, between practical and theoretic education. As some further apology for offering them to the public, we recur to a passage in Dr. Reid's [114] Essays, which encourages an attempt to study minutely the minds of children.

"If we could obtain a distinct and full history of all that hath passed in the mind of a child from the beginning of life and sensation till it grows up to the use of reason, how its infant faculties began to work, and how they brought forth and ripened all the various notions, opinions, and sentiments, which we find in ourselves when we come to be capable of reflection, this would be a treasure of natural history which would probably give more light into the human faculties, than all the systems of philosophers about them, from the beginning of the world."

The reader, we hope, will not imagine that we think we can present him with this treasure of natural history; we have only a few scattered notices, as Bacon would call them, to offer; perhaps, even this slight attempt may awaken the attention of persons equal to the undertaking: if able preceptors and parents would pursue a similar plan, we might, in time, hope to obtain a full history of the infant mind.

It may occur to parents, that writing notes of the remarks of children would lessen their freedom and simplicity in conversation; this would certainly be the case if care were not taken to prevent the pupils from thinking of the *note-book*. [115] The following notes were never seen by the children who are mentioned in them, and though it was in general known in the family that such notes were taken, the particular remarks that were written down, were never known to the pupils: nor was any curiosity excited upon this subject. The attempt would have been immediately abandoned, if we had perceived that it produced any bad consequences. The simple language of childhood has been preserved without alteration in the following notes; and as we could not devise any better arrangement, we have followed the order of time, and we have constantly inserted the ages of the children, for the satisfaction of preceptors and parents, to whom alone these infantine anecdotes can be interesting: We say nothing farther as to their accuracy; if the reader does not see in the anecdotes themselves internal marks of veracity, all we could say would be of no avail.

X— — (a girl of five years old) asked why a piece of paper fell quickly to the ground when rumpled up, and why so slowly when opened.

Y— — (a girl of three years and a half old) seeing her sister taken care of and nursed when she had chilblains, said, that she wished to have chilblains.

Z— — (a girl between two and three) when her mother was putting on her bonnet, and when she was going out to walk, looked at the cat, and said with a plaintive voice, "Poor pussey! you have no bonnet, Pussey!"

X— — (5 years old) asked why she was as tall as the trees when she was far from them.

Z— — (4 years old) went to church, and when she was there said, "Do those men do every thing better than we, because they talk so loud, and I think they read."

It was a country church, and people sang; but the child said, "She thought they didn't sing, but roared, because they were shut up in that place, and didn't like it."

L—— (a boy between 3 and 4 years) was standing before a grate with coals in it, which were not lighted; his mother said to him, "What is the use of coals?"

L——. "To put in your grate."

Mother. "Why are they put there?"

L——. "To make fire."

Mother. "How do they make fire?"

L——. "Fire is brought to them."

Mother. "How is fire brought to them?"

L——. "Fire is brought to them upon a candle and put to them."

L——, a little while afterwards, asked leave to light a candle, and when a bit of paper was given to him for that purpose, said, "But, mother, may I take some light out of your fire to put to it?"

This boy had more exact ideas of property than Prometheus had.

Z——, when she was between five and six, said, "Water keeps things alive, and eating keeps alive children."

Z—— (same age) meddling with a fly, said, "she did not hurt it." "Were you ever a fly?" said her mother. "Not *that I know of,*" answered the child.

Z——'s father sent her into a room where there were some knives and forks. "If you meddle with them," said he, "you may cut yourself."

Z——. "I won't cut myself."

Father. "Can you be sure of that?"

Z——. "No, but I can take care."

Father. "But if you should cut yourself, would it do you any good?"

Z——. "No—Yes."

Father. "What good?"

Z——. "Not to do so another time."

—— (same age.) Z——'s mother said to her, "Will you give me some of your fat cheeks?"

Z——. "No, I cannot, it would hurt me."

Mother. "But if it would not hurt you, would you give me some?"

Z——. "No, it would make two holes in my cheeks that would be disagreeable."

A sentimental mother would, perhaps, have been displeased with the simple answers of this little girl. (Vide Sympathy and Sensibility.)

The following memorandums of Mrs. H——E——'s (dated 1779) have been of great use to us in our chapter upon Toys.

"The playthings of children should be calculated to fix their attention, that they may not get a habit of doing any thing in a listless manner.

"There are periods as long as two or three months at a time, in the lives of young children, when their bodies appear remarkably active and vigorous, and their minds dull and inanimate; they are at these times incapable of comprehending any new ideas, and forgetful of those they have already received. When this disposition to exert the bodily faculties, subsides, children show much restlessness and distaste for their usual plays. The intervals between meals, appear long to them; they ask a multitude of questions, and are continually looking forward to some future good; if at this time any mental employment be presented to them, they receive it with the utmost avidity, and pursue it with assiduity; their minds appear to have acquired additional powers from having remained inactive for a considerable time."

(January 1781.) Z——, (7 years old.) "What are bones made of? My father says it has not been found out. If I should find it out, I shall be wiser in that respect than my father."

(April 8th.) Z——. "What becomes of the blood when people die?"

Father. "It stays in the body."

Z——. "I thought it went out of the body; because you told me, that what we eat was turned into blood, and that blood nourished the body and kept it alive."

Father. "Yes, my dear; but blood must be in motion to keep the body alive; the heart moves the blood through the arteries and veins, and the blood comes back again to the heart. We don't know how this motion is performed. What we eat, is not turned at once into blood; it is dissolved by something in the stomach, and is turned into something white like milk, which is called chyle; the chyle passes through little pipes in the body, called lacteals, and into the veins and arteries, and becomes blood. But I don't know how. I will show you the inside of the body of a dead pig: a pig's inside is something like that of a man."

Z—— (same age) when her father had given her an account of a large stone that was thrown to a considerable distance from Mount Vesuvius at the time of an eruption, she asked, how the air could keep a large stone from falling, when it would not support her weight.

Z——, (same age) when she was reading the Roman history, was asked, what she thought of the conduct of the wife of Asdrubal. Z—— said she did not like her. She was asked why. The first reason Z—— gave for not liking the lady, was, "that she spoke loud;" the next, "that she was unkind to her husband, and killed her children."

We regret (though perhaps our readers may rejoice) that several years elapsed in which these little notes of the remarks of children were discontinued. In 1792 the following notes were begun by one of the same family.

(March, '92.) Mr. —— saw an Irish giant at Bristol, and when he came home, Mr. —— gave his children a description of the giant. His height, he said, was about eight feet. S—— (a boy of five years old) asked whether this giant had lived much longer than other men.

Father. "No; why did you think he had lived longer than other men?"

S——. "Because he was so much taller."

Father. "Well."

S——. "And he had so much more time to grow."

Father. "People, after a certain age, do not grow any more. Your sister M——, and I, and your mother, have not grown any taller since you can remember, have we?"

S——. "No; but I have, and B——, and C——."

Father. "Yes; you are children. Whilst people are growing, they are children; after they have done growing they are called men and women."

(April, '92.) At tea-time, to-day, somebody said that hot chocolate scalds worse than hot tea or hot water. Mr. —— asked his children if they could give any reason for this. They were silent.

Mr. ——. "If water be made as hot as it can be made, and if chocolate be made as hot as it can be made, the chocolate will scald you the most. Can you tell me why!"

C—— (a girl between eight and nine years old.) "Because there is oil, I believe, in the chocolate; and because it is thicker, and the parts closer together, than in tea or water."

Father. "What you say is true; but you have not explained the reason yet. Well, *H——*."

H—— (a boy between nine and ten.) "Because there is water in the bubbles."

Father. "Water in the bubbles? I don't understand. Water in what bubbles?"

H——. "I thought I had always seen, when water boils, that there are a great many little bubbles upon the top."

Father. "Well; but what has that to do with the question I asked you?"

H——. "Because the cold air that was in the bubbles, would cool the water next them, and then"—(he was quite confused, and stopped.)

B—— (a girl of ten or eleven years old) spoke next. "I thought that chocolate was much thicker than water, and there were more parts, and those parts were closer together, and each could hold but a certain quantity of heat; and therefore chocolate could be made hotter than water."

Father. "That is a good chemical idea. You suppose that the chocolate and tea can be *saturated* with heat. But you have none of you yet told the reason."

The children were all silent.

Father. "Can water ever be made hotter than boiling hot?"

B——. "No."

Father. "Why?"

B——. "I don't know."

Father. "What happens to water when it does what we call *boil*?"

H——. "It bubbles, and makes a sort of noise."

B——. "It turns into steam or vapour, I believe."

Father. "All at once?"

B——. "No: but what is at the top, first."

Father. "Now you see the reason why water can't be made hotter than boiling hot: for if a certain degree of heat be applied to it, it changes into the form of vapour, and flies off. When I was a little boy, I was once near having a dreadful accident. I had not been taught the nature of water, and steam, and heat, and evaporation; and I wanted to fill a wet hollow stick with melted lead. The moment I poured the lead into the stick, the water in the wood turned into vapour suddenly, and the lead was thrown up with great violence to the ceiling: my face narrowly escaped. So you see people should know what they are about before they meddle with things.—But now as to the chocolate."

No one seemed to have any thing to say about the chocolate.

Father. "Water, you know, boils with a certain degree of heat. Will oil, do you think, boil with the same heat?"

C——. "I don't understand."

Father. "In the same *degree of heat* (you must learn to accustom yourself to those words, though they seem difficult to you)—In the same heat, do you think water or oil would boil the soonest?"

None of the children knew.

Father. "Water would boil the soonest. More heat is necessary to make oil boil, or turn into vapour, than to make water evaporate. Do you know of any thing which is used to *determine*, to *show*, and *mark*, to us the different degrees of heat?"

B——. "Yes; a thermometer."

Father. "Yes: thermometer comes from two Greek words, one of which signifies heat, and the other measure. Meter, means measure. Thermo*meter* a measurer of heat; baro*meter*, a measurer of the weight of the air; hygro*meter*, a measurer of moisture. Now, if you remember, on the thermo*meter* you have seen these words at a certain mark, *the heat of boiling water*. The quicksilver, in a thermometer, rises to that mark when it is exposed to that degree of heat which will make the water turn into vapour. Now the degree of heat which is necessary to make oil evaporate, is not marked on the thermometer; but it requires several degrees more heat to evaporate oil, than is necessary to evaporate water.—So now you know that chocolate, containing more oil than is contained in tea, it can be made hotter before it turns into vapour."

Children may be led to acquire a taste for chemistry by slight hints in conversation.

(July 22d, 1794.) *Father.* "S——, can you tell me what is meant by a body's falling?"

S—— (seven years old.) "A body's falling, means a body's dying, I believe."

Father. "By *body*, I don't mean a person, but any thing. What is meant by any thing's falling?"

S——. "Coming down from a high place."

Father. "What do you mean by a high place?"

S——. "A place higher than places usually are; higher than the ground."

Father. "What do you mean by the ground?"

S——. "The earth."

Father. "What shape do you think the earth is?"

S——. "Round."

Father. "Why do you think it is round?"

S——. "Because I have heard a great many people say so."

Father. "The shadow.—It is so difficult to explain to you, my dear, why we think that the earth is round, that I will not attempt it *yet.*"

It is better, as we have often observed, to avoid all *imperfect* explanations, which give children confused ideas.

(August 18th, 1794.) Master —— came to see us, and taught S—— to fish for minnows. It was explained to S——, that fishing with worms for baits, tortures the worms. No other argument was used, no sentimental exclamations made upon the occasion; and S—— fished no more, nor did he ever mention the subject again.

Children sometimes appear cruel, when in fact they do not know that they give pain to animals.

(July 27th, 1794.) S—— saw a beautiful rainbow, and he said, "I wish I could walk over that fine arch."

This is one of the pleasures of Ariel, and of the Sylphs in the Rape of the Lock. S—— was not praised for a poetic wish, lest he should have learnt affectation.

(September 3d, 1794.) Mr. —— attempted to explain to B——, H——, S——, and C——, the nature of insurance, and the day afterwards he asked them to explain it to him. They none of them understood it, except B——, who could not, however, explain it, though she did understand it. The terms were all new to them, and they had no ships to insure.

(September 19th.) At dinner to-day, S—— (seven years old) said to his sister C——, "What is the name of that man that my father was talking to, that sounded like Idem, Isdal, or Izard, I believe." "Izard!" said somebody at table, "that name sounds like Lizard; yes, there is a family of the Lizards in the Guardian."

S——. "A real family?"

Mr. ——. "No, my dear: a name given to supposed characters."

M——. "Wasn't it one of the young Lizards who would prove to his mother, when she had just scalded her fingers with boiling water out of the tea-kittle, that there's no more heat in fire that heats you, than pain in the stick that beats you!"

Mr. ——. "Yes; I think that character has done harm; it has thrown a ridicule upon metaphysical disquisitions."

Mrs.——. "Are not those lines about the pain in the stick in the 'Letter [116] to my Sisters at Crux Easton,' in Dodsley's poems?"

Mr. ——. "Yes; but they come originally from Hudibras, you know."

In slight conversations, such as these, which are not contrived for the purpose, the curiosity of children is awakened to literature; they see the use which people make of what they read, and they learn to talk freely about what they meet with in books. What a variety of thoughts came in a few instants from S——'s question about *Idem!*

(November 8th, 1795.) Mr. —— read the first chapter of Hugh Trevor to us; which contains the history of a passionate farmer, who was in a rage with a goose because it would not eat some oats which he offered it. He tore off the wings of the animal, and twisted off its neck; he bit off the ear of a pig, because it squealed when he was ringing it; he ran at his apprentice Hugh Trevor with a pitch-fork, because he suspected that he had drank some milk; the pitch-fork stuck in a door. Hugh Trevor then told the passionate farmer, that the dog Jowler had drank the milk, but that he would not tell this before, because he knew his master would have hanged the dog.

S—— admired Hugh Trevor for this extremely.

The farmer in his lucid intervals is extremely penitent, but his fit of rage seizes him again one morning when he sees some milk boiling over. He flies at Hugh Trevor, and stabs him with a clasp knife, with which he had been cutting bread and cheese; the knife is stopped by half a crown which Hugh Trevor had sewed in his waistcoat; *this half crown he had found on the highway a few days before.*

It was doubted by Miss M. S——, whether this last was a proper circumstance to be told to children, because it might lead them to be dishonest.

The evening after Mr. —— had read the story, he asked S—— to repeat it to him. S—— remembered it, and told it distinctly till he came to the half crown; at this circumstance he hesitated. He said he did not know how Hugh Trevor *"came to keep it,"* though he had found it. He wondered that Hugh Trevor did not ask about it.

Mr. — — explained to him, that when a person finds any thing upon the highway, he should put it in the hand of the public crier, who should *cry it*. Mr. — — was not quite certain whether the property found on the high road, after it has been *cried* and no owner appears, belongs to the king, or to the person who finds it. Blackstone's Commentaries were consulted; the passage concerning *Treasuretrove* was read to S— —; it is written in such distinct language, that he understood it completely.

Young people may acquire much knowledge by consulting books, at the moment that any interest is excited by conversation upon particular subjects.

Explanations about the *law* were detailed to S— —, because he was intended for a lawyer. In conversation we may direct the attention of children to what are to be their professional studies, and we may associate entertainment and pleasure with the idea of their future profession.

The story of the passionate farmer in Hugh Trevor was thought to be a good lesson for children of vivacious tempers, as it shows to what crimes excess of passion may transport. This man appears an object of compassion; all the children felt a mixture of pity and abhorrence when they heard the history of his disease.

(November 23d, 1795.) This morning at breakfast Miss — — observed, that the inside of the cream cover, which was made of black Wedgwood's ware, looked brown and speckled, as if the glazing had been worn away; she asked whether this was caused by the cream. One of the company immediately exclaimed, "Oh! I've heard that Wedgwood's ware won't hold oil." Mr. — — observed, that it would be best to try the experiment, instead of resting content with this hearsay evidence; he asked H— — and S— — what would be the best method of trying the experiment exactly.

S— — proposed to pour oil into a vessel of Wedgwood's ware, and to measure the depth of the oil when first put in; to leave the oil in the vessel for some time, and then to measure again the depth of the oil.

H— — said, "I would weigh the Wedgwood's ware vessel; then pour oil into it, and weigh *it* (them) again; then I would leave the oil in the vessel for some time, and afterwards I would pour out the oil, and would weigh the vessel to see if it had gained any weight; and then weigh the oil to find out whether it had lost any weight since it was put into the vessel." H— —'s scheme was approved.

A black Wedgwood's ware salt-cellar was weighed in accurate scales; it weighed 1196 grains; 110 grains of oil were poured into it; total weight of the salt-cellar and oil, 1306 grs. Six months afterwards, the salt-cellar was produced to the children, who were astonished to see that the oil had disappeared. The lady, who had first asserted that Wedgwood's ware would not hold oil, was inclined to believe that the oil had oozed through the pores of the salt-cellar; but the little spectators thought it was more probable that the oil might have been accidentally spilled; the salt-cellar weighed as before 1196 grains.

The experiment was repeated, and this time it was resolved to lock up the salt-cellar, that it might not again be thrown down.

(April 14th, 1796.) Into the same salt-cellar 100 grains weight of oil was poured (total weight 1296 grains.) The salt-cellar was put on a saucer, and covered with a glass tumbler. (June 3d, 1796.) Mr. — — weighed the salt-cellar, and found that with the oil it weighed precisely the same as before, 1296 grains; without the oil, 1196 grains, its original weight: therefore it was clear that the Wedgwood's ware had neither imbibed the oil, nor let it pass through its pores.

This little experiment has not been thus minutely told for philosophers, but for children; however trivial the subject, it is useful to teach children early to try experiments. Even the weighing and calculating in this experiment, amused them, and gave some ideas of the exactness necessary to prove any fact.

(Dec. 1st, 1795.) S— — (8 years old) in reading Gay's fable of "the painter who pleased every body and nobody," was delighted to hear that the painter put his pallet upon his thumb, because S— — had seen a little pallet of his sister A— —'s, which she used to put on her thumb. S— — had been much amused by this, and he was very fond of this sister, who had been absent for some time. Association makes slight circumstances agreeable to children; if we do not know these associations, we are surprised at their expressions of delight. It is useful to trace them. (Vide Chap. on Imagination.)

S— — seemed puzzled when he read that the painter "dipped his pencil, talked of *Greece*." "Why did he talk of Greece?" said S— — with a look of astonishment. Upon inquiry, it was found that S— — mistook the word *Greece* for *Grease!*

It was explained to him, that Grecian statues and Grecian figures are generally thought to be particularly graceful and well executed; that, therefore, painters attend to them.

(Dec. 1st, 1795.) After dinner to-day, S— — was looking at a little black toothpick-case of his father's; his father asked him if he knew what it was made of.

The children guessed different things; wood, horn, bone, paper, pasteboard, glue.

Mr. — —. "Instead of examining the toothpick-case, S— —, you hold it in your hand, and turn your eyes away from it, that you may think the better. Now, when I want to find out any thing about a particular object, I keep my eye fixed upon it. Observe the texture of that toothpick-case, if you want to know the materials of which it is made; look at the edges, feel it."

S— —. "May I smell it?"

Mr. — —. "Oh yes. You may use all your senses."

S— — (feeling the toothpick-case, smelling it, and looking closely at it.) "It is black, and smooth, and strong and light. What is, let me see, both strong and light, and it will bend—parchment."

Mr. — —. "That is a good guess; but you are not quite right yet. What is parchment? I think by your look that you don't know."

S— —. "Is it not paper pasted together?"

Mr. — —. "No; I thought you mistook pasteboard for parchment."

S— —. "Is parchment skin?"

Mr. — —. "Of what?"

S— —. "Animals."

Mr. — —. "What animal?"

S— —. "I don't know."

Mr. — —. "Parchment is the skin of sheep."

"But S— —, don't keep the toothpick-case in your hand, push it round the table to your neighbours, that every body may look again before they guess. I think, for certain reasons of my own, that H— — will guess right."

H— —. "Oh I know what it is now!"

H— — had lately made a pump, the piston of which was made of leather; the leather had been wetted, and then forced through a mould of the proper size. H— — recollected this, as Mr. — — thought he would, and guessed that the case might have been made of leather, and by a similar process.

S— —. "Is it made of the skin of some animal?"

Mr. — —. "Yes; but what do you mean by the skin of some animal? What do you call it?"

S—— (laughing.) "Oh, leather! leather!"

H——. "Yes, it's made the same way that the piston of my pump is made, I suppose."

M——. "Could not shoes be made in the same manner in a mould?"

Mr. ——. "Yes; but there would be one disadvantage; the shoes would lose their shape as soon as they were wet; and the sole and upper leather must be nearly of the same thickness."

S——. "Is the tookpick-case made out of any particular kind of leather? I wish I could make one!"

M——. "You have a bit of green leather, will you give it to me? I'll punch it out like *H*'s piston; but I don't exactly know how the toothpick-case was made into the right shape."

Mr. ——. "It was made in the same manner in which silver pencil-cases and thimbles are made. If you take a thin piece of silver, or of any ductile material, and lay it over a concave mould, you can readily imagine that you can make the thin, ductile material take the shape of any mould into which you put it; and you may go on forcing it into moulds of different depths, till at last the plate of silver will have been shaped into a cylindrical form; a thimble, a pencil-case, a toothpick-case, or any similar figure."

We have observed (V. Mechanics) that children should have some general idea of mechanics before they go into the large manufactories; this can be given to them from time to time in conversation, when little circumstances occur, which *naturally* lead to the subject.

(November 30th, 1795.) *S——* said he liked the beginning of Gay's fable of "The man and the flea," very much, but he could not tell what was meant by the crab's crawling beside the *coral grove,* and hearing the ocean roll *above.* "The ocean cannot roll *above,* can it mother?"

Mother. "Yes, when the animal is crawling below he hears the water rolling above him."

M——. "Coral groves mean the branches of coral which look like trees; you saw some at Bristol in Mr. B——'s collection."

The difficulty *S——* found in understanding "coral groves," confirms what has been observed, that children should never read poetry without its being thoroughly explained to them. (Vide Chapter on Books.)

(January 10th, 1795.) *S——* (8 years old) said that he had been thinking about the wind; and he believed that it was the earth's turning round that made the wind.

M——. "Then how comes it that the wind does not blow always the same way?"

S——. "Aye, that's the thing I can't make out; besides, perhaps the air would stick to the earth as it turns round, as threads stick to my spinning top, and go round with it."

(January 4th, 1795.) As we were talking of the king of Poland's little dwarf, S—— recollected by contrast the Irish giant whom he had seen at Bristol. "I liked the Irish giant very much, because," said S——, "though he was so large, he was not surly; and when my father asked him to take out his shoe-buckle to try whether it would cover my foot, he did not seem in a hurry to do it. I suppose he did not wish to show how little I was."

Children are nice observers of that kind of politeness which arises from good nature; they may hence learn what really pleases in manners, without being taught grimace.

Dwarfs and giants led us to Gulliver's Travels. S—— had never read them, but one of the company now gave him some general account of Lilliput and Brobdignag. He thought the account of the little people more entertaining than that of the large ones; the carriage of Gulliver's hat by a team of Lilliputian horses, diverted him; but, when he was told that the queen of Brobdignag's dwarf stuck Gulliver one day at dinner into a marrow bone, S—— looked grave, and seemed rather shocked than amused; he said, "It must have almost suffocated poor Gulliver, and must have spoiled his clothes." S—— wondered of what cloth they could make him new clothes, because the cloth in Brobdignag must have been too thick, and as thick as a board. He also wished to know what sort of glass was used to glaze the windows in Gulliver's wooden house; "because," said he, "their common glass must have been so thick that it would not have been transparent to Gulliver." He thought that Gulliver must have been extremely afraid of setting his small wooden house on fire.

M——. "Why more afraid than we are? His house was as large for Gulliver as our house is for us."

S——. "Yes, but what makes the fire must have been *so much* larger! One cinder, one spark of theirs would have filled his little grate. And how did he do to read their books?"

S—— was told that Gulliver stood at the topmost line of the page, and ran along as fast as he read, till he got to the bottom of the page. It was suggested, that Gulliver might have used a diminishing glass. S—— immediately exclaimed, "How entertaining it must have been to him to look through their telescopes." An instance of invention arising from *contrast*.

If the conversation had not here been interrupted, S— — would probably have invented a greater variety of pleasures and difficulties for Gulliver; his eagerness to read Gulliver's Travels, was increased by this conversation. We should let children exercise their invention upon all subjects, and not tell them the whole of every thing, and all the ingenious parts of a story. Sometimes they invent these, and are then interested to see how the *real* author has managed them. Thus children's love for literature may be increased, and the activity of their minds may be exercised. "Le secret d'ennuyer," says an author [117] who never tires us, "Le secret d'ennuyer est celui de tout dire." This may be applied to the art of education. (V. Attention, Memory, and Invention.)

(January 17th, 1796.) S— —. "I don't understand about the tides."

H— — (13 years old.) "The moon, when it comes near the earth, draws up the sea by the middle; attracts it, and as the middle rises, the water runs down from that again into the channels of rivers."

S— —. "But—Hum!—the moon attracts the sea; but why does not the sun attract it by the middle as well as the moon? How can you be sure that it is the moon that does it?"

Mr. — —. "We are not sure that the moon is the cause of tides."

We should never force any system upon the belief of children; but wait till they can understand all the arguments on each side of the question.

(January 18th, 1796.) S— — (9 years old.) "Father, I have thought of a reason for the wind's blowing.

When there has been a hot sunshiny day, and when the ground has been wet, the sun attracts a great deal of vapour: then *that* vapour must have room, so it must push away some air to make room for itself; besides, vapour swells with heat, so it must have a *great, great* deal of room as it grows hotter, and hotter; and the moving the air to make way for it, must make wind."

It is probable, that if children are not early taught by rote words which they cannot understand, they will *think* for themselves; and, however strange their incipient theories may appear, there is hope for the improvement of children as long as their minds are active.

(February 13th, 1796.) S— —. "How do physicians try new medicines? If they are not sure they will succeed, they may be hanged for murder, mayn't they? It is cruel to try *them* (*them* meant medicines) on animals; besides, all animals are not the same as men. A pig's inside is the most like that of a man. I remember my father showed us the inside of a pig once."

Some time afterwards, S—— inquired what was meant by the circulation of the blood. "How are we sure that it does move? You told me that it doesn't move after we die, then nobody can have seen it really moving in the veins; that beating that I feel in my pulse does not feel like any thing running backwards and forwards; it beats up and down."

The lady to whom S—— addressed these questions and observations, unfortunately could not give him any information upon this subject, but she had at least the prudence, or honesty, to tell the boy that "she did not know any thing about the matter."

S—— should have been shown the circulation of the blood in fishes: which he might have seen by a microscope.

Children's minds turn to such inquiries; surely, if they are intended for physicians, these are the moments to give them a taste for their future profession, by associating pleasure with instruction, and connecting with the eagerness of curiosity the hope of making discoveries; a hope which all vivacious young people strongly feel.

(February 16th.) S—— objected to that fable of Phædrus in which it is said, that a boy threw a stone at Æsop, and that Æsop told the boy to throw a stone at another passenger, pointing to a rich man. The boy did as Æsop desired, and the rich man had the boy hanged.

S—— said, that he thought that Æsop should have been hanged, because Æsop was the cause of the boy's fault.

How little suited *political* fables are to children. This fable, which was meant to show, we suppose, that the *rich* could not, like the poor, be insulted with impunity, was quite unintelligible to a boy (nine years old) of *simple* understanding.

(July 19th, 1796.) Amongst *"Vulgar errours,"* Sir Thomas Browne might have mentioned the common notion, that if you take a hen and hold her head down to the ground, and draw a circle of chalk round her, she will be enchanted by this magical operation so that she cannot stir. We determined to try the experiment, for which Dr. Johnson would have laughed at us, as he laughed at Browne [118] for trying *"the hopeless experiment"* about the magnetic dials.

A hen's head was held down upon a stone flag, and a chalk line was drawn before her; she did not move. The same hen was put into a circle of chalk that had been previously drawn for her reception; her head was held down according to the letter of the charm, and she did not move; line or circle apparently operated alike. It was suggested (by A——) that perhaps the hen was frightened by her head's being held down to the ground, and that the chalk line and circle had nothing to do with the business. The hen was carried out of sight of the magic line and circle, her head was held down to the ground as before; and when the person who had held her, gently withdrew his hand, she did not move. She did not for some instants recover from her terror; or, perhaps, the feeling of pressure seemed to her to remain upon her head after the hand was withdrawn.

Children who are accustomed to *doubt*, and to try experiments, will not be dupes to "Vulgar errours."

(July 20th, 1796.) S—— (between 9 and 10) when he heard a lady propose to make use of a small glass tumbler to hold pomatum, made a face expressive of great disgust; he was begged to give a reason for his dislike. S—— said it appeared to him dirty and disagreeable to put pomatum into a tumbler out of which we are used to drink wine or water.

We have observed, (V. Chapter on Taste and Imagination) that children may early be led to reflect upon the cause of their tastes.

(July 24th, 1796.) S—— observed, that "the lachrymal sack is like Aboulcasem's cup, (in the Persian tales.) It is emptied and fills again of itself; though it is emptied ever so often, it continues full."

The power of reasoning had been more cultivated in S—— than the taste for wit or allusion; yet it seems his mind was not defective in that quickness of seizing resemblances which *may* lead to wit. He was not praised for the lachrymal sack, and Aboulcasem's cup. (V. Chapter on Wit and Judgment.)

(August 3d, 1796.) C—— (11 years old) after she had heard a description of a fire engine, said, "I want to read the description of the fire engine over again, for whilst my father was describing one particular part, I recollected something that I had heard before, and *that* took my attention quite away from what he was saying. Very often when I am listening, something that is said puts me in mind of something, and then I go on thinking of *that*, and I cannot hear what is said any longer."

Preceptors should listen to the observations that their pupils make upon their minds; this remark of C——suggested to us some ideas that have been detailed in the "Chapter on Attention."

(August 1st, 1796.) S——, who had been translating some of Ovid's Metamorphoses to his father, exclaimed, "I hate those ancient gods and goddesses, they are so wicked! I wish I was Perseus, and had his shield, I would fly up to heaven and turn Jupiter, and Apollo, and Venus into stone; then they would be too heavy to stay in heaven, and they would tumble down to earth; and then they would be stone statues, and we should have much finer statues of Apollo and Venus than any they have now at Rome."

(September 10th, 1796.) S— — (within a month of ten years old) read to his sister M— — part of Dr. Darwin's chapter upon instinct; that part in which there is an account of young birds who learn to sing from the birds who take care of them, not from their parents. S— — immediately recollected a story which he had read last winter in the Annual Register. Extract from Barrington's Remarks upon singing Birds. "There was a silly boy once (you know, sister, boys are silly sometimes) who used to play in a room where his mother had a nightingale in a cage, and the boy took out of the cage the nightingale's eggs, and put in some other bird's eggs (a swallow's, I think) and the nightingale hatched them, and when the swallows grew up they sang like nightingales." When S— — had done reading, he looked at the title of the book. He had often heard his father speak of Zoonomia, and he knew that Dr. Darwin was the author of it.

S— —. "Oh, ho! Zoonomia! Dr. Darwin wrote it; it is very entertaining: my father told me that when I read Zoonomia, I should know the reason why I stretch myself when I am tired. But, sister, there is one thing I read about the cuckoo that I did not quite understand. May I look at it again?" He read the following passage.

"For a hen teaches this language with ease to the ducklings she has hatched from supposititious eggs, and educates as her own offspring; and the wag-tails or hedge-sparrows learn it from the young cuckoo, their foster nursling, and supply him with food long after he can fly about, whenever they hear his cuckooing, which Linnæus tells us is his call of hunger."

S— — asked what Dr. Darwin meant by "learns it."

M— —. "Learns a language."

S— —. "What does foster nursling mean?"

M— —. "It here means a bird that is nursed along with another, but that has not the same parents."

S— —. "Then, does it not mean that the sparrows learn from their foster sister, the cuckoo, to say Cuckoo!"

M— —. "No; the sparrow don't learn to say cuckoo, but they learn to understand what he means by that cry; that he is hungry."

S— —. "Well, but then I think this is a proof against what Dr. Darwin means about instinct."

M— —. "Why? How?"

S——. "Because the young cuckoo does say cuckoo! without being taught, it does not learn from the sparrows. How comes it to say cuckoo at all, if it is not by instinct? It does not see its own father and mother."

We give this conversation as a proof that our young pupils were accustomed to *think* about every thing that they read.

(Nov. 8th, 1796.) The following are the "*Curiosities of Literature,*" which were promised to the reader in the chapter upon Grammar and Classical Literature.

Translation from Ovid. The Cave of Sleep, *first* edition.

> "No watchful cock Aurora's beams invite;
> No dog nor goose, the guardians of the night."

Dog and *goose* were objected to, and the young author changed them into dogs and geese.

> "No herds nor flocks, nor human voice is heard;
> But nigh the cave a *rustling* spring appear'd."

When this line was read to S——, he changed the epithet *rustling* into *gliding*.

> "And with soft murmurs faithless sleep invites,
> And there the flying past again delights;
> And near the door the noxious poppy grows,
> And spreads his sleepy milk at daylight's close."

S—— was now requested to translate the beginning of the sentence, and he produced these lines:

> "Far from the sun there lies a cave forlorn,
> Which Sol's bright beams *can't* enter eve nor morn."

Can't was objected to. Mr. —— asked S—— what was the literal English. S—— first said *not*, and then *nor*; and he corrected his line, and made it

> "Which Sol's bright beams *nor* visit eve nor morn."

Afterwards:

> "Far in a vale there lies a cave forlorn,
> Which Phœbus never enters eve nor morn."

After an interval of a few days, the lines were all read to the boy, to try whether he could farther correct them; he desired to have the two following lines left out:

"No herds, nor flocks, nor human voice is heard,
But nigh the cave a gliding spring appeared."

And in the place of them he wrote,

"No flocks nor herds disturb the silent plains:
Within the sacred walls mute quiet reigns."

Instead of the two following:

"And with soft murmurs faithless sleep invites,
And there the flying past again delights."

S— — desired his *secretary* to write,

"But murmuring Lethe soothing sleep invites,
In dreams again the flying past delights."

Instead of

"And near the doors the noxious poppy grows,
And spreads his sleepy milk at daylight's close,"

the following lines were written. S— — did not say *doors*, because he thought the cave had no doors; yet his Latin, he said, spoke of squeaking hinges.

"From milky flowers that near the cavern grow,
Night scatters the collected sleep below."

We shall not make any further apology for inserting all these corrections, because we have already sufficiently explained our motives. (V. Chapter on Grammar and Classical Literature.)

(February, 1797.) A little theatre was put up for the children, and they acted "Justice Poz." [119] When the scenes were pulled down afterwards, S— — was extremely sorry to see the whole theatre vanish; he had succeeded as an actor, and he wished to have another play acted. His father did not wish that he should become ambitious of excelling in this way at ten years old, because it might have turned his attention away from things of more consequence; and, if he had been much applauded for this talent, he would, perhaps, have been over-stimulated. (V. Chapter on Vanity and Ambition.)

The way to turn this boy's mind away from its present pursuit, was to give him another object, not to blame or check him for the natural expression of his wishes. It is difficult to find objects for children who have not cultivated a taste for literature; but infinite variety can be found for those who have acquired this happy taste.

Soon after S—— had expressed his ardent wish to have another play performed, the trial of some poor man in the neighbourhood happened to be mentioned; and it was said, that the criminal had the choice of either going to Botany Bay, or being hanged.

S—— asked how that could be. "I did'nt think," said he, "that a man could have two punishments. Can the judge change the punishment? I thought it was fixed by the law."

Mr. —— told S—— that these were sensible questions; and, as he saw that the boy's attention was fixed, he seized the opportunity to give him some general idea upon the subject. He began with telling S——the manner in which a suspected person is brought before a justice of the peace. A warrant and committal were described; then the manner of trying criminals; what is called the court, the jury, &c. the crier of the court, and the forms of a trial; the reason why the prisoner, when he is asked how he will be tried, answers, "By God and my country:" this led to an account of the old absurd fire and water ordeals, and thence the advantages of a trial by jury became more apparent by comparison. Mr. —— told S—— why it is called *empannelling* a jury, and why the jury are called a *pannel*; the manner in which the jury give their verdict; the duty of the judge, to sum up the evidence, to explain the law to the jury. "The judge is, by the humane laws of England, always supposed to be the protector of the accused; and now, S——, we are come round to your question; the judge cannot make the punishment more severe; but when the punishment is fine or imprisonment, the quantity or duration of the punishment is left to his judgment. The king may remit the punishment entirely; he may pardon the criminal; he may, if a man be sentenced to be hanged, give him his choice, whether he will be hanged or *transported*"—(the word was explained.)

"But," said S——, "since the judge cannot *change* the punishment, why may the king? I think it is very unjust that the king should have such a power, because, if he changes the punishment for one thing, why mayn't he for another and another, and so on?"

Mr. ——. "I am inclined to believe, my dear S——, that it is for the good of a state, that a king should have such a power; but I am not sure. If any individual should have this power, I think it is most safely trusted to a king; because, as he has no connection with the individuals who are tried, as he does not live amongst them, he is not so liable as judges and jurymen might be to be prejudiced, to be influenced by personal revenge, friendship, or pity. When he pardons, he is supposed to pardon without any personal motives. But of all this, S——, you will judge for yourself, when you study the law. I intend to take you with me to —— next assizes to hear a trial."

S—— looked full as eager to hear a trial, as he had done, half an hour before, to act a play. We should mention, that in the little play in which he had acted, he had played the part of a justice of the peace, and a sort of trial formed the business of the play; the ideas of trials and law, therefore, joined readily with his former train of thought. Much of the success of education, depends upon the preceptor's seizing these slight connections. It is scarcely possible to explain this fully in writing.

(February 25th, 1797.) S—— was reading in "Evenings at Home," the story of "A friend in need, is a friend indeed."

"Mr. G. Cornish, having raised a moderate fortune, and being now beyond the meridian of life, he felt a *strong desire* of returning to his native country."

S——. "How much better that is, than to say he felt an *irresistible desire*, or an *insupportable desire*, as people sometimes say in books."

Our pupils were always permitted to stop when they were reading loud, to make whatever remarks they pleased upon whatever books they read. They did not, by this method, get through so many books as other children of their age usually do; but their taste for reading seemed to increase rapidly. (V. Books.)

(March 8th, 1797.) H—— (14) told us that he remembered seeing, when he was five years old, some puppets packed up by a showman in a triangular box; "and for sometime afterwards," said H——, "when I saw my father's triangular hat-box, I expected puppets to come out of it. A few days ago, I met a man with a triangular box upon his head, and I thought that there were puppets in the box."

We have taken notice of this propensity in children, to believe that particular, are general causes; and we have endeavoured to show how it affects the temper, and the habits of reasoning. (V. Temper, and Wit and Judgment.)

(March 27th, 1797.) Mr. —— showed little W——(3 years old) a watch, and asked him if he thought that it was alive.

W——. "Yes."

Mr. ——. "Do you think that the fire is alive?"

W——. "Yes."

Mr. ——. (The child was standing at the tea table.) "Do you think the urn is alive?"

W——. "No."

Mr. ——. "Do you think that book is alive?"

W——. "No."

Mr. — —. "The horses?"

W— —. "Yes."

Mr. — —. "Do you think that the chaise is alive?"

W— —. "Yes." Then, after looking in Mr. — —'s face, he changed his opinion, and said *no*.

W— — did not seem to know what was meant by the word *alive*.

Mr. — — called H. (5 years old) and asked her whether she thought that the watch was alive. She at first said Yes; but, as soon as she had time to recollect herself, she said that the watch was not alive.

This question was asked, to try whether Reid was right in his conjecture as to the answers a child would give to such a question. (V. Reid's Essays on the Intellectual Powers of Man.)

We frequently say, that flowers, &c. are dead: we should explain to children that there are two kinds of life; or rather, that the word *life* is used to express two ideas; vegetable life, and animal life.

(July, 1797.) Miss Louisa — — told us, that when a rose bud begins to wither, if you burn the end of the stalk, and plunge it red hot into water, the rose will be found revived the next day; and by a repetition of this burning, the lives of flowers may be fortunately prolonged many days. Miss Louisa — — had seen many surprising recoveries performed by this operation, and several of her friends had adopted the practice with uniform success.

We determined to repeat the experiment. Children should never take any thing upon trust which they can verify. Two roses, gathered at the same time, from the same tree, were put into separate glasses of water. The stalk of one of these roses was burnt, according to prescription; they were left a night in water, and the next day the rose that had been burnt, appeared in much better health than that which had not been burnt. The experiment was afterwards several times repeated; and should be tried by others until the fact be fully ascertained.

(July, 1797.) Little W— — (three years old) was shown Miss B— —'s beautiful copy of the Aurora surgens of Guido. The car of Apollo is encircled by the dancing hours, so that its shape is not seen; part of one wheel only is visible between the robes of the dancing figures. We asked little W— — why that man (pointing to the figure of Apollo in his invisible car) looked so much higher up in the air than the other people?

W— —. "Because he is in a carriage; he is sitting in a carriage."

We pointed to the imperfect wheel, and asked if he knew what that was? He immediately answered, "Yes, the wheel of the carriage." We wanted to see whether the imagination of a child of three years old, would supply the invisible parts of the *car*: and whether the wheel and horses, and man holding the reins, would suggest the idea of a phæton. (V. Chapter on Taste and Imagination.)

We shall not trespass upon the reader's patience with any more anecdotes from the nursery. We hope, that candid and intelligent parents will pardon, if they have discovered any desire in us to *exhibit* our pupils. We may mistake our own motives, and we do not pretend to be perfectly impartial judges upon this occasion; but we have hoped, that only such conversations or anecdotes have been produced, as may be of some use in Practical Education. From conversation, if properly managed, children may learn with ease, expedition, and delight, a variety of knowledge; and a skilful preceptor can apply in conversation all the principles that we have laboriously endeavoured to make intelligible.

[113] Mrs. Honora Edgeworth, daughter of Edward Sneyd, Esq. of Litchfield. As this lady's name has been mentioned in a monody on the death of Major André, we take this opportunity of correcting a mistake that occurs in a note to that performance.

"Till busy rumour chas'd each pleasing dream,
    And quench'd the radiance of the silver beam."
Monody on Major André.

The note on these lines is as follows:

"The tidings of Honora's marriage. Upon that event Mr. André quitted his profession as a merchant, and joined our army in America."

Miss Honora Sneyd was married to Mr. Edgeworth in July, 1773, and the date of Major André's first commission in the Welch Fusileers is March 4th, 1771.

[114] This has been formerly quoted in the preface to the Parent's Assistant.

[115] The anecdotes mentioned in the *preceding* pages, were read to the children with the rest of the work.

[116] Soame Jennings's.

[117] Voltaire.

[118] V. Johnson's Life of Browne.

[119] Parent's Assistant.